CN
C
AN

447164

D1152896

CHOOSE FREEDOM

ROY HATTERSLEY

CHOOSE FREEDOM

THE FUTURE FOR DEMOCRATIC SOCIALISM

MICHAEL JOSEPH
LONDON

First published in Great Britain
by Michael Joseph Ltd
27 Wrights Lane, London W8 5TZ
1987

British Library Cataloguing in Publication Data

Hattersley, Roy
   Choose Freedom: the future for democratic
   socialism.
   1. Socialism   2.Democracy
   I. Title
   335.5   HX73
   ISBN 0–7181–2483–9

Typeset in Great Britain by Cambrian Typesetters
Printed and bound by
Billings and Son, Worcester

To Sparkbrook

'The British version of socialism has democracy as its basis . . . It involves not the curtailment of liberties, but their more general extension, and is, for that reason, denounced as tyrannical by those whose authority is likely, as a consequence, to suffer diminition.'

R.H. Tawney, *The Radical Tradition*

Contents

Preface

The opinions which follow may, in some part, be controversial. It is therefore necessary to be more explicit about responsibiity than would be possible were I simply to express my thanks for help received and to absolve my helpers from blame for the errors which they were unable to prevent.

I wrote the first draft of *Choose Freedom* during 1984. Each chapter was rewritten at least twice – and some chapters rather more often – during 1985 and the early weeks of 1986. On the day that the manuscript was delivered to the publisher, copies were also sent to a number of valued friends with a request for their urgent comments. Professors Anthony King, Maurice Peston and Raymond Plant, Lord Williams of Elvel, Mr Tony Howard and Mr Berry Wilson, together with David Hill (my senior assistant) and Douglas Jones (my economic assistant), all offered improving comments which ranged from the correct spelling of 'Macleod' to the insistence that, in one particular, I had done Friedrich Hayek less than justice. I am deeply grateful for their generous help and for the speed of their response. Thanks to the benevolence of the Amalgamated Engineering Union (who have, for several years, lent a word processor to my office and who arranged for several of the chapters to be typed and retyped) and to the assiduity of my secretary, Joyce Farrell, the advice which I accepted was incorporated quickly enough to avoid a major confrontation with the publisher. Justin Ash confirmed (though he would probably say corrected) the references and the notes.

I am grateful to all of them for their help and repeat the customary absolution and statement of gratitude with more than usual force. The improvements are theirs, the errors and omissions mine.

Roy Hattersley
1987

Acknowledgments

The author is grateful to the following for permission to reproduce quoted material: Wheatsheaf Books Ltd: R. H. Tawney *The Acquisitive Society*; J. M. Dent and Sons: R. H. S. Crossman *New Fabian Essays*; K. Joseph and J. Sumpton *Equality*; Penguin Books Ltd: Geoff Hodgson *The Democratic Economy*, Peter Townsend *Poverty in the United Kingdom*, Mark Abrams, Richard Rose and Rita Hinden *Must Labour Lose?*; Lawrence and Wishart Ltd: Karl Marx *Capital Vol. I*, Engels *Anti-Duhring*; Macmillan Ltd: *Marxism, Socialism and Freedom*, Evan Luard *Socialism Without the State*, H. Pelling *The Labour Government 1945–51*; Yale University Press: T. Mischel *Human Action*; Gower Publishing: P. N. Balchin *Housing Improvement and Social Inequality*; Weidenfeld and Nicolson: Donoghue and Jones *Herbert Morrison*, Harold Evans *Good Times Bad Times*; Methuen and Co: Adam Smith *The Wealth of Nations*; Tavistock Publications: A. Ellis and K. Kumar *Dilemmas of Liberal Democracy*, Bean, Ferris and Whyner (eds) *The Defence of Welfare*; Oxford University Press: Goldthorpe, Llewellyn and Payne *Social Mobility and Class Structure in Modern Britain*, Matthew Arnold *Selected Essays*, John Rawls *A Theory of Justice*, John C. Rees *John Stuart Mill's On Liberty*, Isaiah Berlin *Inaugural Lecture as Professor of Social and Political Theory 1958*; Policy Studies Institute: Colin Brown and Pat Gay *Racial Discrimination: 17 Years After the Act*, No. 646, 1985; Allen and Unwin: R. H. Tawney *Equality* and *The Radical Tradition*, R. H. Titmuss *The Gift Relationship*, A. Nove *The Economics of Feasible Socialism*; Batsford: Enoch Powell *Freedom and Reality*; Routledge and Kegan Paul Ltd: Elizabeth Durbin *New Jerusalems*, F. Hirsch *Social Limits to Growth*, F. S. Hayek, *The Constitution of Liberty*, *Law, Legislation and Liberty*, *New Studies*, *Studies in Philosophy, Politics and Economics*; Secker and Warburg, the estate of the late Sonia Orwell and Harcourt Brace: G. Orwell *The Road to Wigan Pier*; André Deutsch: J. K. Galbraith, *The New Industrial State*.

The Choice of Freedom

The true object of socialism is the creation of a genuinely free society in which the protection and extension of individual liberty is the primary duty of the state. That is a precept which I have instinctively taken for granted since some time in the 1940s; for the idea that the Labour Party was founded to make us all free was firmly embedded in my mind long before I had even heard of the rival theories of socialism. Now – even though I know that different definitions of socialism exist – my primitive assumption still seems self-evidently true. Socialism and the parties which are its practical manifestation have a central and simple purpose: the provision for as many people as possible of rights and opportunities which, in other sorts of society, are limited to a small section of the population. My experiences in the late 1940s taught me that the achievement of that objective requires more than an assertion of liberty. Rights are not, in themselves, enough. They must be accompanied by sufficient economic power to give their theoretical existence a practical meaning. That is the doctrine of 'agency' – a concept which I discovered many years after the Labour government of 1945 had first put it into effect on my behalf.

For I was, in many personally significant ways, the product of the post-war Labour government. I pushed the leaflets of that government through the letter boxes of the Hillsborough constituency in Sheffield. But, more important to my nascent view of socialist philosophy, I benefited from the social revolution which it brought about. I was the sickly recipient of extensive care from the free health service. My education – from grammar school through to university – would have been impossible without the financial support of a Labour city council and a Labour government. I saw the slums which the new housing policy was to replace; and I lived amongst the families which the new system of social security had emancipated. We – the emergent working classes of the 1940s – had not previously been denied the right to health, education and decent housing. There was no statute which forbade us to live in a proper house or accept adequate medical care. In the decades before the war we had simply been unable to afford the price of enjoying such advantages. It was because of that practical experience that I came to regard the idea of negative freedom – liberty as the absence of coercion – as a cruel joke.

Socialism exists to provide – for the largest possible number of people – the ability to exercise effective liberty. Socialists certainly support the minimum intrusion of the state into the lives of its citizens. But unless the state intervenes to protect the poor and the weak, the rich and the powerful will simply exploit them in the name of freedom. The socialists' obligation is to use collective power to protect individual rights. It is a complex and, in some ways, paradoxical objective which cannot be turned into a slogan for shouting through the microphones of mass rallies. That is one of the reasons why the Labour Party – far from enjoying the reputation which it deserves as the true proponent of liberty – is often caricatured as the enemy of freedom.

But at least in part, the Labour Party has acquired that reputation because of the reckless willingness of some of its members to behave in a way which undermines its libertarian credentials. Some petty bureaucrats have equated municipal socialism with town hall regulation. A few weak-minded Labour supporters have openly sympathised with Eastern European autocracies because those tyrannies called themselves 'socialist republics'. But such behaviour has provided no more than the supplementary justifications for Labour's damaging reputation as the party of authoritarianism and control. Its libertarian credentials have been undermined by two related causes. The first is the enthusiasm with which the political right espoused liberty – carefully defining it in a way which entrenched privilege and protected wealth. The theories of von Mises and Hayek possessed, for the already advantaged, the irresistible attraction of legitimising their selfishness and greed. But the second major cause of Labour's reputation as the enemy of freedom is that, for years, British democratic socialists have lacked the intellectual confidence to challenge the establishment's concept of liberty with a radical definition of what freedom really means. That reluctance was the product of the Labour Party's traditional suspicion of ideology, its conviction that British democratic socialism needed no theory with which to justify its practice.

There always has been (and there still remains) a strange reluctance within the Labour Party to set out a clear statement of socialist belief against which to measure programmes and policies. But the time when Labour could take refuge in ideological agnosticism has passed. The philosophical clarity which is now essential to our future success need not be so sectarian as to narrow our appeal. The extension of liberty, as the main aim of socialism, is an ideal which can be traced back through Tawney, Hobhouse and T. H. Green to the radical utilitarianism of John Stuart Mill. It is also to be found in the Marxist 'revisionist' theories of Bernstein and his followers. Both ethical socialists and believers in the creation of socialism by the organisation of socialist institutions see the pursuit of freedom as a primary obligation. For those who have thought about the nature of socialism, the only argument on the subject of liberty concerns the way in which it can be best extended.

Some Labour Party members have, of course, always grasped at clichés as an alternative to the construction of a philosophical framework within which the socialist programme could be developed. The most inadequate is the shibboleth about 'nationalisation' in Clause IV of the 1918 Labour Party manifesto. The most complex and paradoxical is the insistence of Professor Arthur Lewis that 'socialism is about equality'. The problem of that axiom is that it is true – but only partly true. Without extensions of equality – a more even distribution of power and wealth – the generality of men and women will never be able to exercise, in full, the rights which democratic socialism should provide. But equality is a means, not an end in itself. Of course, to provide the greatest amount of freedom for the largest possible number of people requires a limitation of the power enjoyed by the previously privileged minority. That is the inevitable result of any diffusion of rights. The Reform Bills of 1832 and 1866 removed the right of the upper and middle classes to determine the government of Great Britain. But freedom was extended by the gradual movement towards political equality. The same rule applies to economic and social freedom: an equal distribution of power is necessary for its achievement.

The principle – for principle it is – applies to the distribution of real liberty between the races and the sexes as well as between the social and economic groups which make up the hierarchy of our society. The disadvantaged groups all overlap. The ethnic minorities are more likely to be unemployed than are members of the indigenous majority. Women are too often condemned to work in the low-wage industries and in the jobs within them that pay the worst wages. Both groups – the black and Asian minorities and the female majority within the population – are under-represented in all the institutions which form opinion and determine the nature of society within Great Britain. Formally and informally both their views and their values are disregarded and discounted. The creation of sexual and racial equality requires policies specifically directed to that aim. The full emancipation of both women and the ethnic minorities demands special measures to elevate their standing and status. But essential aspects of the march towards racial freedom and sexual equality are directly and inextricably linked with the general thesis to which this book is devoted: the need to give effect to theoretical rights by the provision of resources by which those rights can be exercised. Without the acceptance of that principle, the campaigns for racial and sexual equality will remain morally admirable but meaningless to the lives of most of the people on whose behalf they are fought.

The achievement of a more equal distribution of wealth and power, and the resultant increase in the sum of freedom for the community as a whole, is the principal goal of socialism. Socialism is about the nature of society and – since it is concerned with a social and political system – there are some subjects about which there is no intrinsically 'socialist' position. There is, for example, no such thing as a socialist defence or foreign policy – save only for the support of liberty in both the Soviet Union and South Africa. The argument that follows therefore does not offer an opinion about nuclear defence or collective security. It is possible to be a socialist and in favour of both, one or neither. Those are subjects appropriate only to election manifestos.

What follows is an attempt to assert a simple point – though one which has been scandalously neglected and can now be re-established only by complicated argument. Socialism is 'about freedom'. The achievement of that aim requires the constant pursuit of equality. The Labour Party is most likely to accept those related obligations if it possesses a clear and intellectually convincing philosophical basis for the policies which make up its programme. Without an ethical framework on which to build its programmes, Labour will risk losing its way in the future, as it has lost it in the past.

The ethical framework which can give shape and coherence to our programme was defined for me by Tony Crosland on the Sunday before his fatal illness.[1] We were spending the weekend at Dorney Wood. It was the Foreign Secretary's first and (as it turned out) last visit to his 'official country residence' and it had been organised in a way which paid proper respect to the irreverence that he thought essential to socialism. In the late afternoon we walked in the garden and, as always, talked about a new book on socialism – the book which we were all too busy to write but which was desperately needed.

'Give me,' said Crosland, 'a simple definition of socialism.' Of course, I failed as I was intended to fail. Crosland had a definition which he offered after an extended denunciation of one-sentence descriptions of complicated philosophical concepts. 'Socialism,' he said, 'is about the pursuit of equality and the protection of freedom – in the knowledge that until we are truly equal we will not be truly free.' It is that self-evident truth that *Choose Freedom* seeks to demonstrate.

[1] For a full account of the conversation see S. Crosland, *Tony Crosland* (Jonathan Cape, London, 1982).

THE PRINCIPLES

Chapter One

In Praise of Ideology

Herbert Morrison – Labour's Deputy Leader for over twenty years and putative father of the plan to nationalise coal, gas, electricity and the railways – was not a man beset by philosophic doubts. 'Socialism,' he said, 'is what the Labour Party happens to be doing at any one time.' As a description of a complex and comprehensive ideology, the most that can be said of that definition is that its pragmatic convenience almost compensates for its intellectual inadequacy; and that is exactly what has been said in that definition's favour during the last eighty years.

It was during Harold Wilson's leadership that pragmatism was elevated into a major socialist virtue. But from the day that the Labour Party was born – and partly as a result of its complicated parentage – powerful voices have always insisted that to define the philosophical framework within which its policies could be assembled would only lead to trouble. There would, it was prophesied, be damaging disputations about faith and doctrine – an undesirable state of affairs from which eighty years of ideological evasion has not always protected us. Sometimes, the opponents of doctrine argued, the establishment of firm principles would only lead to the allegation that socialist theory was not always put into practice – another political liability which enthusiastic agnosticism has not always avoided. Beneath the cynicism and the sophistries was the fear that if the floating voters ever discovered what the Labour Party really stood for, they would decide that they did not like it. The result has been that, when the Labour Party establishment has had its way, the loudest voices at party conference (whatever their philosophical authority) and the most strident commentators in Fleet Street (however great their prejudice) have been allowed to announce, unchallenged, the principles on which the Labour Party bases its programmes. Too often, the official reaction to the advocacy of

3

unacceptable ideas was the insistence that the prudent course was to have no ideas at all.

So after the period in which the Wilson pragmatists downgraded, denigrated and denied the idea that British socialism should have an ideological foundation, the army of political riffraff who infiltrated the Labour Party in the late sixties and early seventies were allowed to claim that every half-digested Trotskyite notion (and each nonsense which they invented for themselves) was wholly consistent with the socialist ethic. Meanwhile, socialism's opponents had a clear field in which they could advance arguments which would have been dismissed as intellectual garbage had the Labour Party made its ideological basis clear. Sir Keith Joseph built his reputation as a 'thinker' on the assertion of an unchallenged absurdity:

> Almost half the population of the world is ruled by those who prefer to act in the name of egalitarian ideals, whether of the Marx or Tawney variety. It is, therefore, a matter of some interest that with the exception of the Scandinavian countries, they have produced a parade of totalitarian dictatorships which have not even succeeded in suppressing inequality but have, on the contrary, magnified it in almost every case.[1]

It is not enough to say that the Scandinavian countries are a considerable exception. The important point (conceded by the authors of that diatribe in other parts of their text) is that Marx (on whom they blame the Soviet system) advocates equality in none of his major works. Yet, because of its fear of ideological clarity, Labour allows itself to be held responsible for the excesses of those who claim to build their tyrannies upon his doctrine – even though it is not, and never has been, a Marxist party.

The fear that ideology is an electoral liability stretches right back to the Party's foundation. It was the early Independent Labour Party that G. D. H. Cole had in mind when he wrote of 'socialism almost without doctrine – so undefined in its doctrinal basis as to make recruits readily amongst people of quite different types.'[2] The rejection of an alliance based on

[1] K. Joseph and J. Sumpton, *Equality* (John Murray, London, 1979), Ch. 3, 'Equality and Liberty', p. 42.
[2] C. A. R. Crosland, *The Future of Socialism*, (Jonathan Cape, London, 1980) Ch. 3, 'The Traditions of British Socialism' (quoting G. D. H. Cole, *A Short History of the British Working Class Movement, Vol. III*), p. 49.

doctrine in favour of 'a broad movement on behalf of the bottom dog'[3] was thought to have great popular appeal. The prejudice persisted in 1952, a year after the defeat of the Attlee government. R. H. S. Crossman, writing what amounted to a plea for a statement of democratic socialist philosophy, nevertheless conceded that 'it was largely because the Party accepted the unphilosophic Fabian approach that it was able to become a national party and assume the national responsibilities of government more easily than any other socialist party in Europe'. But he went on to insist that the 'absence of a theoretical basis for practical programmes of action is the main reason why the post-war Labour government marked the end of a century of social reform and not, as socialist supporters had hoped, the beginning of a new epoch'.[4] Crossman argued that 'the development from the liberalism of 1906 to the modern welfare state' was not 'explicitly socialism' and, therefore, needed neither socialist doctrine for justification nor socialist vision to reveal the way ahead. But he insisted that in 1950 socialism had to stand on its own ideological feet. For, with the establishment of a universal health service, the introduction of comprehensive national insurance and the nationalisation of the public utilities, it was not possible further to improve society without fundamentally changing it.

The men and women who wrote Labour's post-war manifesto – like the ministers who implemented it – rejected the notion that *Let Us Face The Future* was anything less than a full-blown socialist programme. But one implication of Crossman's judgment was undoubtedly true. The 1945 manifesto won the support of voters who were not theoretical socialists and therefore attracted around it a coalition of objectives, if not of ideas. The creation of a national health service, free at the point of use, appealed to ideologues and ameliorators alike. The ideologues believed that its creation would contribute to the achievement of a more equal society. The ameliorators knew – for the evidence was all around them – that the cost of private medicine prevented millions of families from receiving essential medical care.

The ameliorators – numerically by far the larger of the two

---

[3] *ibid.*
[4] R. H. S. Crossman (ed), *New Fabian Essays*, (J. M. Dent, London, 1980) 'Towards a Philosophy of Socialism', p. 4.

groups – were little concerned about the political labels that were pinned on Labour's programme, either by the delegates who supported it at the Party Conference or by Conservative critics who warned that its implementation would produce a state in which the Gestapo would feel at home. The need for social reform was so obvious – and the memories of pre-war deprivation were still so vivid – that there was a natural consensus for compassion. And since the war had been won by collective, rather than private enterprise, co-operation seemed common sense. In 1945, the Labour Party polled 47.8 per cent of the total votes cast. Twenty-one years later, Harold Wilson was elected for a second term with 47.9 per cent of the poll. The two decades between those victories was the period when Labour could – to a greater or lesser degree, depending on the items included in its programme – rely on the coalition of objectives. Ameliorators and ideologues could work together in satisfied partnership; the objection to ideas was not a liability.

The coalition of objectives can be recreated; but it will not be built again in its original form, for the political world has changed. If the Labour Party is to attract the support that will ensure a working majority, we cannot allow the voters to have any doubt about the ethical principles on which democratic socialism is based. Paradoxically, unless we stake out our ideological boundaries and defend them against external assault and internal subversion, we will not attract to our cause the millions of unideological supporters who are necessary for our victory. A clear statement of our philosophy is essential to our success and perhaps even to our survival as a major political force.

The problem for democratic socialists is not so much finding their ideological origins as choosing a suitable philosophical basis from the wide variety on offer. One of the reasons why the ethical framework of Labour Party policy has always been in doubt is that the federation of progressive belief has never been able to agree on its primary aim and principal purpose. Indeed, British socialists have argued about their destiny and duty since long before the Labour Representation Committee decided, in 1900, to 'establish a distinct Labour Group in Parliament who shall have their own organisation and agree upon their own policy'. In 1880, the Social Democratic Federation used to meet in a little basement room in a block of buildings in Westminster. There was always a good deal more friction than fraternity. The type of man who had the intellectual and moral courage to join a new and unpopular movement has also fully developed the faults of his qualities – obstinacy, vanity, a sort of prickly originality.[5]

In 1886, Anne Besant, taking up the position which has come to characterise the Fabian Society, attacked the SDF call for violent action with the insistence that society could only be changed 'by a slow process of evolution, not by revolution and bloodshed'. It is, she said, 'you revolutionaries who stem and block the revolutionary process'.[6] Bernard Shaw wrote in the *Workman's Times* for autumn 1892 that 'the only vital difference between the Fabian Society and the SDF is that the Fabians want to grow the plums first and make the pies afterwards whilst the Federation wants to make the pies first and find the plums afterwards'. At the end of the inaugural conference of the Independent Labour Party in Bradford in 1893, the organisers proclaimed that the meeting had been 'a great and unqualified success', but the failure to include the word 'socialist' in the new Party's title convinced fundamentalists that although the ILP was 'a perfectly honest and disinterested attempt . . . to help forward the emancipation of the workers . . . The attempt will fail'.[7] The Labour Party was born arguing with itself and it has gone on arguing ever since.

If the Labour Party had a major source to which all the other early socialist movements acted as tributaries, it was the Labour Representation Committee which assembled under the auspices of the Trades Union Congress Parliamentary Committee in the Memorial Hall, Farringdon Street, London EC4, on Tuesday, 27 February 1900. The Social Democratic Federation was there; as was the ILP, with a delegation that included P. Snowden of 28 Cotton Street, Keighley, and Alderman Fred Jowett of 4 Grantham Place, Bradford – representing respectively the non-conformist conscience and the spirit of municipal enterprise

[5] H. Bland, *Sunday Chronicle* 26.5.1895 (quoting H. Pelling in *Origins of the Labour Party*, Quartet, London, 1972), Ch. 2, 'The Socialist Revival', pp. 27–8.
[6] T. Bolam, *The Practical Socialist* (quoting N. and J. McKenzie in *The First Fabians*, Ch. 5, 'England Arise', p. 78.
[7] H. W. Lee, *Justice* 21.1.1883 (quoting H. Pelling, *ibid.*), Ch. 6, 'The Emergence of the National ILP', p. 124.

which were to play such a prominent part in the future of the Party which they helped to form. The Fabian Society, with only 861 members, had a single delegate and 1 vote to contribute to the total of 22 cast by the three overtly political associations. The trades union (numbering amongst their delegates Ben Tillett of the Dock Labourers, J. R. Clynes and Will Thorne of the Gas Workers, and John Burns MP of the Engineers) cast 540 votes. The pattern of trades union numerical dominance was thus established at the start. So was the pattern of argument which has persisted for almost ninety years. Will Thorne carried the Conference for the LPP's right to control the list of Parliamentary candidates. The ILP assisted in the defeat of a resolution which committed the new movement to the pursuit of socialism and 'a recognition of the class war'. The eventual decision was unequivocally pragmatic. It promised no more than the creation of a distinct organisation ready 'to co-operate with any party which for the time being may be engaged in promoting legislation in the direct interests of labour'. The crucial sentence was drafted and proposed by J. Keir Hardie of the ILP. Being the forerunner of the Labour Party, the Labour Representation Committee gave its support to that historic decision by endorsing an amendment to the original motion on its agenda. It seemed that the idea of ideological clarity had been abandoned from the start.

The Labour Party's disparate origin – and the dominance within its councils of the essentially pragmatic trades union – accounts only in part for the historic reluctance to agree on the ethical framework against which to measure the principles of policies and the basis of programmes. The reasons why Labour has always shied away from statements of philosophical position are also concerned with the British character and intellectual tradition – within which the temperament of the typical radical dissenter played a special part. It is the nature of the dissentient to dissent – against almost everything; and the radical's traditional belief sometimes turned into a preference for railing against the elements rather than attempting to build a temporary and imperfect shelter against the storm. Opposition is, in any event, easier than the construction of an alternative philosophy – since it can never be proved conclusively wrong. 'Every revolutionary opinion,' said George Orwell at his most cynical, 'draws part of its strength from the secret conviction that nothing can be changed.'[8] Meanwhile, whilst life (or at least Liverpool) remains the same, some socialists have fallen into the trap of which Heine accused William Cobbett, likening him to a guard dog, who was said

> to fall with equal fury on everyone who he does not know, often bites the best friend of the house on the calves, barks incessantly and just because of this incessantness of his barking cannot get listened to, even when he barks at a real thief.[9]

But the confusion which comes from permanent and vocal opposition has been only a minor deterrent to the creation of a comprehensive statement of ideological foundation. Much more important has been the British instinct which preferred action to words and, in the phrase of R. H. S. Crossman, 'repudiated socialist theory as dangerous Teutonic verbiage', and believed that 'ideological speculation is best left to the exponents of American free enterprise and Russian Communism'.[10] The Labour Party has been anti-intellectual not so much in theory as in practice. It became a Benthamite movement which insisted that its members could recognise human happiness when they saw it and did not need any theoretical justification for arguing in favour of its extension. The victory of 1945 was the triumph of general principles described and advocated in the language of individual practical necessities. After the defeat of 1951, the underlying principles became submerged under the arguments about the merits of the programme which it prompted. Tony Crosland complained that Labour deteriorated into 'a party for the defence of the 1951 position with perhaps a few minor questions thrown in'.[11] R. H. S. Crossman took an even more critical view of the ideological black hole into which the Party disappeared, claiming that Labour 'lost its way not only because it lacks maps of the new country it is crossing, but because it thinks maps unnecessary for experienced travellers'.[12] So between 1901 and 1964, Labour swung wildly between gestures

---

[8] G. Orwell, *The Road to Wigan Pier* (Penguin, London, 1973), p. 102.
[9] Quoted in M. Arnold, *Selected Prose* (Penguin, London, 1982), pp. 163–4.
[10] R. H. S. Crossman (ed), *New Fabian Essays* (J. M. Dent, London, 1970), 'Towards a Philosophy of Socialism', pp. 4–5.
[11] C. A. R. Crosland, *Can Labour Win?* (Fabian Society Pamphlet, 1960).
[12] R. H. S. Crossman (ed), *New Fabian Essays*, (J. M. Dent, London, 1970) 'Towards a Philosophy of Socialism', p. 2.

of its socialist integrity – like the promise to nationalise the sugar and cement industries – and attempts to propitiate the gods of financial probity – like the 1964 decision to hold the exchange rate at a level which prejudiced the interests of the real economy. And throughout that entire period, the Labour Party was accused by its opponents of being obsessed with dogma to the exclusion of the real world's necessities. That was largely because although the Party was (and remains) deeply suspicious of ideology, it possesses a deep enthusiasm for constructing clichés about the ideology which it regards itself as too sensible to define. The question, 'Is it really socialist?' is still constantly asked, as if it is possible to give any sensible answer without an agreed definition of what socialism is.

There are, of course, a very large number of clichés which pass for philosophical definition and act as an alternative to thought. Many of them are based on a linear theory of politics and politicians which suggests that ideology can be measured along a straight line, beginning at a point philosophically adjacent to anarchy, syndicalism or Soviet communism (or lumped together by socialism's critics under the meaningless title of 'Marxism') and ending at the far end of the spectrum of belief in various forms of fascism. On the way from extremism to extremism, the line passes through socialism, radicalism, social democracy, liberalism and conservatism. The whole concept, as well as being intellectually ridiculous, encourages the Labour Party to judge its programme not against a yardstick of its own, but according to its relationship with the policies of its opponents. Thus, to advocate the public ownership of a clearing bank is to flirt with communism, whilst to support membership of the European Economic Community is to embrace conservatism. Judging policies against the criteria laid down by opponents is, at best, not conducive to coherence and consistency. But it is not the most dangerous way to answer the question 'Is it really socialist?'. Nor is it the easiest.

The swiftest way to become 'a socialist' (and the certain way to demonstrate a position on the left wing of the movement) is to subscribe to the school of political philosophy pioneered by Humpty Dumpty. ' "When I use a word," he told Alice, in a rather scornful voice, "it means just what I choose it to mean." ' So, a Labour Party member can usually become a left-wing socialist simply by announcing that he or she is a left-wing socialist and that their beliefs and instincts are left-wing. Self-definition rarely fails, especially if it is reinforced by membership of groups made up by other self-defined left-wing socialists. After the status is acquired, it is almost impossible to lose.

Once 'left-wing' sympathies or support are announced it becomes possible to assist totalitarian régimes abroad, oppose minimum wage legislation at home, reject positive discrimination in favour of the ethnic minorities, and take up close associations with groups on the wilder shores of politics and still maintain a 'left-wing' reputation. If British democratic socialism were properly defined, its adherents would be judged against a sterner test than self-estimation, self-esteem and self-interest.

Clearly, that definition must concern the nature of society, its economic organisation and the relationship between its members. One traditional test of 'real socialism' which observes that rule is the often instinctive belief in what is generally termed 'public ownership' and a related opposition to what is loosely described as 'free-market economics'. Opponents wrongly relate these complementary attitudes to support for something which they call Marxism. In fact, support for the Marxist doctrine has always been minimal within the Labour Party. A movement which prides itself on its practicality is not likely to embrace wholeheartedly a doctrine that asserts the historical inevitability of an outcome which it urges its adherents to achieve by struggle and sacrifice, it concerns itself with a theory of value which is wholly meaningless in the real world and insists that 'freedom consists of converting the state from an organ superimposed upon society into one completely subordinate to it'; but, when applied in practice, produces an authoritarian régime supported by an all-powerful bureaucracy. People call themselves Marxists without knowing what Marxism is. But there is sometimes a half-developed idea at the back of the democratic socialist mind that Marx – who also defined socialism as the 'nationalisation of the means of production, distribution and exchange' – at least produced some of the theoretical background to the contention that everything would change for the better once 'capital' was publicly owned and 'markets' were replaced with 'planning'. Paradoxically, Marx was given credit for the possession of something that Labour despised – ideas.

That idea was incorporated into *Labour and the New Social*

11

Order, the manifesto on which the Party fought the 1918 Great Election. The following year, Sydney Webb – the manifesto's author – drafted a new Party constitution. The notion of public ownership was enshrined in Part 4 of Clause IV and the idea that socialism and public ownership are synonymous (largely unknown until the 1920s) slipped into the hearts and minds of Labour Party members. Its popularity lay, in part, in the history of the time. The Great War had been won by public enterprise and the Webbs had been much impressed by the organisation of the Ministry of Munitions under Neville Chamberlain, its Director General. The commitment to 'the common ownership of the means of production, distribution and exchange' had a comfortably tangible meaning which was more attractive to practical men and women than was the idealistic aspiration of Clause V, 'generally to promote the Political, Social and Economic Emancipation of the People and more particularly of those who depend directly upon their own exertions by hand or brain for the means of life'. It is not, however, clear that Sydney Webb himself was as unequivocally committed to the wholesale application of the promise which he drafted as are the Clause IV disciples within the modern party.

Writing in *The Observer* of 21 October 1917, he was at pains to clarify the meaning of the passages on public ownership which he had prepared for the manifesto.

> This declaration of the Labour Party leaves it open to choose from time to time whatever form of common ownership (from Co-operative store to nationalised railway) and whatever form of popular administration and control of industry (from national guilds to ministers of employment and municipal management) may, *in particular cases*, commend themselves.[13]

The italics are Sydney Webb's, and the single phrase '*in particular cases*' invalidates at least the insistence that the author of the famous constitutional commitment regarded an overall transformation from private to public ownership as the essential ingredient of progress towards a socialist society. Nor have any of the real philosophers of democratic socialism ever regarded public ownership, of any sort, as providing a sufficient definition of either socialism's purpose or socialism's existence. Tawney is typically succinct:

[13] Quoted by Lisanne Radice in *Beatrice and Sydney Webb* (Macmillan, London, 1984).

Whether in any particular instance it is desirable or not is a question to be decided in the light, not of resounding affirmations of the virtues of either free enterprise or of socialisation, but on the facts of the case.[14]

Tony Crosland dismisses the notion with equally typical disdain. 'Marx appropriated' the word socialism and used it as a description of 'the collective ownership of the means of production'. Crosland's distaste for Marx's definition stems from a belief not that Marx and all his works were wicked, but the judgment that many of Marx's conclusions were wrong. For Marx worked 'on the false assumption . . . that the pattern of ownership determined the character of the whole society and that collective ownership was a sufficient condition of fulfilling the basic aspirations'.[15] In that sentence lies, only half hidden, the fundamental objection to equating public ownership with socialism. The real objection is not that public ownership is too extreme a remedy for society's ills, but that it is, in itself, an inadequate solution. It may sometimes be a necessary – even important – part of the prescription. But it is not a complete cure, and talking of it as if it were can only result in the real changes which socialists should wish to see being either ignored or rejected as less than the full gospel of the true faith. The problem with equating socialism with nationalisation is not that the connection produces too extreme a definition of that political ideology. Equating socialism and nationalisation is the easy alternative to thought. It is philosophically meaningless. It can also lead to terrible heresies.

> Thus if, for example, socialism is defined as the nationalisation of the means of production, distribution and exchange, we produce solutions which are impossible to reconcile with what the early socialists had in mind when they used the word: such as that Soviet Russia is a socialist country (much more so, for instance, than Sweden) – even though it denies almost all the values which Western socialists have normally read into the word.[15]

The Labour Party has – for quite extraordinary historical reasons – put a special gloss on the supposed connection

[14] R. H. Tawney, *The Radical Tradition* (Penguin, London, 1964), Ch. 10, 'Social Democracy in Britain', p. 158.
[15] C. A. R. Crosland, *The Future of Socialism* (Jonathan Cape, London, 1980), Ch. 4, 'The Meaning of Socialism', p. 66.

between state ownership and socialism. Marx equated socialism with at least an initial period of centralised ownership. Some Labour Party members see socialism as synonymous with nationalisation, simply because that was the form of public ownership which Herbert Morrison decided was right for the public utilities. A few activists may consciously believe and openly argue that the government monopoly offers the best prospect of 'planning' and is therefore essential to the command economy of targets, quotas and regulations in which they believe. But most of the advocates of the national corporation – owned by the state and run from London – support that view of socialist ownership for the most reactionary of reasons: that is the way in which we did it before, and it is, therefore, the way in which we should do it again. There is a splendid irony in the fact that Herbert Morrison, these days the object of so much hatred on the far left, was the only true begetter of the central plank in the fundamentalist programme – nationalisation. Morrison himself (with the experience of the London Passenger Transport Board behind him) was clearly right to advocate the simple state corporation as the proper model for the public ownership of the utilities. But as a formula for the implementation of socialism in our time, nationalisation is worse than inadequate. Indeed, it does not even answer most of the questions about how social ownership – itself only a small part of socialism – should be approached in the future. The time has come at least to ask such questions – and to go on to attempt an intellectually respectable definition of what socialism is really about.

For the first eighty years of its existence, it was possible for the Labour Party to stumble along unencumbered by ideology, openly sceptical of ideas and wholly untainted by the allegation that – like the continental socialist parties – we based our policies for each election on coherent ethical principles. But pragmatism is no longer enough. The old coalition of objectives, which shared aims without worrying about motives, has disappeared for ever. To become, once more, the dominant force in British politics, Labour has to win converts to the philosophy of socialism. For the world has changed in four distinct ways.

First, the political and social map of Britain bears very little resemblance to the charts on which we plotted our 1945 election victory.

14

In that year, we knew the groups whose allegiance was unchanging. We could be certain of support from those – particularly young and middle-aged men – who worked in unskilled or semi-skilled occupations. Their class loyalty and self-interest were reinforced by the feeling of solidarity with a party which was created by the trades unions on which they relied for real material protection. Families in the north of England, Scotland and Wales were more likely to vote Labour than their southern counterparts; tenants' enthusiasm for Labour was three or four times greater than that of owner-occupiers. Of course, the existence of these bedrocks of support never guaranteed Labour victory. Aneurin Bevan – Deputy Labour Leader but still the hero of the left – told the 1959 Party Conference that

> I was in this movement in between the war years when there were two million unemployed and still the Tories got a majority. You would have thought that there was some spontaneous generation of socialist conviction, but we lost before the war years. Even the unemployed voted against us. Even in the areas where there was as much as 20 or 30 per cent of unemployment we lost seats.[16]

But, apart from the years of self-inflicted catastrophe, like 1931, there were always stable foundations of traditional support on which to build. The key voters who made up the volatile marginal increment necessary for victory were a comparatively small part of the electorate. The bedrock has not changed its characteristics: the same people, from the same areas, with the same jobs, still vote Labour. There are simply fewer of them. The British population has drifted to London and the south-east; employment is manual and semi-skilled industry has decreased in both absolute and relative terms; owner-occupation has grown both absolutely and relatively; trades unions membership – particularly in the manual unions, affiliated to the Labour Party – has shrunk. The position was put into absolute perspective by the fieldwork done in preparation for the political fund ballot carried out (wholly successfully) by the National Union of Railwaymen. Fewer men worked on the railways in 1983 than were employed by the private companies when the Labour Representation Committee met in 1900; a

[16] A. Bevan, speech at 1959 Labour Party Conference.

third of them owned their own houses; over half lived south of Watford.

Second, the economy no longer invariably behaves in the way which we once anticipated would be the case under governments of all persuasions.

Thirty years ago, we all took growth for granted. Keynes had demonstrated how it could be done; and the new Tory Party, stripped of its nineteenth-century dogmatism by the Butler reforms, shared the commitment to expansion and, to some degree, the belief in extended equality. The argument was largely about how much and how fast. The difficult questions about how to achieve continuous improvement for the least advantaged members of society, under conditions of stagnation or even slump, could be put aside; so could the fundamental arguments about the propriety of greater equality and the utility of the free enterprise system. A quarter of a century before Margaret Thatcher became Prime Minister, Tony Crosland announced that capitalism was dead. It had, he said, been replaced by a new form of economic organisation which he called 'statism':

> with its arrival the most characteristic features of capitalism have all disappeared – the absolute rule of private property, the subjection of all of life to market influences, the domination of the profit motive, the neutrality of government, typical *laissez faire* division of income and the ideology of individual rights.

Crosland detected a major shift in power from management to labour and rejoiced that 'through fiscal policy and a variety of physical, legislative and financial controls the state now consciously regulates (or seeks to regulate) the level of employment, the distribution of income, the rate of accumulation'.[17] Every assumption contained within that paragraph has been challenged by Milton Friedman or F. A. Hayek. And many of the 'irreversible changes' which Crosland observed have been reversed by Margaret Thatcher's government. We can no longer rely on an instinctive consensus in favour of the compassionate society. Some voters will behave as Per Albin Hansson observed the Swedes behaving in 1946. 'A people with political liberty,

---

[17] *ibid.*, Ch. 2, 'Is This Still Capitalism?', p. 30.

16

full employment, and social security has lost its dreams.'[18] Others have been encouraged to see government spending, high levels of welfare provision and economic intervention in the working of the market as a nightmare. Either way, the case for compassion has to be argued again from first principles.

Third, the changes in population which diminished the Labour Party's areas of natural support also changed the characteristics of the typical Labour Party member.

The new middle classes – very largely the product of the free milk, full employment and universal secondary education introduced by the Attlee government – did not all espouse conventionally bourgeois values. Some of the new generation of mortgage-holding, car-owning, pension-contributing, continental-holidaying sons and daughters of old Labour supporters felt that their recently acquired status automatically alienated them from the Labour Party. But many of the recently well housed, securely employed and highly educated recruits to property and prosperity retained a radical enthusiasm which they expressed in ways that complicated rather than clarified Labour's claim to be a national party which deserved national support. For they directed their enthusiasm towards special interest groups. Men and women who, in previous years, would have employed their reforming zeal within the Labour Party itself turned instead to the support of individual issues: nuclear disarmament, sexual equality, pollution and the protection of the environment, animal rights and law reform. Many of them, if they joined the Labour Party at all, made it clear that their membership was contingent on its continued support of their favourite cause. They professed views not on the general organisation of society, but only on the treatment and management of one of its parts. Whatever the merits of their individual enthusiasms, their treatment of Labour as a vehicle for the promotion of their particular passions blurred the sharp image of socialism and increased the difficulty of portraying and popularising a coherent and consistent strand of policy. The need to emphasise support for a wide variety of essentially minority causes (which, even when added together, could not make up a plurality of votes) made successive manifestos look

---

[18] C. A. R. Crosland, *The Future of Socialism* (Jonathan Cape, London, 1980), Ch. 2, 'Is This Still Capitalism?', p. 30.

like a rag-bag of unrelated side issues. Floating voters want their political parties to concentrate on what they regard as the central issues of the time.

The other new phenomenon – wholly unknown until the late 1960s – was a second group (or combination of groups) which also chose to use the Labour Party as a vehicle for their own ideas, most of which were alien to Labour's tradition: the Militants, the International Marxists, the Socialist Workers and the rest. They, too, were partly the product of the changes in society which the Attlee government had begun. Many of the new revolutionaries were the sons and daughters of the new middle classes who had obtained an education, half-digested an idea, found a grievance but had been unable to relate their criticisms of society to the processes of democratic politics. Some of them believed that the old Labour Party was not worth fighting for because it had come, so closely, to resemble its Conservative opponents with an apparently identical commitment to full employment, collective security and the mixed economy. They either rejected or lacked the sophistication to consider the idea that traditional Tories had been dragged to the left by the pressures of socialism and kept there because the Labour Party stood by, ready to implement nationally popular policies if the Tories turned their back on the health service, the pensioners and full employment. Not until the early 1980s – by which time the Labour Party was so debilitated that it could not act as a deterrent to the far Tory right – did it become clear how wide the gulf between the parties would become, once the Conservatives realised that they could govern without concern for the popularity of the socialist alternative. Paradoxically, the Trotskyites claimed as justification for advocating their extremism within the Labour Party the same excuse as some other traditionals gave as their reason for leaving the Party altogether. Democratic socialism seemed out of fashion.

Fourth, ideological politics came back into fashion in the 1970s.
For thirty years, the voters wanted a combination of economic growth and conspicuous compassion, and the patrician concern of Harold Macmillan joined with the earthy understanding of Harold Wilson to make up a clear consensus against the dangerous notion that political parties might base their policies on philosophical principles rather than on the instincts of good

regimental officers and highly qualified technicians. Even before the growth began to fade, the politics of common sense and decency had grown boring. Margaret Thatcher, advocating the saloon-bar version of Hayek and Friedman, seemed to offer something which was both new and exciting. First, the small-circulation weeklies noticed that theories were coming out of the Conservative Research Department and the Institute of Economic Affairs. Then the serious newspapers began to describe the ethical basis of modern Toryism, its major prophets and the institutions which had been set up to examine the application of new remedies to old problems. Fleet Street is in permanent thrall to anything which can be described as new or different. So it was not long before the tabloids, which would normally only print a story about political theory if they could persuade a pretty philosophy student to take her clothes off, began to announce that the Conservative Party had won the war of ideas. They were joined – as is so often the case with the most damaging of assaults on Labour – by allies from the far left. The *Sun* and *Militant* combined to argue that there were only two coherent and consistent political theories and that the choice had to be between the neo liberalism of the Conservative Party and the Marxism of the fringe groups which hover at the edges of the Labour Party. The Labour Party made no intellectual response to the claim, and therefore lost the ideological argument by default. For too long the mainstream of the Labour Party believed that it was possible to combat bad ideas by opposing ideas in general.

It would be easy to argue that the emergence of the Social Democratic Party is the fifth reason why Labour must assert its ideological identity. In one sense, such an argument would be wholly justified, for their existence means that, although Labour remains the only party that can offer an alternative government, the SDP (and their Liberal allies) now offer an alternative name on the ballot paper. It is no longer possible for the Labour Party to sit back and wait for the political pendulum to swing its way as electors grow tired of Conservatism and decide to give 'the other lot' a chance: there are two 'other lots' now. The Liberals and the SDP cannot win an election, and will not win many individual seats, but they can win enough votes to spoil Labour's chances of becoming a majority government.

We can defend ourselves against that threat only by attempting to win back from the Alliance those natural Labour supporters who have abandoned their allegiance since 1981. In theory, that might best be done by the imitation of their ideological incoherence, an attempt to make Labour the Mugwump Party of the left which – like the SDP – stands for no consistent view of society but attempts to mobilise all sorts of political emotions into a coalition of frustration and optimism, hope and resentment. But if the British people were – at some time during the 1970s – advertising for a wholly unideological party, the position is no longer vacant. The Alliance does the job. It would not even be expedient to copy them. So the morality of the Labour Party adopting such a course need not detain us. Despite the traditional incoherence of our ideological position, the *formal* abandonment of ideology would be impossible. Our activists would not accept an entrenchment of unconvincing pragmatism of the late sixties and early seventies. Some clear ideological foundation is essential. We had better make sure that we choose the right one.

For many new Labour supporters, the assertion that Labour is a party of principle is more important than a clear statement of what the principle is. And, to a degree, they are right to place the priorities in that order, for a formal rejection of philosophy would mean a formal rejection of socialism. In any case, the political market can only bear one party which relies on political agnosticism for its strength and the position is already taken.

So there is no doubt that the existence of the SDP-Liberal Alliance as a sort of national political force is, in itself, an important reason why Labour must redefine and defend its ideological boundaries. But they are not a *primary* cause. The existence of the Alliance is the result of four phenomena which make up the fundamental argument for a clear statement of our philosophical position. The SDP is a product of the affluence and security which the Attlee government pioneered – and of the new middle classes which that revolution created. The collapse of confidence in constant growth obliged a re-examination of the comfortable old arguments about the speed of universally accepted social improvements. As the realities of politics grew harsher, it was inevitable that a movement would develop which urged conciliation, compromise and coalition as

20

an alternative to facing the hard alternatives. The Marxists of the new, hard left (and the rough working-class habits of the residual trades unionists) inevitably offended the political and social susceptibilities of many voters who, in the forties and fifties, automatically assumed that their opinions and their class had a natural home within the Labour Party; and as the Tory Party moved right to embrace the scientifically uncompassionate theories of neo liberalism, it was only natural that fundamentally decent men and women should look for a non-ideological alternative to both the major parties. The Labour Party's failure was not its refusal to offer them its own non-ideological alternative, but its inability to convert them to an ideology which they would have seen as practical, compassionate and relevant to their daily lives. The SDP is an essentially secondary phenomenon of British politics. Its success – indeed, its existence – depends on the behaviour of its opponents. If, for the fundamental reasons which justify our argument, the Labour Party were to define its philosophical position in a way which increases its electoral popularity, the whole Alliance might not disappear; but it would certainly shrink to proportions which make it no more politically significant than the old Liberal Party. The Alliance would then become a party of Siamese pygmies, locked together by their inability to rise individually even to a height that makes them more than an irrelevance in British politics.

For all those reasons, a clear definition of our ideological position is now essential – particularly if that definition can give the Labour Party a new and broad appeal that transcends classes, races and regions. Democratic socialism, properly defined, is a philosophy with an immense natural appeal, for it is the gospel of personal emancipation, and much of our past unpopularity has been the product of the fear that we stand either for regulation rather than emancipation or for nothing at all.

What we stand for is freedom. That is the ultimate objective of socialism. The immediate intention of socialist policies is the creation of a more equal society within which power and wealth are more evenly distributed. But socialism's fundamental purpose – indeed, the purpose of the equality which we seek – is

21

the extension of liberty.[19] Socialists may, in the short term, be concerned with the problems of property, wealth, earnings and economic organisation – but they are concerned with them only as a means by which a more fundamental aim may be achieved. The true measure of socialism is not the extent of public ownership, the degree of central planning or the degree of government regulation. Indeed, in some cases, central planning and government regulation may limit freedom, and thus be the enemies of socialism. *A socialist society is judged by the extent to which it succeeds in providing, for the largest possible number of its citizens, the power to exercise rights which, under other forms of organisation, are either denied or made available only in theory. Socialism is the promise that the generality of men and women will be given the economic strength which makes the choices of a free society have meaning. It is a commitment to organise society in a way which ensures the greatest sum of freedom, the highest total amount of real choice and, in consequence, the most human happiness. It is the understanding that the collective power should be used to enhance individual liberties.*

To socialists, freedom is not the absence of restraint on the rich and the powerful, but the ability of the generality of men and women to exercise their inherent rights. A socialist society sees liberty 'not as a possession to be defended but as a goal to be achieved' and its achievements depend upon the creation of rights – social and economic, as well as political – 'which must be such that wherever the occasion for their exercise arises, they can in fact be exercised'.[20] It is, to paraphrase Keynes, *effective* freedom which socialists seek.

Yet, despite socialism's traditional ideological dependence on a highly developed theory of liberty, Labour has increasingly allowed itself to be caricatured as the 'We Know Best Party' when we are (or ought to be) the 'We Will Make You Free Party'. We have failed to proclaim our purpose and describe our destiny largely because of intellectual reticence – the lack of self-confidence which prevented us from moving liberty out of our

---

[19] Throughout what follows, liberty and freedom are regarded as synonymous. There are distinguished precedents for that practice. Sir Isaiah Berlin adopted it in his Inaugural Lecture, as Professor of Social and Political Theory in the University of Oxford.

[20] R. H. Tawney, *The Radical Tradition* (Penguin, London, 1964), Ch. 10, 'Social Democracy in Britain', pp. 166–7.

opponents' ground by insisting that their definition of that ideal condition is prejudiced, and perverse. We should not have been afraid to argue that extending choices as widely as possible makes inevitable the removal of those exclusive rights which have previously been the prerogative of privilege. Every public footpath is an infringement of the landlord's right to fence his property. We all know that and accept the limitation on landlords' liberties as a feature of a free society. Yet by espousing the landlords' cause, the Conservatives have represented themselves as the freedom party and successfully pretended that those who would protect the footpath are dictators, whilst those who proclaim the right of way are tyrants. It is in our failure to be visibly the party of liberty that our careless unconcern about a proper ideological framework for policies is most damagingly reflected. There have, of course, been other contributory reasons for our damagingly authoritarian reputation – reasons concerned with petty town hall tyrannies, Soviet friendship societies and trades union restrictive practices. But the prime cause has been our willingness to argue about liberty in the language of our opponents, to contend that freedom amounts to no more than the removal of restraints. Instead of arguing for a better definition of freedom, we have stayed silent as if we either had nothing better to put in its place or actually accepted the phoney notion and chosen to neglect what passes, within it, for liberty in the hope of creating greater equality. *As we evangelised for equality, we should have made clear that without it, for a majority of the population, the promise of liberty is a cruel hoax. Liberty is our aim. Equality is the way in which it can truly be achieved. It is time that we made our ideological purpose clear.*

Chapter Two

Is Equality Outdated?

Those who oppose the creation of a more equal society base
their defence of inequality on a variety of related propositions.
Those assertions are central to the philosophies of the neo-
libertarian right whose followers believe that equality is the
enemy of liberty, and that a high level of inequality is necessary
for both the economic success of a society and the highest level
of consumption to be secured for all classes within it. But there
are two plain man's objections to equality with which we must
deal first. They are the instinctive beliefs that:

> 1. Equality is – in anything but the attenuated version
> popularly described as 'equality of opportunity' – a utopian
> dream, rendered impossible of achievement by the naturally
> diverse qualities and characteristics of human beings.

> 2. Equality is an ideal which, whatever its ethical validity
> in the years of grinding poverty, is a wholly inappropriate
> aspiration for a motor-car owning, owner-occupying, tele-
> vision-renting, package-holiday-touring society.

These objections to equality are closely connected and need
to be refuted together. They have the force common to the plain
man's argument. For, if repeated on the top of an omnibus,
bound for any destination, they are likely to elicit the response
that 'of course' we cannot achieve real equality and 'of course'
those who urge us to attempt its attainment are living in the
poverty-stricken pre-war past. We need, therefore, to examine
those propositions before we turn to the philosophical and
economic objections to the pursuit of equality.

The case for equality (whatever the current gross domestic
product and its annual growth rate) and the possibility of its
attainment are closely related, for both objectives are dependent
on a sensible definition of the sort of society which socialists

seek. It is not a society in which we all think, act or are even paid the same. Such a condition is as undesirable as it is unattainable. It is, however, a community which is organised in a way which diminishes rather than accentuates the differences in prospects that flow from sex, origin and income; one which is committed to a reduction in those disparities of wealth and power which are the product of entrenched privilege; and one which – since, in the truest sense, it is concerned with economic and social emancipation of all its citizens – is more concerned with liberty than the neo-libertarianism of the far right could possibly be. Since it is concerned with such fundamental ethical objectives, the case for equality is not altered by the economic condition of the time. Had Britain been a more equal society, there is little doubt that our recent decline would, at least, have been less rapid. Further, greater equality would certainly improve our future economic performance. But that is its subsidiary justification; it is right in itself, as well as necessary.

Thirty years ago, when Harold Macmillan was proclaiming with justifiable conviction that Britain had 'never had it so good', Tony Crosland wrote that Lord Attlee had recently explained that he 'joined the socialist movement because I did not like the sort of society that we had, and I wanted something better'. Crosland went on to ask: 'Why should anyone say the same today?' Then, in the middle of an era of unparalleled economic expansion and unmitigated social optimism, he gave three answers.

> First, for all the rising material standards and apparent contentment, the areas of avoidable social distress and physical squalor are still on a scale which narrowly restricts the freedom of choice and movement of a large number of individuals. Secondly (and perhaps more intractable) we retain a disturbing amount, compared with some other countries, of social antagonism and class resentment, visible in both politics and industry, and making society less peaceful and contented than it might be. Thirdly, the distribution of rewards and privileges still appears highly inequitable, being poorly correlated with the distribution of merit, virtue, ability and brains; and in particular, opportunities for gaining top rewards are still excessively unequal.[1]

[1] C. A. R. Crosland, *The Future of Socialism* (Jonathan Cape, London, 1980), Ch. 4, 'The Meaning of Socialism', p. 80.

Tony Crosland's statement about British society in 1956 is equally applicable to British society today. Thirty years on, his complaints about the inequitable distribution of rewards is certainly couched in the language of the fifties and perhaps even implies an acceptance of that decade's values. Today, radicals are less certain that virtue can be measured and merit defined. The competitive nature of equality of opportunity is no longer regarded as possessing the power to emancipate a majority of the people. Nor is the alleviation of social distress regarded amongst socialists as any more than the first skirmish in a long campaign. Crosland's argument – at least, in that passage of *The Future of Socialism* – is the minimalist's argument for equality. But it is also the classic case for changing the nature of society, rather than rearranging the membership of the hierarchies within it. The Labour Party, said Tawney, 'forgets its mission' when it 'seeks not a social order of a different kind . . . but a social order of the same kind in which money and power will be somewhat differently distributed'[2]. Tawney and Crosland are joined by Hugh Gaitskell in their insistence that socialism is about the reorganisation of society with the specific object of creating a more equal distribution of power and wealth – not an equal chance to become one of the minority who are both powerful and wealthy. As a young economics lecturer at London University – and whilst feeling his way towards a theory of socialism – he wrote in an unpublished treatise on wages that

> to remove the injustice implicit in capitalist society is the ideal which all socialist movements have in common. This injustice is in part caused by, in part identical with, economic inequality. Hence the destruction of this inequality, the creating and maintaining of a society in which it cannot exist, become the essential and direct purpose of all socialist policy.[3]

After the war, when capitalism had changed (not least as the result of the Labour government's historic impact on British society) the case against the divided community was just as strong.

> Under welfare capitalism (i) though the national income is rather more fairly distributed than before, the concentration of

[2] R. H. Tawney, *The Attack* (Spokesman Books, London, 1981), 'The Choice Before the Labour Party'.
[3] E. Durbin, *New Jerusalems* (Routledge & Kegan Paul, London, 1985), Ch. 6, 'Cole and the New Fabians Attack Traditional Policy', p. 127.

capital (and so of economic privilege) remains unchanged (ii) profits, wages and salaries are still determined not by any conditions of natural interest or social justice but by traditional methods of *laissez faire*. Under conditions of full employment this must result in inflationary pressure which undermines our standard of living (iii) though certain basic industries are transformed into public corporations and private industry is subject to some control, effective power remains in the hands of a small managerial power elite.[4]

The cause of the more equal society – as a matter of principle and as a pragmatic necessity – has been espoused by socialists during every phase of the economic cycle and during moods of national optimism as well as of generalised despair. Crosland argued the case when both left and right believed that growth would go on for ever. Then the left hoped that the increased confidence, as well as the greater wealth, that came from expansion would make equality easier to achieve as relative material disparates were diminished whilst the rich simultaneously grew richer. Attlee and Gaitskell, before the war, both understood that in times of intolerable deprivation (and the subjugation that inevitably follows poverty) the need for a more equal distribution of wealth was all the more urgent and obvious – though less likely to be accepted by the prosperous. Socialists will argue that the pursuit of equality – being right, in itself – is a moral obligation, irrespective of the circumstances of the time. What is beyond doubt is that Britain is no more equal a society today than it was a hundred years ago.

In 1931, R. H. Tawney reported that

> the last Decennial Census of the Registrar General . . . dividing the whole population into five social classes and representing the general level of infantile mortality by 100, found that the infantile mortality rate in what he called the 'independent class' was 48, in the middle class 70, and in the poorest labouring class 123.[5]

In the later editions of *Equality*, he wrote that

> more recent investigations underline the same point. It has been shown – to quote only one example – that in Stockton-

---

[4] R. H. S. Crossman (ed), *New Fabian Essays* (J. M. Dent, London, 1970), 'Towards a Philosophy of Socialism', pp. 26–7.
[5] R. H. Tawney, *Equality* (Allen & Unwin, London, 1952), Ch. 4 (iii), 'The Extension of Social Services', p. 148.

upon-Tees the standardised death rate during the years 1931–4
was 11.5 per 1,000 for better-off families and more than twice as
much – 26 per 1,000 – for the poorest.[6]

Since then, tuberculosis has been virtually eliminated from our
society; healthier mothers are having healthier babies, which are
now almost always born in the germ-free security of maternity
hospitals; smallpox vaccination is no longer necessary, for
smallpox has almost disappeared; clean air has reduced the
incidence of bronchitis; and a free health service offers the
benefits of constantly developing medical science to the generality of men and women. But the disparities between the classes
persist in almost exactly the same numerical proportion to that
which Tawney observed between the wars.

Official statistics now divide the population into five social
groups. According to the most recent figures, infant mortality
per 1,000 live legitimate births in England and Wales was 6.2 in
Class 1 and 12.8 in Class 5.[7] The poorest and the most deprived
20 per cent of the population still had an infant mortality rate
which was more than twice as high as that endured by the most
fortunate 20 per cent of the population. *Social Trends* confirms
that the pattern of general mortality rates recorded in Stockton
during the early 1930s has not changed: 'variations in the
standard mortality rate by social class were as high in recent
years as they were 50 years ago'.[8] And when the figures are
revised (as Tawney revised his figures for the second edition of
Equality) it seems certain that the divergence in the 'class
chances' – the prospect of the different social groups – will have
widened as it did between his first and second calculation.
Unemployment, deprivation in the inner cities, cut-backs in
pre-, post- and peri-natal care, discrimination – intentional and
unconscious – against the ethnic minorities have all made that
outcome certain.[9]

Since Edwin Chadwick's reports first persuaded Parliament

[6] *ibid.*, Ch. 2 (ii), 'The Economic and Social Contours', pp. 70–1.
[7] *Office of Population and Census Statistics Monitor*, 1983.
[8] *Social Trends*.
[9] On 1 August 1986, *The Lancet* confirmed the gloomy prediction: 'There has been an
overall fall in all-cause mortality for both manual and non-manual occupational classes,
but the rate of decline has been greater in non-manual groups. Thus the social gap has
widened. Widening inequalities between social groups are evident in mortality from lung
cancer, coronary heart disease and cerebrovascular disease, each of which already
differed markedly by social class in 1970–72. For coronary heart disease the regional
differences within manual and non-manual groups are undiminished.'

that public health was its proper responsibility, the incidence of death and disease amongst the social classes has been regarded as the classic measurement of divisions within our society. And since Chadwick's time, we have believed that we know the way to improve the life expectancy and medical prospects of the most vulnerable groups within the population. Chadwick himself believed in redemption through sanitation; and the cholera maps of northern cities confirmed that where money was spent on sewers and drainage, the contagion was contained. It was reasonable to assume that a higher volume of public spending on medical care would improve the general level of health.

And so it has. To pursue our example, infant mortality rates have declined. But the spending has failed to reduce the difference in class chances. It might have been assumed, from the simple application of marginal analysis, that the most underprivileged section of society who, before the mid-point of the nineteenth century, received virtually no medical treatment, would be those whose health record improved most dramatically – shifting their relative position in the table of disadvantage. When the Public Health Act in 1848 stipulated that a death rate of 23 per 1,000 from cholera entitled a borough to apply to the Central Commission for the installation of minimal sanitary arrangements, it was envisaged that the cost, per life saved, would be comparatively small. It would certainly be far less than the cost that would have been necessary to improve the life expectancy of the Harrogate citizens, who refused to pay the rate increase necessary to finance a clean water supply on the grounds that they possessed private wells. Keeping Howard Hughes alive for an extra day or two would have been more expensive than saving the life of a sub-Saharan malnutrition victim. The theoretically equal distribution of public funds ought to have changed the relative position of the most disadvantaged. It did not do so. If they benefited by what is called the 'trickle-down effect' – the gradual extension of all forms of prosperity from the fortunate few to the grateful majority – the benison has not flowed freely. In fact, advantage (even publicly financed advantage) has been dammed up for the benefit of the middle class. Only a few drops have trickled down to the lower income groups.

That is clear from an analysis of public spending patterns, even during the last twenty-five years – the age of the common man. *From Birth to Seven*, the National Children's Bureau's Child Development Study examination of the 'abilities and attainments, behaviour, physical development, health, home environment and birth history' of 16,000 children born between 3 and 9 March 1958, concluded that for the 'underprivileged or deprived child, enriching or compensating education needs to be provided during the pre-school years and confirmed during the school years'. That can be dismissed as a value judgment, as can the Bureau's conclusion that 'some direction of scarce resources to those children at higher risk of handicap seems prudent', and will be the subject of discussion in later chapters. What is beyond dispute is that 'those sections of our community which, in general, have the most need of statutory services, tend to use those services least'. Those in greatest need receive the smallest share of help. The pattern of distribution can easily be described.

The rule 'to them that hath shall be given' applies throughout the allocation of state funds. Owner-occupiers have always received (through tax concessions) much greater assistance than that provided for tenants of rented property – a group generally on low incomes. The pattern is the same in the allocation of other forms of housing finance.

> Although in West London generally, improvement grants were found to be distributed mainly to areas with a high proportion of residents in the lower socio-economic groups, it is suggested that these residents failed to benefit from rehabilitation and, indeed, suffered from the loss of their accommodation. The conversion of low-income dwellings into owner-occupied properties or high-rent luxury accommodation has forced the poor to consume less housing space, often within the same borough. and homelessness and council waiting lists are increasing.[10]

The net result of such a pattern of distribution has been to widen the gulf between the classes. The National Children's Bureau's *From Birth to Seven* survey went on in a second volume, *Born to Fail*, to describe children who were born to fail because they were born into deprivation. These children received so little help from the welfare state that their relative position deteriorated – their reading ages falling further and

---

[10] P. N. Balchin, *Housing Improvement and Social Inequality* (Saxon House, Farnborough, 1979) , Ch. 8, 'Conclusions', p. 227.

further behind their natural age, their physical development increasingly failing to conform with the norm of weight and height, and even their teeth decaying at a faster than average rate. These examples are, of course, taken from the bottom of the social scale; but an examination of the whole class relationship shows the same pattern. Relative positions and prospects have not changed since the industrial revolution. The *Oxford Social Mobility Survey* – in which the origins and post-war progress of 10,000 men aged between 20 and 64 were examined – came to a conclusion which its two volumes of analysis and evidence made irrefutable.

> Even in the presumably very favourable context of a period of sustained economic growth and of major changes in the form of occupational structure, the general underlying processes of class mobility – or immobility – have apparently been little altered and indeed have, if anything, tended in certain respects to generate still greater inequalities.[11]

Of course, during that time the working-class child's chance of 'getting on' improved with changes in the economy and increases in the gross domestic product. But when we compare the relative prospect of individuals at different points on the social scale, we discover that relative class chances have hardly changed at all. The *Oxford Social Mobility Survey* – examining educational prospects – concludes that the 'inequalities which prevail are often of a quite gross kind'. The *Mobility Survey* was, of course, considering the inequalities between men in different social groups. If the position of women had been examined the divergence would have been even greater. That should not surprise us; for we know that the pattern of success and failure is determined early in life, according to the circumstances of a child's birth and upbringing, and that once a pattern is established, only the most exceptional individual will be able to break out. We also know that the pattern of government spending, far from concentrating on the areas of greatest need, usually allocates the largest share of national resources for families who are already thrusting, determined and middle-class. The middle classes have received more than their proportional share, partly because of their superior ability to

[11] Goldthorpe, Llewellyn and Payne, *Social Mobility and Class Structure in Modern Britain* (Clarendon Press, Oxford, 1980), Vol. 1, Ch. 3, 'Trends in Class Mobility', p. 85.

obtain the maximum level of help that the state provides. But that is not the only reason. Part of the cause is the subject of the opening passage of R. H. Tawney's *Equality*: 'Discussing some sixty years ago the text "Choose Equality and Flee Greed", Matthew Arnold observed that in England inequality is almost a religion.' Over a century later, Arnold's judgment still applies; although, these days, we find excuses for our insistence that the rich man in his castle and the poor man at his gate occupy their relative positions by divine will. One of the excuses is called equality of opportunity.

John Gray, perhaps Britain's leading academic exponent of the Hayekian view of society and concept of virtue, is endearingly frank about the distributive outcome of a system which combines the welfare state and equality of opportunity. Not for him the sentimentalism of the reformist right.

> The greatest net beneficiaries from the welfare state in Britain have been the professional middle classes, whose political pull and social skills have enabled them to create and to exploit a vast range of services largely sustained by tax subsidies derived from the poorer minority.[12]

The neo liberal concludes from that observation of undisputed fact that the provisions of the welfare state ought to be more strictly circumscribed. Socialists will argue that they ought to be redirected according to a more acceptable system of social justice. But whatever moral conclusion is thought to follow, the fact of maldistribution of resources is undeniable.

When equality is taken to mean 'equality of opportunity' its supporters, whether they know it or not, advocate an essentially competitive view of society, an organisation of our affairs which is based on the naturally strong contesting with the naturally weak for a share of scarce national resources. The notion is naturally most attractive to those men and women who have won or are equipped to win society's competition: the frogs of Tawney's famous analogy whose success is such a comfort to their less fortunate contemporaries.

> Intelligent tadpoles reconcile themselves to the inconvenience of their position by reflecting that though most of them will live

[12] J. Gray, in A. Ellis and K. Kumar, *Dilemmas of Liberal Democracy* (Tavistock, London, 1983), Essay 9, 'Classical Liberalism', p. 180.

to be tadpoles and nothing more, the more fortunate of the species will one day shed their tails, distend their mouths and stomachs, hop nimbly onto dry land and croak addresses to their former friends on the virtues by means of which tadpoles of character and capacity can rise to be frogs.[13]

It is essentially a nineteenth-century aspiration which conforms to the first Victorian rule of reform and philanthropy: the alleviation of suffering and injustice up to the point at which further acts of compassion and social justice might begin to disturb the accepted social order and threaten the entrenched privileges of the establishment. Equality of opportunity is also wholly consistent with the nineteenth-century view of liberty: the fallacy that it is no more than the absence of restraint. Both ideas fitted neatly together with the theory that free competition and the unfettered operation of market forces would produce the most efficient and prosperous society. Indeed, the theory of equality of opportunity was easily translated into economic terms, with human beings treated as resources which could only be used to best advantage when various market imperfections – like artificial barriers to entry into the professions – are removed. The Victorians were admirably consistent political philosophers. Their ideas on society and human progress, individual liberty and economic efficiency were all of a piece, mutually dependent, and wrong.

Samuel Smiles brought all three ideas together in his biography of George Stephenson. The engineer of genius, Smiles explained, was able to rise above all other engineers because engineering was an open profession. Had Stephenson hoped to become a soldier or civil servant of equal eminence, his ambition would have been frustrated. Entry into both those professions was limited by formal, indeed statutory, limitations. During the lifetime of the first Gladstone administration, the purchase of commissions in the army and recruitment into the civil service by personal patronage were both ended. But the class composition of both professions was barely changed; the chances of the son of an artisan becoming an army or navy officer remained negligible, and the prospects of the daughter of a labourer becoming a civil servant continued to be virtually non-existent. The introduction of equality of opportunity is the

[13] R. H. Tawney, *Equality* (Allen & Unwin, London, 1952), Ch. 3 (ii), 'Historical Background', p. 108.

classic response of the establishment to assaults upon their advantaged position. Domination is sufficiently relaxed to allow the gullible to believe that the old order has begun to change. It has changed a little, but it has not changed so much that power passes out of the hands which have traditionally held it so tightly.

Equality of opportunity is best defined as the removal of artificial barriers to progress, and is best illustrated – as it is most often exemplified – in the periodic reorganisation of the education system. The idea of liberating the pupils of talent who are, or were, denied the chance to fulfil their academic potential is intrinsically attractive. It has interested romantically inclined writers as diverse as Thomas Hardy, with *Jude the Obscure*, and Emlyn Williams in his play *The Corn is Green*. The Trades Union Congress demanded as long ago as 1896 that 'our education system should be completely remodelled on such a basis as to secure the democratic objective of equality of opportunity.' In the half-century which followed, the Hadow, Spens, Norwood and Fleming reports all suggested ways in which the educational prospects of the selected few could be improved. The apotheosis of equality of opportunity was the Butler Education Act which actually enshrined that objective in its preamble. But all the schemes – admirable as they were in their attempts to prevent poverty being a barrier to talent's progress – had a similar defect. By concentrating on the demands of gifted pupils, they directed attention away from the needs of the generality of children. So, for fifty years, the organisation of education concerned itself with 15 or 20 per cent of the school population; and the chosen 20 per cent were chosen on the results of a social steeplechase in which the ditches and hurdles were environment and heredity. Most of the eleven-plus losses could have been identified before the race began from the addresses on their entry forms.

The majority were disadvantaged, and further downgraded by movement from unsegregated primary schools to selective secondaries, because the system was not designed to meet their needs. Any system of separate development reduces (both relatively and absolutely) the prospects of the least favoured groups. As long ago as 1916, the Bradford Charter (drafted by a partnership of radicals and non-conformists) insisted that 'No longer should education be administered on the assumption that only a small minority are fit to be educated or that education is for the few'. The Conservative Party does not, and never has, accepted that opinion. Its view on education reflects its view on life. Progress is said to be dependent on the progress and performance of the élite. The most charitable interpretation of that notion is a patronising theory of progress that depends on the belief that as men and women of talent steam ahead at full speed, they will tow their old and inferior fellow citizens along in their wake. That is classical Conservatism; and it is foolish as well as uncharitable to blame Conservatives for being Conservative. What is more difficult to understand is how anyone who genuinely wanted 'universal secondary education' which involved 'parity of esteem' and equality of any sort could possibly have believed that they could achieve such a result from the selective system of secondary education. Understanding how the mistake was made will help us to untangle the real confusion between equality and equality of opportunity.

Today, it seems impossible that anyone ever honestly believed that children from the slums – badly housed, badly fed, badly protected from disease and enjoying little or no acquaintance with books – could be said to have acquired any sort of equality with their well provided suburban contemporaries, just because they took the same examination on one or two mornings of their mutually twelfth year. The built-in advantages possessed by the candidates from secure and prosperous homes were reflected in the pattern of their eleven-plus results. Jean Floud, when Principal of Newnham College, Oxford, described the situation with proper scholastic clarity: 'Social as well as academic selection is at work in schools.'

Tawney made the same point by analogy and at greater length:

> opportunities to 'rise' are not a substitute for a large measure of practical equality, nor do they make immaterial the existence of sharp disparities of income and social condition. On the contrary, it is only the presence of a high degree of practical equality which can diffuse and generalise opportunities to rise. The existence of such opportunities, in fact, and not merely in form, depends not only upon an open road but upon an equal start.[14]

[14] R. H. Tawney, *Equality* (Allen & Unwin, London, 1952), Ch. 3(ii), 'Historical Background', p. 109.

In fact, we now know that even the equal start and open road are not enough. Certainly, for the open road of, say, the competitive examination to have any relevance to equality at all, the many travellers must set out from the nearest to a common starting line that society can organise. That requires an assault on environmental deprivation, inadequate housing, domestic poverty, second-rate health care, and overcrowded primary schools, which imperfectly teach English as a second language. It requires minimum-wage legislation and an improvement in those conditions which fashion a child's prospects even before it is born. For the National Children's Bureau has taught us that physical and emotional disadvantage acquired *before* birth is impossible to shake off. But however we struggle to create an equal start, the results will be far from perfect. There will never be a contest at any point in life – whether it is competition for a nursery or secondary school place, search for first job or first house (either ownership or tenancy), or pension application – at which every contestant will stand on the same starting line. Life is an endless competition, as anyone who has applied for a discretionary benefit, a council-house transfer or non-mandatory student grant will testify. It is a race which – as presently organised – places the least advantaged at the back of the starting grid, ensuring that at each stage they fall further and further behind. So, as well as attempting to provide an equal start, early in life, we have to decide how to deal with the natural stragglers. Simply removing artificial obstacles from their path is not enough. There ought to be pre-school help for the children from homes in which books are unknown or English is a second language; post-school encouragement for young people who left full-time education without fulfilling their full potential; a national minimum wage to provide a decent standard of living for families previously dependent on income below the poverty line; extra domiciliary medical care for areas of overcrowded or inadequate housing. Tawney taught us that it is not an equal race if some of the contestants are lame. Now we have to argue that the competitors who, despite all our efforts, start out with a handicap or develop disabilities *en route* are given positive assistance to make further progress.

Attempts to argue for a system which compensates for those disadvantages that are imposed on an individual or family by society itself have been prejudiced by the name that has been given to that desirable process. 'Equality of outcome' sounds like a process by which we are all squeezed into the same mould. It is no such thing. At any one moment a snapshot of society confirms that inequalities are forced upon us by the way in which we distribute our resources and organise our institutions. Inequalities are not the 'natural' outcome of blind chance. They are often the result of the conscious decision of our forefathers (who invented the institutions of inequality) or of groups within present-day society which have a vested interest in maintaining vast disparities of wealth and power. As society is now organised, inequalities are likely to breed upon themselves and be intensified. The divergence between the social groups constantly widens. All that 'equality of outcome' demands is that society should attempt to replace those 'imposed' and ever-increasing inequalities with a conscious effort to remove or to reduce them. Equality of outcome is, in reality, a just distribution of the nation's resources – not the chance to grab something extra (which is equality of opportunity) but the real prospect of receiving a fair share of wealth and power.

Attempts to produce 'equality of outcome' have been described by some of its critics as the utopian pretence that men and women are the same or can be made identical. Egalitarians in fact, argue quite the opposite. True egalitarians know that we are all different. But they do not confuse difference and inequality. Inequality is almost always the product of society itself – the organisation of society and the standards of value which society accepts. Michael Rutter and Nicola Madge, in *Cycles of Disadvantage*, listed the extensive causes of deprivation which can be attributed to 'social structure and institutional factors', and their careful research confirms the accuracy of that conclusion to all but the most prejudiced reader. Everyone who has lived or worked in the decaying central areas of our old cities will, for example, confirm their judgment on the life chances of the

> black people [who] are subject to various forms of stigma and discrimination. This may be the result of individual attitudes and practices, but it is also important to examine the way in which society's structure leads to, or perpetuates, such discrimination. For example, certain local authorities have demanded a long period of residence before newcomers are placed on the housing list. The result of this policy is to exclude immigrants

37

from council housing and force them into private rented accommodation. When the immigrants are relatively poor and there is a period of high immigration this can lead to ghettos and immigrants' poor-quality housing. Not only does this tend to segregate immigrant families but also it leads to schools with a high proportion of immigrants and hence often schools with many children with language problems and educational retardation.[15]

The result of that can be seen today in the inner city of Birmingham. Originally the immigrants were forced to occupy low-cost and poor-quality private houses. There was then a reluctance to rehouse them – sometimes the result of overt unconscious prejudice, sometimes the product of the hard reality that clearing a house in multi-occupation required the compensating construction of half a dozen new dwellings, whereas the rehousing of a single family living in a whole, though inadequate, house allowed one property to be demolished at the expense of a single new unit. Having been driven into low-quality housing (and kept there) the immigrants (and their children, who are not immigrant at all) believed that help would come with the public purchase of their properties and the prospect of radical improvement schemes. The properties were purchased, but the cost of improvement proved too much for the government to finance adequately, and the administrative intricacies of organising what few funds were available were beyond the management skills of the Housing Department bureaucrats. Locked into the pattern of underprivilege, the immigrant families found escape wholly beyond them. Each deprivation bred the next disadvantage. The only escape would have been a massive allocation of resources specifically earmarked for the purpose of the relief of specific areas of need. Such problems demonstrate the truth of the cliché that simply spending money solves none of the problems of inequality. Money has to be directed towards the exact need, and money alone is not enough. But without the *extra* money, the inequalities will remain.

In *Cycles of Deprivation*, Rutter and Madge go on to explain how 'the existing framework of society shapes the distribution of wealth and job opportunities'. To recognise that fact is not to

[15] M. Rutter and N. Madge, *Cycles of Disadvantage* (Heinemann, London, 1976), Ch. 11, 'Conclusions', p. 314.

neglect the influence of heredity. The concept of a *cycle* of deprivation implies that it is impossible to determine where nature begins and nature ends. We are the product of our parents' genetic union. But the characteristics which we inherit are, themselves, in part the product of the environment in which our parents lived. The relative importance of the two factors cannot be measured. But the relationship was at least put into proper perspective by the National Children's Bureau. In its first report, *From Birth to Seven*, it demonstrated that, as society is presently organised, children born into disadvantage are less likely to be able to escape than to sink further and further into the abyss of deprivation. The cause is not the innate ability with which they entered the world. It is the conditions which society provides thereafter. The point is dramatically demonstrated by *Born to Fail*, the second volume of the National Children's Bureau study. Children from underprivileged homes made dramatic progress when fostered with or adopted by families who lived in more comfortable circumstances. Our progress through life is largely determined by the conditions in which we live and it is possible, by making changes in those circumstances, to improve the chances of even the least socially and intellectually endowed individual. When Matthew Arnold wrote that inequality 'on the one side . . . harms by pampering',[16] he was reminding us of what the concentration of resources can achieve – even amongst the 'barbarians' of British upper-class society. We live in an unequal society because we choose inequality. We could, if we chose to do so, organise society so as to, at least, reduce the levels of inequalities that society itself either creates or perpetuates. And if we accept that much inequality is the direct result of how society is organised, then we cannot accept the Hayek/Friedman contention that discrepancies in rewards, esteem, health and even mortality rates are the natural product of random forces – unintentional and haphazard and therefore not a matter about which it is reasonable either to complain or make moral judgments. If it is our chosen form of society which causes inequalities. Those of us who support present values and present hierarchical organisation are responsible for a social outcome which is both predictable and intended. Changing the organisa-

[16] M. Arnold, *Selected Essays* (Oxford University Press, Oxford, 1964), 'Equality'.

tion of society – to produce the most equal outcome – is what is meant by 'equality of outcome'.

A fairer distribution of resources – 'equality of outcome' as it was once called – does not depend on the pretence that human beings are born with equal endowments or in the hope that they can be moulded into identical shape. Nor do socialists hope for such dull uniformity. Socialists should rejoice in human diversity. But doing so does not require the acceptance of the divisions which are imposed on groups of diverse individuals and often – whatever sentimental Conservatives claim – results in the suppression, not the liberation, of the human spirit. The diversity of the human race and spirit is infinite and 'to criticise inequality and to desire equality is not, as is sometimes suggested, to cherish the romantic illusion that men are equal in character and intelligence.'[17] Nor is it an attempt to subvert the rôle and rights of the family – an institution of such historical strength that, even if there were a predisposition to undermine its authority, the task would be beyond the social engineers. Equality of outcome can be simply defined. To support it

> is to hold that, while natural endowments differ profoundly, it is the mark of a civilised society to aim at eliminating such inequalities as have their source, not in individual differences but in its own organisation and that individual differences which are the source of social energy, and more likely to ripen and find expression if social inequalities are, as far as practicable, diminished.[18]

There is not, in that statement, the slightest hope, hint or expectation of a society composed of identical mediocrities. It is an outright rejection of the possibility of uniformity as well as of the idea that uniformity might be desirable. It is a celebration of individuality and an insistence that, if every individual is to achieve his or her true potential, the institutional barriers to the progress of members of disadvantaged groups must be removed and an atmosphere must be created in which individuals who were previously assumed to fail are encouraged to succeed; and (most important of all) resources are allocated in a way which maximise the chances of the largest number of people achieving

[17] R. H. Tawney, *Equality* (Allen & Unwin, London, 1952), Ch. 11, 'Inequality and Social Structure', p. 49.
[18] *ibid.*

their full potential. That is not a condition which can be imposed on society; and it will not therefore achieve complete equality in any numerical or literal sense of that term. For that would be to deny liberty.

> A régime devoted to equality in its literal sense would have to be authoritarian, ready to crush inequalities wherever they reasserted themselves as they inevitably and constantly would.[19]

A fairer distribution of the nation's resources would reduce not crush differences. That is no more difficult to achieve – and no more in conflict with the natural order of things – than to organise society and distribute resources in a way which promotes inequality.

Defined in those terms – the terms on which its advocates have always insisted – real equality is an attainable aim, sneered at only by 'practical' men and women who hide behind their ignorance to disguise their prejudice. Tawney provided the perfect answer to those down-to-earth cynics who urge the prophets of change to understand that no two children come into the world with identical attributes. That is agreed, wrote Tawney, but what is our opinion of the father who lavishes family income exclusively on his healthiest son, or the mother who cares only for her cleverest daughter? That is how we distribute our resources and esteem within society. Caring parents know – if we can pay respect to the practical men and women by pursuing their homely metaphor – the *differences* in the talent, strength, potential and perhaps even virtue of their children. But they do not treat them *unequally*. They know that nature (they may call it God) makes us different, but that society makes us unequal. It can never be reorganised in a way which eliminates inequalities completely; but it can be changed in a way which reduces inequality and enormously increases the life chances of millions of families. That is irrefutable. And once the fact is conceded, it requires some quick-footed casuistry to explain why the higher levels of practical equality should be rejected. But one objection can be disposed of at once. It is the contention that growth makes equality *unnecessary*; that it is tolerable to be held in an inferior position to one's neighbour as long as there is an absolute improvement in material well-

[19] R. Norman, *Radical Philosophy*, Spring 1985, p. 85.

being. Growth – even if we ever achieve it again to the degree which we believed to be possible in the 1950s – may actually result in the least advantaged sections of society not only falling further and further behind, but being permanently denied the chance even to enjoy the absolute levels of satisfaction which their more prosperous contemporaries have long taken for granted. Michael Young and Peter Willmott considered society as a moving column in which the leaders are, naturally enough,

> the first to wheel in a new direction. The last rank keeps its distance from the first and the distance between them does not lessen. But as the column advances, the last rank has passed some time before . . . The people in the rear cannot, without breaking rank and rushing ahead reach where the van *is*, but since the whole column is moving forward they can hope to reach where the van *was*.[20]

That image – more than Tawney's famous analogy of tadpoles and frogs – represents the popular justification of inequality. It is the 'trickle-down effect', the best way, yet discovered, to legitimise a market distribution of resources which, by its nature, spreads material rewards unevenly. If we can demonstrate that, by allowing the favoured few to surge ahead, the generality of men and women will be pulled along behind them, the moral case for inequality is far less difficult to argue. According to Schumpeter, capitalism has brought the silk stocking that was once the privilege of queens to every shop girl. And if we could believe that market allocation eventually benefited everyone, the argument about relative levels of reward and different levels of prosperity would largely be about timing, and the whole case for equality might be out of date as its critics suggest. But socialists, observing the empirical evidence of the way in which benefits have trickled down, have to ask themselves the question: if the progress for which we argue concerns more than material goods, will the rear ranks in the column of life ever receive the benefits which were enjoyed by the front ranks when they travelled over new and virgin ground? Twenty years ago Fred Hirsch questioned the very concept of continual growth. Commenting on the Young–Willmott metaphor he insisted that 'growth is a substitute for redistribution of resources for the worse off only in its early stages'.

[20] F. Young and P. Wilmott, *The Symmetrical Family* (Penguin, London, 1975).

. . . by the time that the sought-after ground is reached by the rear of the column, that ground will have been affected by the passage of the column itself. These effects are not only psychological. . . . More extensive proliferation of particular commodities also affects their characteristics in an objective, non-psychological way, by affecting the environment in which they are used. . . . For the family in the tail end of the Young–Willmott march that acquires its automobile after the luxury of pleasure-driving has been qualified by congestion and parking restrictions (while the necessity of car ownership has been established by the decay of public transport) . . . passing the once vaunted milestones of car-ownership . . . may appear less a release from its old subordinate position than a new facet of an unchanged subordinate reality.[21]

We cannot, in honesty, argue that growth will even one day solve the problems of the poor, or take refuge in the fashionable pretence of the 1960s that economic expansion will be continuous and that it absolves us from worry about how our national income is distributed. Tony Crosland has often been accused of falling into both traps – of believing that growth would go on for ever and of hoping that growth in itself would absolve all democratic socialists from determining a morally just theory of distribution. What Crosland wrote, as distinct from what he was accused of writing, is more a statement of the obvious than a philosophical error.

The achievement of greater equality without intolerable social stress and probable curtailment of liberty depends heavily upon economic growth. The better-off have been able to accept with reasonable equanimity a decline in their relative standard of living because growth has enabled them (almost) to maintain their absolute standard of living despite redistribution.[22]

That contention is, in itself, correct. In the absence of economic expansion, greater equality is more necessary and more difficult. But, even in the wholly propitious conditions of continual increase in national income, the achievement of a more equal society requires specific action to achieve that end. Indeed, the alleviation of the suffering which comes from

---

[21] F. A. Hirsch, *Social Limits to Growth* (Routledge & Kegan Paul, London, 1978), Ch. 12, p. 167.
[22] C. A. R. Crosland, *The Future of Socialism* (Jonathan Cape, London, 1980), Pt 5, 'Economic Growth and Efficiency'.

relative poverty will not come about without a conscious determination to achieve greater equality. The equality we seek is equality of outcome – the state organised to reduce rather than to accentuate natural differences. That pattern of social organisation is both practical and necessary. Indeed, it is so obviously right for our society that the vested interests which oppose equality have to invent objections to its extension. They are the first two defences of inequality which were listed at the beginning of this chapter – its alleged malign effects on individual liberty and economic efficiency. It is because socialists have been so reticent about advancing the theory of equality that its opponents have been allowed to propagate, largely unchallenged, the dangerous nonsense which they set out as the theory of distribution within the competitive and unequal society.

Chapter Three

Do the Poor
Need the Rich?

Equality is more easily promoted at times of economic growth, but during times of economic stagnation or decline the promotion of equality becomes all the more necessary. As the economy expands, the rich and powerful can enjoy an increase in the level of their absolute income, whilst at the same time suffering the relative decline that equality demands – and the absolute increase makes the relative decline tolerable. The confidence which comes from enjoying the benefits of a buoyant economy breeds the generous spirit which is necessary if the men and women with influence as well as wealth are to support those policies which adversely affect their relative position. Conversely, when there is a shortage of resources – when, for instance, the financial demands made by an ageing population and improved medical techniques outstrip the government's estimate of what can be spent on health and hospitals – it seems, to most civilised and compassionate people, essential that the limited resources be distributed according to some notion of social justice.

That assertion illustrates the classical objection to equality – indeed, to any social system other than the operation of an unhindered market: it is impossible to argue that *everyone* believes in the distribution of limited resources according to the same, or indeed to any, notion of social justice. It is the basic tenet of the new libertarian right that since there is no generally agreed concept of how anything – scarce or not – should be distributed, it would be wrong to impose any one pattern on the population as a whole and thus oblige some people to accept a standard of values to which they do not subscribe. The application of such a principle leads to the conclusion that since, for example, there is no agreement about the way in which the use of scarce dialysis machines are allocated, it would be wrong to impose any pattern of allocation on society, other than the right of those who can afford them to buy life and health, whilst the less well-off suffer and die.

That is, of course, a central pillar in the philosophical edifice built around F. A. Hayek. It is a ramshackle construction, derelict behind its elegant façade. But its influence on contemporary politics is undeniably immense. A philosophy which, twenty years ago, was regarded as a joke, has become the guiding light of the new right in Britain and America. Margaret Thatcher makes passing obeisance to the theories of *The Road to Serfdom*, whilst the Centre for Policy Studies, which her supporters created to make the Conservative Party conservative again, spends much of its time and energy translating Hayek's principles into what passes for political practice. In the United States, the Reaganite right has always aspired to translate the Hayek theories into the day-to-day business of government.[1] This philosophical edifice poses three attractions. First, it claims to be complete and consistent, offering an answer to every political question. Second, it masquerades as a defence of freedom, and therefore enjoys the appearance of a doctrine which liberates and emancipates. Third, it justifies great disparities in power and wealth – an attribute which is always attractive to the powerful and wealthy.

It is important (before we examine his work in detail in later chapters) to have a clear picture of the policies which flow from the acceptance of Hayek's philosophy. Hayek himself usually propounds generalities. It is his disciples who examine the specific implications of the doctrine that society should not impose on its members a standard of values to which some of them do not subscribe. In his essay 'Classical Liberalism, Positional Goods and the Politicisation of Poverty', John Gray could hardly be more frank; and his frankness is reinforced by the provision of examples to bolster up a theory which Hayek himself is normally wise enough to leave in the area of abstract generalities.

---

[1] For a glimpse into the Washington argument about whether or not President Reagan fulfilled his free-market destiny see David A. Stockman, *The Triumph of Politics* (Bodley Head, London, 1986).

Not all basic needs are even in principle satiable. Think only of medical needs connected with senescence. These are surely basic needs in that their non-satisfaction will result in death or a worthless life, but (contrary to the quietly apocalyptic hopes which inspired the writers of the Beveridge Report) there is no natural limit on the resources which could be devoted to satisfying them.[2]

Having established – at least, to his own satisfaction – the inability of modern society to meet the medical needs of its members, Mr Gray then goes on to suggest how the limited resources should be distributed; health and housing no less than any other commodity. His answer is, of course, through the market – though he has the grace to admit, by implication, that even the market is a social system and that it might be difficult to overcome 'the obstacles encountered in gaining general assent to procedural principles of market justice'. But he does not allow such intellectual fastidiousness to divert him from his central thesis. 'The traditional defence of market freedom – that it permits different cultures and value systems to live in peaceful co-existence – has never been more relevant or more neglected than it is now.'[3]

Philosophers of the free-market system ought to choose their words more carefully. In the example quoted above, market freedom does not encourage all members of society to live in either peaceful co-existence or in anything else. It encourages them to die if they cannot afford necessary medical treatment; and when they resent being left to die, they are accused by Conservative propagandists of succumbing to the sin of envy. Like so many of the arguments of the libertarian right, the argument upon which that accusation is based is wholly circular. For if – as socialists claim – a man or woman has the right to a decent level of medical care, resentment at not receiving it is properly described not as envy but as righteous anger. That is particularly true in a society which could allow such elementary rights to be respected, if its members agreed to its being organised in a way which promoted that moral aim.

For readers who feel some astonishment at the blandness with which the new right advocate a system which leaves the poor to

---

[2] J. Gray, *Dilemmas of Liberal Democracy* (Tavistock, London, 1983), 'Classical Liberalism, Positional Goods and the Politicisation of Poverty', p. 182.
[3] *ibid.*, p. 183.

die – and invests it with a moral justification – Mr Gray provides a clue to the cause of the tortuous reasoning of the libertarian right when he writes that 'The traditional defence of market freedom has never been more necessary and never been more neglected.'[4] He means that the legitimacy of market distribution has now to be defended in new terms. When growth was continuous in Western Europe, and thought to be capable of replication in Asia, Africa and South America, the iniquities of market distribution were blurred. Even the poor were doing slightly better than last year and the year before, and it was hoped that the expanding economies of Europe, North America and the Soviet bloc would finance the improvements which would end famine in India and sub-Saharan Africa. Indeed, it was argued that the market system was bringing benefits to the poor which other economic régimes could not provide – and that those benefits were actually *dependent* upon the inequalities inherent within it. Hayek could not have been more explicit.

> If today in the United States or Western Europe the relatively poor can have a car or refrigerator, or aeroplane trip or radio at the cost of a reasonable part of their income, this was made possible because in the past others with large incomes were able to spend it on what was then a luxury. The path of advance is greatly eased by the fact that it has been trodden before.[5]

The images of political philosophy are repeated over and over again in different forms. For it will be remembered that Hirsch – extending the metaphors of echelon advance – concluded that after the front ranks in the column had trampled on the ground of new prosperity, it would not prove so fertile for the rest of the formation. But Hayek has no doubts.

> It is because scouts have found the goal that the road can be built for the less lucky and the less energetic . . . Many of the improvements would indeed never have become a possibility for all if they had not long before been available for some. If all had to wait for better things until they could be provided for all, that day would, in many instances, never come. Even the poorest today owe their relative material well-being to results of past inequality.[6]

[4] *ibid.*, p. 182.
[5] F. A. Hayek, *The Constitution of Liberty* (Routledge & Kegan Paul, London, 1960), p. 44.
[6] *ibid.*, p. 44.

It is difficult to imagine a more seductive moral justification for the persistence of inequalities. Indeed, it is so elegant and persuasive an argument for the propriety of immediate poverty that it is difficult not to regret that it suffers from the one simple defect of being wrong – or at least of having less and less validity as the developments of an increasingly complicated society encourage the men and women in the rear ranks of the marching column to aspire to more than the simple material possessions. For the 'trickle-down', 'echelon', or 'spread-out' effects of the progress made by the privileged minority in an unequal society are diminishing. And as they decline, the moral justification for a market theory of distribution declines as well.

It is one thing to defend manifest inequalities if, as a direct result of the initiatives which they generate, the disadvantaged and the dispossessed are eventually dragged along behind the prosperous chariots of their more fortunate contemporaries. But it is quite another to justify inequalities which are permanent, self-perpetuating and likely to entrench rather than eventually diminish the disadvantages suffered by the generality of men and women. It has been fashionable, amongst the new right, to scoff at the socialist revisionist theories of Tony Crosland because they are dependent upon – or at least hypothesise – continuous growth. But the post-war Conservatism of Butler, Macleod and Macmillan had an equally vested interest in permanent economic expansion, for it was what legitimised the hierarchical social system which they supported. Once the certainty of growth no longer offers the promise of general and continual – if socially protracted – improvement, it becomes no longer possible to justify a system of market allocation as the best possible way of eventually benefiting every group within society. In such circumstances, the task of justifying the unregulated economy becomes infinitely more difficult. Indeed, it requires the construction of an acceptable theory of distribution – a task which the optimists of free enterprise have until recently found unnecessary since, in the fifties and sixties, they were able to argue complacently that the poor, as well as the rich, were obviously benefiting from a still largely *laissez faire* economy and an organisation of society calculated to preserve rather than eliminate inequalities.

This chapter has largely been concerned with the effects of markets on the distribution of resources and the result such a system of allocation has for the poor and low-paid. Future chapters will return to the subject of markets and consider their importance for economic efficiency and their rôle in securing a state which is free from bureaucratic control. Such considerations are best carried out with the assistance of evidence and example. The attitudes towards markets demonstrates a difference in intellectual method (perhaps even in psychology) between the philosophers of the new right and their genuinely libertarian opponents. The new right believes in – perhaps even has an emotional need for – philosophic iron laws: rules which can be constantly applied with certain moral and economic effect. So the philosophers argue that market allocation is *always* right – even though it may have to be abandoned in time of war, pestilence or plague (though significantly not famine which only affects the poor). Socialists should not attempt to mirror their absolutism by insisting that market allocation is always wrong. In some areas it is essential; in others it is intolerable. What is certain is that years of expansion obscure the need to decide when market allocation is necessary and where it is undesirable.

The assertion – backed up by some evidence during the post-war years – that material growth had produced eventual advantage for even the lowest income group enabled the moderate right to answer the questions concerning the morality of their social system with unbounded confidence. For, of course, there is no doubt that in conditions of sustained growth the material condition of the lower-income groups did improve. Nothing else was possible. It would have been truly amazing had the richest 10 per cent of the population *all* acquired both town and country houses with electronically controlled garage doors and sunken baths whilst *all* the poorest 10 per cent had remained in shared accommodation and property unfit for human habitation. The real world is not like that. What has happened is that *most* of the top 10 per cent live in relative splendour whilst most of the *lowest* decile exist in absolute poverty. What matters is whether or not the success of the most advantaged group promotes, or is responsible for, improvements lower down the income scale. The evidence suggests that it is not. On the elimination of poverty and the promotion of equality, the evidence is categorical. As we have become a more prosperous nation we have not become a more equal society. In the ten years since 1976 the number of families below the DHSS poverty line has steadily increased, irrespective of movements in gross national income. Indeed the evidence confirms that whenever the general level of prosperity is threatened (or even the rate of growth slows down) the rich find excuses for protecting themselves at the expense of the rest. During the Thatcher years taxation policy has redistributed income by taking from the poor and giving to the wealthy. There has been a trickle-up effect. If we are to end poverty, we must proceed directly and effectively to decide how best to identify social justice and then to promote what we have defined.

John Rawls, the most fashionable proponent of the notion that social justice is a condition which can be identified and measured, actually laid down principles by which those who believe in equality should relate it to the practical needs of the poor.

> All social values, liberty and opportunity, income and wealth and the bases of self respect are to be distributed equally *unless equal distribution of any or all of these values is to everyone's disadvantage.*[7]

To that assertion, the moderate right, in the years in which we never had it so good, would have indicated assent – qualified only by their empirical judgment that in most instances the 'unequal distribution of any or all' of such values *is* 'to everyone's advantage', as it encourages and promotes the trickle-down effect. To them the National Health Service was a product of private medicine and compassion. The new right of Hayek and Friedman would argue differently, insisting that the provision of state-funded welfare – to say nothing of the pursuit of equality – was always and automatically detrimental to society as a whole since it invariably diminishes liberty and impairs allocative efficiency. Democratic socialists, not enjoying the dubious certainties of support for an absolute and universally applicable principle, do not expect to achieve – nor do they strive to create – 'complete equality'. The socialist obligation is to regard equality as the ideal condition, the state for which they should strive, since it is essential to the achievement of the liberty which is socialism's aim. But there will be times when the promotion of further equality is either impossible or undesirable.

---

[7] J. Rawls, *A Theory of Justice* (Oxford University Press, Oxford, 1972), Vol. 2, Ch. 11, 'The Principles of Justice', p. 62.

It was in an attempt to draw the boundary line between desired equality and necessary inequality that Rawls drew up his 'Difference Principle':

> It must be reasonable for each relevant representative man defined by this structure (i.e. the socially just level of inequality), when he views it as a going concern, to prefer his prospects with the inequality to his prospects without it.[8]

It is by the application of these two imperatives that Rawls answers the question: what can possibly justify the 'initial inequalities in life prospects' which distinguish the property owner from the unskilled labourer? According to the difference principle, such inequalities are only justified 'if the difference in expectation is to the advantage of the representative man who is worse off'. At least Rawls takes the presumption of equality as his first principle – the 'natural state' of Matthew Arnold and the nineteenth-century egalitarians. But although he describes the circumstances which would justify a departure from the pursuit of equality, he describes them in a way which makes it impossible for practical politicians to recognise the moment when it arrives. He provides a formula without numbers which gives no hint about how much inequality is likely to promote the absolute interests of the worse-off. And, against the background of a popular belief that inequality is the necessary precursor to economic growth, the 'Difference Principle' offers to those who choose so to interpret it little more than a sophisticated justification for a large degree of inequality. Rawls holds the view that 'a theory of justice depends on a theory of society'; and it is difficult to believe that there would be general support for a theory of society which permanently relegated a majority of citizens to second-class status without offering them the compensation of absolute, if not relative, advance. It is impossible to imagine a theory of justice which would defend inequalities between its citizens (of a sort which is within society's power to eradicate) if those inequalities were not at least represented as in some way improving the lot of the least advantaged men and women. Rawls's 'Difference Principle' possesses all the charm of the blossoms and fruits which flourish on the middle ground of politics. The new right can accept it

[8] *ibid.*, p. 69.

with the observation that 'of course' the rational man at the bottom of society's heap realises that he would be even more deprived were it not for the existence of the millionaire at the apex above him. The sentimental radical can embrace it with the comment that 'of course' sentimental radicals would be wholly opposed to inequality, were it not for its beneficial effects on the depressed and dispossessed.

To express reservations about the indicative importance of the difference principle is not to dismiss, or even to disagree with, the critique of modern society which appears in Rawls's *Theory of Justice*. Rather it is an expression of fear that such an eminently reasonable analysis will be intentionally misinterpreted by vested interests and changed from the opposition to inequality (unless it can be proved, positively, to benefit the less well-off) into the assertion that inequality does benefit the less well-off and is, therefore, to be encouraged. Rawls himself knows better. Indeed, in one paragraph, he brilliantly sums up the essential socialist contention that economic and political freedom are indivisible.

> Historically one of the main defects of constitutional government has been the failure to ensure the fair value of political liberty. The necessary corrective steps have not been taken, indeed they never seem to have been seriously entertained. Disparities in the distribution of property and wealth that far exceed what is compatible with political equality have generally been tolerated by the legal system . . . Moreover the effect of injustices in the political system are much more grave and long-lasting than market imperfections. Thus inequalities in the economic and social system may soon undermine whatever political equality might have existed under fortunate historical conditions.[9]

The connection between economic and political equality is central to the democratic socialist view of society and is reflected in the Crosland aphorism that until we are equal we cannot be free. But it is difficult to believe that the fashionable radicals' acceptance of the difference principle has helped us to remedy the state of affairs which Rawls describes. For the difference principle says that in a decent society we should accept inequalities only when they are positively beneficial to the whole

---

[9] *ibid.*, Vol. 4, Ch. 36, 'Equal Liberty', p. 226.

community. And we can all endorse that view. Socialists, believing in freedom as well as equality, do not support the rigid bureaucratic imposition of equality that impairs liberty as well as efficiency. The libertarian right believe in the intrinsic propriety of inequality, see its trickle-down effects as a supplementary justification, and welcome any theory which gives general legitimacy to a doctrine which, by the generality of citizens, would be regarded as unacceptable were it not for its real or imagined saving graces.

The socialist task is to examine three opinions about the consequences of inequality. The first is the contention that inequality is to the direct benefit of the least advantaged sections of society, since it produces an eventual improvement in their absolute condition. The second is the view that a large measure of inequality is necessary for economic efficiency and material growth – irrespective of how the product of that efficiency and growth is distributed. The third is that inequality is essential to freedom. All three assertions are diametrically wrong. But each is desperately necessary to give a moral justification to a theory which allows, indeed encourages, vast riches to exist alongside grinding poverty. The legitimacy of inequality is crucially dependent on the demonstration of its general, rather than particular, benefits. It would be unfair to suggest that Keith Joseph and Jonathan Sumpton represent the most intellectually distinguished advocates of inequality, but in their little book they do demonstrate how a politician, preparing for government, justifies his belief in the necessity to reduce the higher rate of personal taxation.

> Not only is there no benefit to the poor, but to the extent that confiscatory rates of tax discourage the creation of wealth, the poor are actually worse off than they would be in a society of sharp contrasts . . . Ultimately the capacity of any society to look after its poor is dependent upon the total amount of its wealth, however distributed . . . Human motivation is illusive. No one can demonstrate conclusively what is the effect of redistribution on economic effort. But the proposition that its effect is damaging rather than beneficent is so plainly consonant with common sense as to require from those who would deny it a convincing body of evidence which has not been forthcoming.[10]

[10] K. Joseph and J. Sumpton, *Equality* (John Murray, London, 1979), Ch. 2, 'Equality and the Public Interest', p. 23.

That is a rag-bag of sophistry, half-truths, and logical errors. But it is slightly better than simply saying that the rich should retain their wealth and be damned to the consequences upon others. The free market system needs a theory of distribution which gives it a moral legitimacy.

Moral legitimacy is a noble description of a noble condition, but the concept has its practical applications. If, in a democracy, the people believe that the economic system which governs their lives and prospects cannot be defended or justified by any ethical agreement, they are likely to vote for a change in that system – particularly if that system effects an organisation of society which is detrimental to the material interests of a majority of its citizens. The new libertarians of the far right, as well as being deeply contemptuous of democracy, have no illusions about the consequences for their ideology if they are unable to represent their beliefs as being in the *general* public interest. Hayek sets out the dangers of letting the people decide on how a nation's wealth is spent. Those dangers he regards as so threatening to the social order in which he believes that he openly asserts the superiority of non-elective government (working within the framework of legal or constitutional restraints) over unlimited democracy. As is so often the case with the philosophers of the libertarian right, general theories are not illuminated by practical examples of their application. But the obvious instance of non-elective – but limited – government is Franco's Spain, in which the Caudillo's powers were constrained within boundaries laid down by the army. To Hayek and his followers, such a system avoids the excesses which are certain now that a 'wholesome method of arriving at widely acceptable political decisions has become the pretext for enforcing substantially egalitarian aims.'[11] They do things differently in autocracies, and at least they avoid the dangers of democracy which worry Hayek and his followers most. It is an attribute of the democratic process that is central to socialist ideology. Democracies have a built-in tendency to pursue the greatest good of the greatest number, an inclination to support the masses against the classes and, from Hayek's point of view, a fatal inclination to confuse the liberty of the subject with the subject's ability to exercise the rights that liberty theoretically

[11] F. A. Hayek, *New Studies* (Routledge & Kegan Paul, London, 1978), Ch. 10, 'Whither Democracy?'), p. 152.

provides. 'It is only too easy to pass from defining liberty as the absence of obstacles to the realisation of our desires or even more generally the absence of external impediments. This is equivalent to interpreting it as the effective power to do what we want.'[12]

It is the habit of the new right to extend arguments to their illogical conclusions. The contention that freedom, defined as the power to act, is an unattainable ideal since it requires absolute power for every individual is dealt with in detail in the next chapter. But it is necessary to deal with each of the new libertarian right's *reductio ad absurdum* as they appear. Perhaps complete freedom is 'the power to do what we want'. Certainly that is the definition usually accepted by absolute monarchs and millionaires. And that complete freedom is clearly not available to everyone. But that is not an argument for refusing to extend *any* powers and *any* freedom. We should attempt to increase powers and increase freedom as much as possible for as many people as possible.

In the piping days of post-war prosperity, it was believed by politicians of both the moderate left and moderate right that no theory of distribution was necessary. Economic growth – as well as potentially facilitating the greater equality for which Crosland argued – seemed to render the case for equality outdated. For life was seen to be gradually improving at every level of income and within every section of society, and calls for a change in the pattern of distribution were seen as the fetishes of radical intellectuals, stoical aesthetes who attempted to exploit what was vulgarly called 'the politics of envy'.

The philosopher's stone is no longer turning lead into gold. Expansion is no longer seen as certain and unremitting; and, despite variable levels of increase in gross domestic product, thirty years after the Macmillan boom convinced us all that we would never have it bad again, many of the problems of the underprivileged remain unresolved. The comparative position of the classes was examined in the previous chapter. But even in absolute terms, the condition of the least advantaged has not so much failed to improve but literally deteriorated. Unemployment remains at a level which, three decades ago, would have

[12] F. A. Hayek, *The Constitution of Liberty* (Routledge & Kegan Paul, London, 1960), p. 17.

been dismissed as both intolerable and inconceivable; a million families live in inadequate accommodation; the health service no longer meets all the needs of its potential patients; the earnings-related pension scheme, which during the 1970s seemed to be a natural development of the diffusion of prosperity, is judged to be beyond the nation's means. For a large part of the population, the old hopes of economic expansion's automatic benefits have not been realised. There are colour television sets in more living rooms, and continental holidays enliven the existences of the middle as well as the upper classes; but the major boons of house, health, job, income and pension have not trickled down from the chairman of British Oxygen, on a salary of £700,000 a year, to the unemployed steelworker whose redundancy has reduced the consumption of industrial gas without causing a similar cut in the salary of the chief executive of Britain's premier industrial gas producer.

It would be easy to argue that our present failures to meet the needs of the least privileged 30 per cent of the population is the transient result of government policy. But government policy is to let the market determine the difficult questions of distribution. What Thatcherism has proved is that a combination of market allocation and the trickle-down effect does not automatically benefit the lower-income groups – especially when economic growth is neither spectacular nor continuous. Indeed, the real achievement of economic growth has been to mask the unequal distribution of resources and give a spurious moral validity to a system which always allocated most to the rich and least to the poor. Yet the failure of Western Europe economies to expand at the regular rate which Crosland anticipated is said to demonstrate that egalitarian socialism is outdated. Had not egalitarian socialists combined intellectual diffidence and distaste for ideology in equal measure, the neglect of a third of the population would have been properly accepted as the failure of a market system of allocation *alone* (the qualification is important), either under conditions of growth, when only the appearance of social justice is created, or under conditions of stagnation when the illusion is shattered.

Indeed, it may well be that by *definition* even continuous growth cannot provide increasing benefits for a widening circle of recipients in any other area than that of a limited number of what Fred Hirsch describes in *Social Limits to Growth* as 'unmet biological needs'.[13] In conditions of unremitting growth and technical innovation, chickens and pocket calculators may become available at points further down the income scale. But some goods – 'positional goods' – remain permanently unavailable despite growth, or even because of it, for the value of positional goods depends on their scarcity. The possession of a motor car in 1955 was – for the daily commuter into Central London from Kent or Surrey – an asset of an order quite different from that of a motor car owned by a commuter today. The extended possession of a once rare commodity has not only reduced the esteem which its ownership provides. It actually reduces its utility – leaving workers who cannot afford commuter fares to struggle in their low-capacity cars through London traffic jams whilst better-off travellers choose to buy first-class season tickets on Southern Railways.

The paradigm of the positional good is the single man in a crowd standing on tip-toe and thus gaining an advantage over the rest. Once the whole crowd stands on tip-toe, his positional advantage is lost. An example, at once more realistic than standing on tip-toe and socially more appealing than the possession of a motor car, is higher education. Half a century ago, it was the preserve of either the wealthy and well connected or the prodigiously talented. When the eleven-plus successes of the Butler Education Act took their places in the expanded red-brick universities of the 1950s, a degree seemed (and usually was) the passport to security and prosperity – and possibly even wealth and power. But the creation of new universities and the extension, through the binary system, of higher education opportunities within the polytechnics, has not offered the new generation of students all the advantages which their predecessors (generally known as undergraduates) possessed. They know no less about Shakespeare or Rousseau and probably more about biochemistry and glass technology. But they are not guaranteed the place in society which a degree once made certain. 'In the positional sector,' says Hirsch, 'there is no such thing as levelling up. One's reward is set by one's position on the slope and the slope itself prevents a levelling from below as well as from above.'[14] It is as well, at this point, to recall the evidence from

[13] F. A. Hirsch, *Social Limits to Growth* (Routledge & Kegan Paul, London, 1960), Ch. 12, 'The Liberal Market as a Transition Case', p. 175.
[14] *ibid.*, p. 176.

the *Oxford Social Mobility Survey* quoted in the previous chapter. The chances of a working-class man or woman obtaining a higher education place are – as compared with the chances of their middle-class contemporaries – no better today than they were fifty years ago. And those working-class students who graduate from universities or polytechnics discover that the material benefit which they receive from their enhanced status is considerably less than that which was engaged by persons of similar academic attainment in their parents' or grandparents' generation. It is difficult to argue that growth time and natural progress have solved all their problems without politicians needing to work out an acceptable system of distribution. We are, in a very real sense, back to Tawney's tadpoles. It is *impossible* for everyone to become a frog. What Hirsch calls the 'bourgeois objective' of middle-class levels of remuneration and security 'spreading down' is an unattainable aspiration. Alfred Marshall's dream of 'the official distinction between working men and gentlemen' being replaced by a society in which 'by occupation at least every man is a gentleman'[15] is not going to come true. There is no easy or automatic road to utopia. The idea that growth and technology are going to solve all the problems of distribution and equality is a chimera. It is a chimera which the currently rich and powerful have a vested interest in preserving, but it is a chimera nevertheless.

Hirsch – though not Hirsch alone – saw developments in modern society which 'qualify both the priority and the promise of economic growth in two major ways'. The first is the existence of positional goods, which means that expansion fails to deliver its anticipated potential because it 'runs into social scarcity'. The second reason why growth is not and cannot be an indefinite and permanent panacea is of greater importance to socialists who believe that the state must operate according to acceptable ethical principles. The 'continuation of the growth process', says Hirsch, 'rests on moral preconditions that its own success has jeopardised through its individualistic ethos'. By 'the growth process' Hirsch means, of course, more than an annual increase in gross domestic product. Growth has become 'a substitute for redistribution of resources for the worse-off'[16] and

[15] Quoted in A. C. Pigou, *Memorials of Alfred Marshall* (Macmillan, London, 1925), pp. 101–118.
[16] F. A. Hirsch, *Social Limits to Growth* (Routledge & Kegan Paul, London, 1960), p. 175.

has allowed twentieth-century governments to 'duck' in practice

> the issue that nineteenth-century liberals mostly ducked in their theories – the choice of preserving the full fruits of individual opportunity and unrestricted individual choice available to a minority, as against making the adaptations necessary to extend these fruits to the majority.[17]

For years, the social limits to growth were implicitly recognised and accepted by a willingly hierarchical society. Then, as education and increasing political power made the admission of a fixed class system impossible, came the notion that the natural processes of the market would end all social evils.

It has not done so, and few people now honestly believe that it will or ever can. And the people who possess the power to remedy the ills of poverty and deprivation do not possess the will to use the market system to bring an end to those conditions. The concept of restraint – for the skilled worker, no less than the managing director – has been removed by the development of an individualistic, as distinct from a co-operative, ethic. Income has become a measure of worth as well as the means to material abundance. Frogs grew increasingly reluctant to stretch down from their lily pads and use their energies and resources to give competing tadpoles a helping hand towards higher status. By its nature – philosophical and psychological, as well as economic – the increasingly competitive society could not exhibit the virtues of community and compassion.

Without the veneer of community and compassion, the free-market system was left in desperate need of moral legitimacy. One refuge was the notion that the market rewards merit. But that idea is fatally undermined by the advantages gained from inherited wealth and the windfall gains which are an essential feature of the free-market system. Indeed one aspect of market operation which is wholly predictable is the way that it rewards wealth in general: those who go into the market system with most are likely to come out of it with most. Indeed, they are likely to come out of it with more. The market is predictable in its ability to perpetuate the existing pattern of distribution; changing no more than disparities of wealth and power, and

---

[17] *ibid.*, Ch. 13, 'Inferences for Policy', p. 188.

changing them by widening the gaps between rich and poor. It is difficult to see the market as some sort of omnipotent method of helping the virtuous and punishing the wicked – unless being heir to a fortune or winning the pools is, in itself, a mark of virtue. Even Hayek, who came to the rescue of the market system of distribution, did not believe in what appears to be Margaret Thatcher's view – namely, that the godly prosper and the sinful go bankrupt.

> It is probably a misfortune that, especially in the USA, popular writers like Samuel Smiles and Horatio Alger and later the sociologist W. G. Sumner have defended free enterprise on the ground that it regularly rewards the deserving . . .[18]

For, according to Hayek's view, markets allocate benefits according to only one principle – unpredictability. Indeed, it is the unpredictable quality of market distribution that makes it central to Hayek's economic theories. We must assume that he (erroneously) believes market behaviour to be impossible to forecast. But when he turns to politics, he is prepared to *pretend* that the market has a moral validity. What is more, he is absolutely open in his admission of the necessary pretence. Whether his supporters, who appear genuinely to believe that what Hayek says about markets deserves to be represented as the truth, make their error out of ignorance of the master's work or sheer expediency hardly matters. For Hayek is explicit in the need to disguise the market's real effects for the sake of good order and discipline.

> It is therefore a real dilemma to what extent we ought to encourage in the young the belief that when they really try they will succeed, or should rather emphasise that inevitably some unworthy will succeed and some worthy fail – whether we ought to allow the views of those groups to prevail with whom the over-confidence in the appropriate reward of the able and the industrious is strong and who, in consequence, will do much that benefits the rest and whether, without such partly erroneous beliefs, the large number will tolerate actual dif-

---

[18] F. A. Hayek, *Law Legislation and Liberty* (Routledge & Kegan Paul, London, 1982), Vol. 2, Ch. 9, 'Social or Distributive Justice', p. 74. For an example of the misfortune to which Hayek refers (and for a little innocent amusement) it is worth reading George Gilder's *The Spirit of Enterprise*. He concludes that 'bull headed, defiant, tenacious, creative entrepreneurs continue to solve the problems of the world even faster than the world could create them. The achievement of enterprise remained the highest testimony to the mysterious strength of the human spirit.'

ferences in rewards which will be based only partly on achievement and partly on mere chance.[19]

So much for the justice of the free-market system, and so much for either the honesty or the understanding of many of its supporters. A system based on a deceit cannot possess any intrinsic moral legitimacy. And it cannot be made permanently acceptable simply by abusing those who expose its dishonesty with the accusation that they propagate the politics of envy.

Socialists ought to support and advocate the extension of equality as a matter of principle, which, if not an end in itself, is so closely related to the ultimate goal of freedom that – like life, liberty and the pursuit of happiness – it needs no justification. But socialists should also remember themselves and remind others that a community in which a high proportion of the population doubts the validity of the principles by which they receive society's rewards is likely to be in constant turmoil. Inner-city riots, the alienation of the young, apparently point-less industrial disputes, and teenage violence are all the visible products of a society which allocates its rewards by chance rather than on principle – a society which has recognised that most tadpoles will not become frogs, not least because the existing frogs wish to keep the immergent members of the species permanently submerged. And for every public manifes-tation of resentment and rejection, there are a thousand other examples of disenchantment sublimated and disillusion subdued. Habermas asked the crucial – if ponderously-worded question:

> How would the members of a social system, at a given stage in the development of productive forces, have collectively and bindingly interpreted their needs (and which norm would they have accepted as justified) if they could and would have decided on the organisation of social intercourse through discursive will formation with adequate knowledge of the limiting conditions and functional imperatives of society?[20]

In translation that means: if the people knew, first, that even the most passionate proponents of free market distribution made no claims for the moral validity of the way it allocated resources; second, that the hope of market-created inequalities

---

[19] ibid.
[20] J. Habermas, *Legitimation Crisis* (Heinemann, London, 1976), p. 113.

eventually benefiting the generality of men and women in any way other than the satisfaction of immediate material wants was a chimera; and third, that in the absence of growth (which has proved a far more illusive condition than we once believed it to be) not even the basic material needs of all society would be satisfied by market allocation; then how many votes would actually be cast in a referendum for such a society? An honest description of what pure market allocation provides would encourage a majority of men and women to look for a more socially just system of distributing our resources.

F. A. Hayek's disciples do not agree, insisting that no commonly accepted principle of social justice could be agreed within a heterogeneous population. John Gray is typical.

> Criteria of desert and merit, such as enter into popular conceptions of social justice, are not objective or publicly corrigible, but rather express private judgments grounded in varying moral traditions. Conceptions of merit are not shared as a common moral inheritance, neutrally available to the inner-city Moslem population of Birmingham and the secularised professional classes of Hampstead.[21]

I am uncertain about the intimacy of Mr Gray's acquaintance with Birmingham's Islamic community. My years representing an increasingly Muslim constituency lead me to a different conclusion. From the fundamentalists who attend the mosque each day to the token believers who pay only passing respect to the faith of their forebears, there is general agreement that families should be decently housed, that the incidence of ill health and the likelihood of early death should not be dependent upon financial status, that young people should not leave school at sixteen and remain unemployed for the next five years, and that 20 per cent of the population should not live below the poverty line. There is also a general feeling that a system of allocation which is, in Hirsch's phrase, 'in principle unprincipled' and which its own supporters do not claim possesses any moral justification, is a wholly inadequate basis for the distribution of a nation's wealth. No doubt the secularised professional classes of Hampstead hold similarly enlightened views. Socialists can be reinforced in that optimism

---

[21] J. Gray, *Dilemmas of Liberal Democracy* (Tavistock, London, 1983), 'Classical Liberalism, Positional Goods and the Politicisation of Poverty', p. 181.

by the knowledge that F. A. Hayek – if not all of his disciples – is honest enough to concede that the inequalities that are the natural consequence of the market system are likely to be so unpopular that a crisis of legitimacy is bound to follow a frank description of the true pattern of distribution which it produces.

The pattern of distribution which unrestricted market forces produce automatically and inevitably creates a hierarchical society in which the needs of the less well-off are neglected in the interest – the immediate financial interest – of the prosperous. A hierarchical society will not create and sustain an adequate health service; nor will it provide all the nation's families with adequate housing or education. In a society that accepts inequality, the primary incomes of the lower-paid will, by definition, be at or below the poverty level – and the secondary distribution through taxation and benefits will do too little to redress the balance. That is the sort of society which we may choose and prefer as a result of our espousal of what Matthew Arnold called 'the gospel of inequality'.

Arnold detected that doctrine deeply entrenched in the British character. But no one should pretend that a choice does not have to be made. A nation is more or less equal according to the wishes of its people. Socialists who believe in freedom, and the real liberty which it makes possible, are determined to pursue freedom and, unless its application frustrates the aims it intends to promote, will argue for its positive promotion. That means that on the crucial issue of market allocation, judgments have to be made about the result of its application to different sectors. In large parts of the economy, the obligations to freedom from state control and to efficiency oblige democratic socialists to support the operation of the market. But there are large parts of the system which cannot be governed by those 'unprincipled' forces. (The proper boundaries of the free market are discussed in Chapter 8.) But one ingredient in every sector of the economy cannot be treated like a commodity which is to be bought and sold on a purely commercial basis. For socialists do not accept that labour is just another ingredient in the equation of production. Social considerations have to temper the usual economic calculation. The same rule has to be applied when the cost is calculated for the provision and organisation of basic services – housing, hospitals and schools. The democratic socialist contention is that intervening in the market as it operates in these areas, with the deliberate intention of promoting equality, will also directly promote freedom. It is an intrinsically appealing proposition, which offers emancipation to the mass of mankind and the security that comes from general contentment even to the most privileged. It is for that reason that so many phoney arguments have been invented in an attempt to discredit it. The most corrupt amongst them is the insistence that liberty and equality are incompatible and that every attempt to establish a pattern of social justice is an infringement of what ought to be inalienable rights. Socialists ought to have met that argument head on instead of allowing the reputation for defending liberty to pass into the hands of the neo liberalism of the far right.

Chapter Four

The Organisation
of Liberty

The neo liberals of the far right have claimed to be the sole defenders of personal liberty by perversely defining that human aspiration in a way which entrenches the privileges of the rich and preserves the power of the strong. The new right insists that a choice has to be made between two incompatible goals – liberty and equality. That is an assertion which depends more on the passion with which it is advocated than on the evidence by which it is reinforced. Yet socialists, instead of insisting that no such choice has to be made, have often accepted the false dichotomy and rashly announced that they choose equality in preference to liberty. The willingness of socialists to accept the philosophical framework laid down by their enemies has allowed them a change in attitude to the theories of Hayek and Friedman in twenty years from considering them interesting and eccentric to accepting them as received wisdom. Opinions which were once derided for their obvious absurdity are now tacitly accepted by politicians from every point on the right of the political spectrum. Even Ian Gilmour (sacked from Margaret Thatcher's government because of his inability to support her ideological passions) claims that

> If everybody, because of egalitarianism approved and imposed by social democrats, has to use the same medical services, has to use the same school services . . . the citizen will be increasingly regulated by monopolies and increasingly at their mercy.[1]

The Hayek–Friedman theories advance the most extreme

---

[1] I. Gilmour, *Inside Right* (Hutchinson, London, 1973), p. 183.

66

interpretation of the idea that a choice must be made between freedom and equality. Bentham believed that every law was an infraction of individual liberty. But he did not conclude from that self-evident proposition that there was some sort of legislative slippery slope, down which a nation would slide into totalitarianism if it began the descent by stumbling over the brink with nothing more authoritarian than state medicine or national pension schemes. Nor did he suggest that the gradual extension of state power would end with inevitable damage to the people for whom the state intended protection. Yet Ian Gilmour, writing at a time when the term 'social democrat' was taken to have a different meaning – for David Owen was then abolishing pay beds within the National Health Service and Shirley Williams was expanding comprehensive education at the expense of the direct grant schools – argues that a universal public health 'monopoly' would reduce the quality of medical care for a majority of the population. That view is, of course, manifest nonsense. But the progressive wing of the Tory Party has, if it is to remain in anything like ideological fashion, to invent such pragmatic justifications for the obeisances that it makes to neo liberalism. The real neo liberals do not need to perform such intellectual gymnastics. Hayek himself relies on unsubstantiated assertions based on meaningless theology, in his description of

> the growing recognition that the application of uniform or equal rules to the conduct of individuals (who are, in fact, very different in many respects) inevitably produced very different results for different individuals; and that in order to bring about, by government action, a reduction in these unintended but inevitable differences in the material position of different people, it would be necessary to treat them not according to the same but according to different rules.[2]

That truism could be regarded as the undeniable argument in favour of positive discrimination: the acceptance that if the loose framework of law provides equal opportunities for poor blacks and rich whites alike, the rich whites are likely to benefit from the system more than the poor blacks. But the conclusion

[2] F. A. Hayek, *Studies in Philosophy, Politics and Economics* (Routledge & Kegan Paul, London, 1967), p. 170.

drawn by Hayek from that statement of the obvious is not that which would commend itself either to egalitarians or, indeed, to anyone who believed in the concept of social justice.

> While equality before the law – the treatment of all by government according to the same rules – appears to me to be an essential condition of individual freedom, that different treatment which is necessary in order to place people who are individually very different into the same position seems to me not only incompatible with personal freedom, but highly immoral.[3]

The allegation of 'immorality' must be examined in detail. But, in addition to this major charge, Hayek condemns the imposition of systems of social justice for supplementary – and more down-to-earth, if barely more convincing – reasons. He claims that efficiency is impaired by any interference with the market system of allocating rewards and resources to what the classical economists insisted would automatically be their most productive use. And he judges that the acceptance of social justice (however defined) as an attainable goal would arouse expectations which could not be met and would, in consequence, undermine respect for the legitimate authority of the state. But these pseudo-practical considerations are essentially his supplementary criticisms of the conscious promotion by government of coherent ethical values. His real objection is that, in the absence of a universal consensus for a specific system of social justice, the imposition of moral values on free enterprise imposes an intolerable level of coercion upon those members of society who do not support the ethical system endorsed by the majority. The dissenting minority is then required to subscribe to the implementation of principles with which it does not agree. Indeed, it will be obliged to make material contributions to the application of those principles through the taxes which its members pay. In the end, the principles turn out (like so much of the philosophy of the right) to be vulgar notions dressed up in pretentious language. Hayek simply believes that the least government is the best government.

---

[3] F. A. Hayek, *New Studies* (Routledge & Kegan Paul, London, 1978), Ch. 10, 'Whither Democracy?', pp. 157–8.

> It is due to the fact that we do not enforce a unitary scale of
> concrete ends, nor attempt to secure that some particular view
> about what is more or what is less important governs the whole
> of society, that the members of . . . a free society have as good
> a chance successfully to use their individual knowledge for the
> achievement of their individual purposes as they in fact have.[4]

The social system which Hayek prefers is a sort of economic
natural selection, the elevation of the choice to sink or swim into
a moral precept. But if the doctrine of social *laissez faire* which
he advocates were to be adopted by some socially primitive
society, nobody could reasonably argue that its acceptance
marked the rejection of any concept of ethics or system of
justice. The state cannot be neutral. Even to adopt neutrality is
to take up a position. What Hayek really demands is acceptance
of his prejudices.

Whether or not the government intervenes, the market
operates according to rules which can be described and which
produce results that can be predicted. And, very often, the
acceptance of these rules requires the government of the state in
which they operate to allow, if not to organise, levels of
suffering and deprivation which should be unacceptable in
civilised countries. To accept Hayek's view that there is nothing
that can be done (or that there is nothing *better* that can be
done) is to take refuge in a convenient moral bolt-hole, which
can comfortably accommodate all those who want the rich and
powerful to be unrestricted in their use of wealth and power.
Whatever his academic intentions, Hayek provided a desperately
needed intellectual legitimacy for parties and people with a
vested interest in inequality. In a free society, there is an
inalienable right to advocate great disparities of income and a
system which allows immense riches and desperate poverty to
co-exist within the same society. But in an intellectually
respectable community, it is impossible to defend that system by
pretending that for the state to do nothing absolves it from all
the consequences of those disparities and inequalities. The state
has a responsibility for its own inaction. No one would seriously
argue that a man who saw a child fall into a canal and simply

---

[4] F. A. Hayek, *Studies in Philosophy, Politics and Economics* (Routledge & Kegan
Paul, London, 1967), p. 165.

hurried on home to the comfort of a blazing fire and hot meal would have no responsibility for that child's fate.[5]

Yet that is exactly what Hayek argues when he considers the responsibilities of the state. It is cynicism elevated into moral philosophy.

> It has, of course to be admitted that the manner in which the benefits and burdens are apportioned by the market mechanism would, in many instances, have to be regarded as very unjust if it were the result of a deliberate allocation to particular people. But this is not the case. These shares are the outcome of a process, the effects of which on particular people are neither intended nor foreseen. To demand justice from such a process is clearly absurd and to single out some people in such a society as entitled to a particular share is evidently unjust.[6]

Readers of Hayek learn to accept such subjective assertions as a feature of the unquestioning conviction that his personal standards of value are self-evidently right. The immediate task is to define his position rather than be irritated by his smug mannerisms or amused by the way in which he abandons logic when intellectual rigour becomes inconvenient. So it is only necessary to note that he regards it as unreasonable to complain about the weather and immoral to suggest that society should not be organised in such a way that some of its members have several topcoats and numerous umbrellas whilst others have none at all. For, within his philosophy, it is unreasonable to complain about forces which – being unguided by man's positive involvement – have purely random effects on both their victims and their beneficiaries. Natural forces cannot produce coercion or injustice since, according to Hayek's definition, both these conditions can exist only as the result of human intention. The hardship caused by the operation of these random and motiveless forces has to be borne – by their victims – with fortitude, for attempts to remedy their injustices would infringe the natural rights of those who benefit from their effects. Distaste for a

[5] In the knowledge that the neo liberal right is inclined to extend argument to its illogical conclusions it is, perhaps, necessary to explain that what follows is not a plea for 'good neighbour laws' which make the failure to rescue drowning children a legal offence. It is a plea for voting like good neighbours when decisions about distribution have to be made.
[6] F. A. Hayek, *Law Legislation and Liberty* (Routledge & Kegan Paul, London, 1982), Vol. 2, 'The Mirage of Social Justice', p. 64.

doctrine which accepts the necessity of injustice should not distract us from the other failings of Hayek's theory. As an exercise in logic, it is absurd; for it relies upon self-justifying definitions of all the terms on which the argument depends. If the Hayek view of 'natural', 'coercion', and 'justice', is wrong, the whole argument collapses.

The Hayek view of democracy is similarly dependent upon his definitions of sovereignty and the duties of representative government. The legislature – within Hayek's model of the good society – does not possess supreme legislative powers, but has its sovereignty limited by superior authority. What that superior authority may be – supreme monarch or supreme court – is never altogether clear. Hayek's undisguised contempt for democracy (as it is popularly conceived) has already been noted. He argues that in

> an omnipotent assembly decisions rest on a sanctioned process of blackmail and corruption . . . Majorities are not based on agreement of opinions but are formed by aggregations of special interests, mutually assisting each other . . . Most members of the majority often know that a measure was stupid and unfair, but . . . consent to it, in order to remain members of a majority.[7]

It is for that reason that Hayek and Milton Friedman actually assert that free markets are a better vehicle for the expression of popular will than are free elections. Free markets have, for Hayek, a second advantage over the ballot box. They do not have any truck with egalitarianism.

> Agreements by the majority on sharing the booty gained by overwhelming a minority of fellow citizens or deciding how much is to be taken from them is not democracy. At least it is not that ideal of democracy which has any moral justification. Democracy is not egalitarian. But unlimited democracy is bound to become egalitarian.[8]

To Hayek, any theory of government which seeks to change the natural pattern of resource allocation is coercive. In his more compassionate moods, he concedes that a minimum

[7] F. A. Hayek, *New Studies* (Routledge & Kegan Paul, London, 1978), Ch. 10, 'Whither Democracy?', pp. 156–7.
[8] *ibid.*, p. 156.

provision of welfare may be organised without the state suffering irreparable harm. But he insists that even a low-slung safety net must be put in place as an act of spontaneous benevolence on the part of the well-to-do. He cannot accept that it is the natural right of every citizen to live above the poverty line, for that would require the imposition of a system of values on the minority of citizens who do not accept its moral validity.

If Hayek simply preached against elective tyranny – the subjugation of minorities by the majority – we would need to applaud and endorse rather than to question his views. But that is not the Hayek argument. Elective tyrannies deny rights to religious minorities, suppress freedom of speech, prohibit dissent and deny individual rights. That is a fundamentally different political objective from attempting to increase the sum of human happiness by arranging a more equal distribution of resources. Hayek is only uniting in a single argument political freedom and social freedom – two concepts which many philosophers insist are semantically rather than intellectually related. The relationship between 'freedom to' vote, pray, speak, and 'freedom from' hunger, illness and ignorance, is the subject of later chapters and is central to our principal contention. If socialism is concerned with human emancipation, the right to provide one's children with a decent education is no less a feature of a free society than the freedom to provide those children with an education which is related to a freely chosen religious conviction. The socialist concern with the equal ability of all citizens to use the freedom which the state provides is the subject of later discussion. It is mentioned here only to emphasise that Hayek regards the patterns of wealth and income distribution as matters which are directly related to the concepts of liberty. A free society is, to him, that in which the state does not interfere with the patterns of property ownership and relative earnings. Socialists must assert, with equal conviction, that the free society is that in which the state consciously and intentionally interferes with these things in order that a maximum number of its citizens are able to enjoy to the greatest possible extent their full capacities. It is worthwhile looking at some practical examples of the truth, which seem to have escaped Hayek.

Socialists ought, by definition, to be champions of the classic liberal view of liberty, protecting the right to disagree and dissent, the sanctity of private action, freedom from persecution when in disagreement with majority opinion or under pressure to conform to it. The greater freedoms which socialists seek are not alternatives to political and legal rights, but complementary to them. Indeed, the regard for extensions of those freedoms which the new right despise and deride is essential if the traditional concept of freedom is to have any real meaning.

The text which is most usually quoted as the gospel of unfettered individualism deserves careful attention. John Stuart Mill, the nineteenth-century philosopher, is opposed to the imposition of restraints on an individual's conduct because 'all errors which he is likely to commit against advice and warning are far outweighed by the evil of allowing others to constrain him for what they deem to be *his* good'.[9] The italics – though inserted in this text – are important, for the reference to the *subject*'s 'good' is a rejection of the paternalistic state which imposes (on individuals) society's collective judgment as to what is personally best for all and each of its citizens. Mill argued against prohibiting the sale of alcohol, but he advocates harsh penalties for those who distress their neighbours or damage their neighbours' property as a result of drunkenness. The Mill argument is 'do as you like, as long as it does not prejudice the interests of the rest of society'. Those who claim to follow Mill but claim that liberty is no more than the absence of coercion must explain why that rule applies to the amount a man drinks but not to the amount he owns. 'A person who shows rashness, obstinacy, self-conceit, who cannot live within a moderate means, who cannot restrain himself from hurtful indulgences, who pursues animal pleasures . . . should suffer the penalties subsequent upon his actions.'[10] All this is far removed from the notion of a state which neither accepts nor attempts to implement any concept of social justice. Mill does not argue that the state should be agnostic about all matters except the framework of laws and justice which it needs for its coherent existence. The same philosophy characterises his view on the freedom of worship and conscience. Society, he insists, should not attempt to impose a uniformity of belief or to penalise those who,

[9] J. S. Mill, *On Liberty* (Parker, London, 1859), IV, 'The Limits to the Authority of Society over the Individual', pp. 137–8.
[10] *ibid.*, p. 139–40.

without disadvantage to their neighbours, worship unfamiliar gods.

But none of these libertarian rules apply to conduct which harms society as a whole. Mill was arguing from within a society which still denied its citizens the individual rights which we now take for granted. He demanded that the state abdicate all interest in personal conduct and conscientious dissent. But he did not suggest that the state could be agnostic about the way in which that conduct might adversely affect the interests of the whole community. Indeed, he was explicit in his insistence on the observances of 'specific duty to the public' and the obligation to avoid the 'constructive injury' which a person causes to society.

> The distinction here pointed out between the part of a person's life which concerns only himself and that which concerns others, many persons will refuse to admit . . . But with regard to the merely contingent or, as it may be called, constructive injury which a person causes to society by conduct which neither violates any specific duty to the public nor occasions any specific hurt to any assignable individual except himself, the inconvenience is one which society can afford to bear for the sake of the greater good of human freedom.[11]

Mill was, in fact, arguing that the state should not concern itself with actions which affect only the individuals who perform them or offend others to a minor degree. And, writing at a time when Catholics and non-conformists were denied the full rights of citizenship, his essay *On Liberty* amounted to a call for an authoritarian state to abandon its intrusion in matters of private conduct and personal conviction.

But the abandonment of the state interest in matters which are properly left to individual decision does not and cannot mean that there is no rôle for it to play in the regulation of those matters which involve a conflict between the chosen actions (and, therefore, the personal freedom) of different members of society. 'Clearly,' wrote John Rawls, 'when liberties are left unrestricted they collide with one another.'[12] And the most libertarian philosopher has to decide how to minimise the

---

[11] *ibid.*, pp. 327, 329.
[12] J. Rawls, *A Theory of Justice* (Oxford University Press, Oxford, 1972), Ch. 32, 'The Concept of Liberty', p. 203.

damage done by those collisions. In the less complicated society of the nineteenth-century, radical opinion could rally around a man's right to get drunk in private, whilst taking it for granted that the fighting drunk would be punished for the damage that he did. It was easier then to escape the question of why we should punish the drunken landlord who bullies his tenants but allows the sober extortionist to continue to brutalise his victims by imposing rents which they cannot afford. Nor, until the end of the century, did philosophers begin to wonder if even the basic civil liberties could be properly observed in a society characterised by vast disparities of power and wealth. Whatever the legal framework, 'liberty is unequal when one class of person has greater liberty than another', says John Rawls.[13] And liberty is bound to be distributed unequally if economic power is disproportionately divided. Indeed, without a fair measure of economic equality, genuine liberty – the equal rights of every citizen to the greatest amount of freedom compatible with the good order of society – is impossible.

That is true if only political and legal freedoms – the right of adult suffrage, freedom of expression and equal treatment under the law – are considered. To extend the argument into the field of social and economic freedom – the 'right' to be educated to the point of full intellectual capability and the 'right' to enjoy the level of financial security which is provided by permanent employment as a living wage, reinforces the relationship between liberty and equality. Even in the limited, but crucial field of political and legal freedom, those who pretend that the two conditions can legitimately be separated either delude themselves or deceive others. Far from being the enemy of freedom, equality is its essential companion. Rawls's judgment is worth repeating.

> Historically, one of the main defects of constitutional government has been the failure to ensure the fair value of political liberty. The necessary corrective steps have not been taken, indeed, they never seem to have been seriously entertained. Disparities in the distribution of property and wealth that far exceed what is compatible with political equality have generally been tolerated by the legal system . . . Moreover the effects of injustices in the political system are much more grave and

[13] *ibid.*

longer lasting than market imperfections. Thus inequalities in the economic and social system may soon undermine whatever political equality might have existed under fortunate historical conditions.[14]

In Gladstone's Irish Land Act of 1870 there is an example of how a practical increase in real liberty is dependent on legal and economic equality. Mr Gladstone, in a letter to Cardinal Manning, described it as preventing 'the landlord from using the terrible power of undue and unjust eviction . . . And if [we] extinguish unjust eviction, [we] will also extinguish unjust augmentations of rent'.[15] That Act prohibited landlords from including in their leases clauses which enabled them to renegotiate tenancy agreements within brief periods after their original negotiation and on terms which were injurious to the farmers who rented the land. It brought to an end 'rack-renting', the process by which tenant farmers had previously been obliged either to pay exorbitant rents or leave, without compensation, land which had improved its yield and increased its value because of their labours.[16] For fifty years, Irish farmers had been forced to accept an annual rent increase (and consequent pauperisation) because they were already so near to bankruptcy and eviction that no other choice was open to them. The Irish Land Act would not have been acceptable to the followers of F. A. Hayek, for it involved an interference with market mechanisms which was intended to assist 'people who are individually very different' in achieving 'the same material position as each other'. It also involved 'agreement by the (parliamentary) majority on the sharing of the booty gained' by effectively removing from the Irish landlords the extra rent (or foreclosed property) which they might have obtained from their leaseholders. It was certainly based on the conviction that the state could and should advocate and impose a system of social justice. But, according to Hayek, emancipating the Irish serfs was in fact a step down the road to serfdom; and his philosophical predecessors in the House of Commons opposed

[14] *ibid.*, Ch. 36, 'Political Justice and the Constitution', p. 226.
[15] J. Morley, *Life of Gladstone* (Macmillan, London, 1903), p. 294.
[16] For a discussion of the Irish Land Act 1870 and the general principle of legal freedom and political power, see the lecture given by T. H. Green, 'Liberal Legislation and Freedom of Contract', published in Green's *Collected Works* (edited by R. L. Nettleship and published by Longman, London, 1888).

the Irish Land Act for reasons of which he would have thoroughly approved.

By any standards, the Irish Land Act was an 'infraction of liberty', in so far as it applied to the Irish landlords – and it was opposed as such by the landlords' representatives in Parliament. Jeremy Bentham's description of *every law* as an 'infraction of liberty . . . even if the infraction leads to an increase in the sum of liberty'[17], was not an analysis on which the Tory MPs of 1883 wasted much time. Those whose chief interest is the retention of wealth and privilege are not usually attracted by the subtleties of paradox. They do, however, like to dress up greed to look like an ethical principle. So they insisted that in a free society the undoubted restraint placed on the landowner's freedom of action was intolerable. We can accept that the landlord was no longer free to rack-rent his tenants without beginning to concede the apologists' general case. *Indeed, our case – the connection between liberty and equality – is based on the belief that the unfettered right of the rich to use their economic power has to be limited in order to increase the liberties of the poor and thus increase the sum of liberty*. That was the net result of the Irish Land Act. It created for tenant farmers a freedom which they had not previously enjoyed – the freedom to negotiate long-term leases at rents which they could afford. The state had wilfully circumscribed the behaviour of some of its members; it had imposed upon society a system of social values which, by definition, not all of them accepted. But it is impossible, by any sensible definition of freedom, to argue that the result was not an increase in the sum of liberty.

Green himself offered a definition of freedom: 'a positive power, a capacity of doing or enjoying something worth doing or enjoying'[18]. It is a definition which Hayek would wholly reject, for he held that 'once this identification of freedom with power is admitted there is no limit to the sophisms by which the attraction of the word "liberty" can be used to support measures which destroy individual freedom'.[19] That is an intellectually corrupt response to Green's assertion. We are required to

---

[17] J. Bentham, quoted in I. Berlin, *Inaugural Lecture as Professor of Social and Political Theory* (Clarendon Press, Oxford, 1958), p. 33.

[18] T. H. Green, *Liberal Legislation and Freedom of Contract*, lecture 1880, quoted in G. H. Saline, *A History of Political Theory* (Harrap, London, 1952), p. 357.

[19] F. A. Hayek, *The Constitution of Liberty* (Routledge & Kegan Paul, London, 1960), p. 133.

follow truth wherever it leads, irrespective of the inconvenience that is sometimes caused by taking that path. The relationship between power and freedom may cause discomfort to the powerful who want to retain their power but claim a belief in generalised liberty; but it is undeniable. 'Socialists,' wrote R. H. Tawney, 'interpret [freedom] as implying the utmost possible development of every human being and the deliberate organisation of society for the attainment of that objective.' That definition fulfils the essential socialist requirement that freedom should be seen (in Tawney's words again) 'not as a possession to be defended, but as a goal to be achieved' in real terms which have meaning in the real lives of real people. It is only concerned with rights which 'must be such that whenever the occasion for their exercise arises, they can, in fact, be exercised'.[20] It is a wholly realistic description of 'effective freedom' which requires us to resolve those dilemmas which make our theory inferior to new liberalism in only one way: their system, possessing all the simple charm of a single self-fulfilling iron law, is easier to develop into a set of political slogans.

Socialists must wrestle with the genuine problems and unavoidable difficulties of complex real societies. How do we ensure that the power to exercise the rights provided by a framework of law can be equally exercised by all citizens? How do we make certain that our freedoms are anything more than the ability of the rich and powerful to use their power and riches to their own advantage, but to the detriment of others? Perhaps most practically of all, how – besides the abdication of all interests in social justice – does the state reconcile the inevitable conflicts of one freedom impeding another?

Those conflicts impose particularly severe problems when two individuals – theoretically equal before the law but financially grossly unequal – face each other in court. A man who enjoys an income above the legal-aid limit but below £30,000 a year would be unwise to contest a libel case against a millionaire. The Rent Acts were created to improve the legal prospects of poor tenants in their disputes with rich landlords. The families so grievously affected by Thalidomide faced an impossible task in the prosecution of the Distiller's Company until they were assisted

---

[20] R. H. Tawney, *The Radical Tradition* (Penguin, London, 1964), Ch. 10, p. 167.

and supported by the *Sunday Times*. The equal access to the civil liberties which a liberal state provides is only possible in a society in which wealth and power are equally divided.

Tawney made the two essential points:

> . . . when liberty is construed, realistically, or implying not merely a minimum of civil and political rights, but securities that the economically weak will not be at the mercy of the economically strong and that the control of those aspects of economic life by which all are affected will be amenable, in the last resort, to the will of all, a large measure of equality, so far from being inimical to liberty, is essential to it . . . Economic liberty implies, not that all men shall initiate, plan, direct, manage or administer but the absence of such economic inequalities as can be used as a means of economic constraint.[21]

In that passage Tawney rightly connects political and economic freedom and demonstrates the indisputable relationship between 'freedom from' and 'freedom to'. Without a degree of equality, the dilemma of conflicting rights will always be resolved in the interests of the rich. When freedom is defined as the absence of restraint on such practices as rack-renting, men and women will continue to starve. The case for adopting a more positive view of liberty – freedom to work, freedom to be well housed and educated, freedom to enjoy a fair share of national resources – will be discussed in the next chapter. With vast disparities of wealth such conventional liberties as the freedom of contract are not truly possible, as T. H. Green demonstrated in the case of the Irish Land Act.

The same rule applies in the labour market, where (whatever the neo liberals may say) an equal bargain depends on either a degree of state regulation or the combination of working men and women to create a countervailing force to the strength of even a single employer. The neo liberals should know that to be true. For the man whose portrait many of them wear on their ties was explicit on the point of master and man being incapable of striking a free and equal bargain in an unregulated market.

> The masters can hold out much longer. A landlord, a farmer, a master manufacturer or merchant, though they did not employ

---

[21] R. H. Tawney, *Equality* (Allen & Unwin, London, 1952), Ch. 5, (ii), 'Liberty and Equality', p. 186.

a single workman could generally live a year or two on the stock which they had already acquired. Most workmen could subsist a week, few could subsist a month and scarcely any a year without employment. In the long run the workman may be as necessary to his master as his master is to him, but the necessity is not so immediate.[22]

Yet the landlord, farmer, merchant and master manufacturer will join together in complaint if their power over employees or potential employees is restricted. And, in crude libertarian theory, they will be right to do so. For if the state restricts their powers, there is an undoubted 'infraction' of liberty. And if the trades unions mobilise the collective power of individual workers, an already imperfect market will be made still more imperfect. The freedom of the employer to use his strength is in direct collision with what any reasonable person would regard as the right of a working man and woman to obtain a fair day's pay for a fair day's work. Acceptance of the need to resolve the conflict has, in itself, impeccable socialist origins. For, in earlier times, it was generally accepted, as apparently the neo liberals accept today, that the rival demands would be reconciled according to the strength of the individual parties. The state, holding no view on social justice and allowing the market to answer all its questions about the distribution of wealth, was described by Matthew Arnold a hundred years ago as 'a peculiarly British form of atheism, a peculiarly British form of quietism'. But Arnold detected a growing problem.

> Every Englishman doing what he likes was convenient enough so long as there were only Barbarians or Philistines [his not altogether complimentary terms for the upper and middle classes] to do what they liked . . . [it has] become inconvenient and productive of anarchy now that the populace wants to do what it likes too.[23]

A hundred years after *Culture and Anarchy* was published, John Rawls addressed himself to the dilemma of how to organise society when 'the populace wants to do what it likes too'. When he wrote of unrestricted liberties 'colliding with each other', he described the problem in more prosaic language than

---

[22] A. Smith, *The Wealth of Nations* (Methuen & Co, London, 1930), p. 169.
[23] M. Arnold, *Culture and Anarchy* (Cambridge University Press, Cambridge, 1960), Ch. 3, 'Barbarians, Philistines, Populace', p. 313.

that which Arnold employed. Consider, he suggested, a debating assembly devoted to free speech. Within its rules order may be enforced which, at the time of their use, limits the freedom of some individuals to speak in the manner and at the moment of their choice. But those rules are necessary if freedom of speech is to be preserved for the whole assembly – especially, a socialist will add, if the rights of those with soft voices and diffident manners are to be protected from the demands for time and attention made by the more voluble and self-confident speakers. 'Liberty', says Rawls, 'is unequal when one class of person has greater liberty than another or liberty is less extensive than it should be', and 'a basic liberty can be limited only for the sake of liberty itself, that is only to ensure that the same liberty and different basic liberty is properly protected'. Liberty was obviously extended in the southern states of America by the emancipation of the slaves. But there is a second consideration. 'The worth of liberty to persons and groups is proportional to their capacity to advance their ends within the framework (of liberties) which the system defines.'[24] The right to make a free choice of employer was – to many emancipated slaves – a liberty of very little value; for economic circumstances made it impossible for them to alter their conditions of work from the long hours, low wages, and obligatory subservience which amounted to bondage. The new liberty possessed some value – self-esteem, the right to risk starvation in the new factories of the north. But the value of even the most basic of civil liberties was circumscribed by economic incapacity. There is no definition of liberty which does not encompass the right of men to live free from slavery. But if the difference between slavery and emancipation is indistinguishable because, once freed, the liberated bondsmen are forced to act as if slavery was still allowed in law, the purpose of freedom so defined will be questioned by ex-slaves, if not by political philosophers.

Hayek answers all questions about the relative value of liberty by insisting that equal rights under the law are, themselves, the sole criterion of freedom and that the so-called value of those rights is simply another way of describing unequally distributed power, not liberty. And the argument continues that since the shares in national income are determined by the motiveless

[24] J. Rawls, *A Theory of Justice* (Oxford University Press, Oxford, 1972), Ch. 32, 'The Concept of Liberty', p. 204.

81

market it is unreasonable to complain about 'the outcome of a process, the effect of which on particular people was neither intended nor foreseen'. The assertion that it is unreasonable to complain about unintended or unforeseen distribution of resources is, in itself, open to question. And the notion that we should not try to regulate patterns of distribution which are neither intended nor foreseen is equally arbitrary and similarly indefensible.

The hypothesis that the distribution of wealth and power is wholly random is clearly absurd. The best that can be said about that contention is that it is naïve. Individuals may enter into a market transaction with no intention other than to sell what they have produced. But they are consciously taking part in a process which they must realise invariably results in millions of other people being denied basic resources. They know (indeed most of those engaged in market operations triumphantly declare) that the process has one predictable outcome. The great disparities between rich and poor will be certainly preserved and probably extended. If freedom is concerned with the ability to perform those acts which liberty allows, the market system invariably and unavoidably denies millions of people the resources which would make them truly free. It can be predicted that the individuals who enter the market with the least share of resources will generally leave it with the least share of resources. Inherited wealth is neither unintended nor unforeseen. The prospects of success and advancement are greatest amongst the children of parents who are, themselves, successful. Indeed, it is rarely possible to argue honestly that individuals are the beneficiaries or victims of unintended actions which could not have been foreseen. Low wages may be the result of employers' wilful refusal to pay what they can afford and employees' inability to apply the pressure necessary to increase their earnings; and the low wages which are the consequence may result in the employees and their families being unable even to take advantage to the full of the political liberties and legal rights which are the hallmark of the free nation. They will be unable to afford the political publicity which gives their ideological opinions the same chance of being accepted by a democratic electorate as those which are promoted by parties with greater resources. They will be unable to pay the legal fees necessary to develop a new view of liberty – the chance to work, the freedom to be decently educated, and the ability to obtain the highest quality of medical treatment. If we conceive liberty in a wholly negative sense, the *value* of the rights we provide will certainly be far less than if we define them in a positive fashion. In his lecture 'Government and Opposition', Professor Raymond Plant quotes G. Macallum's algebraic formulation of the two alternatives: freedom equals freedom of X from Y to do or become Z. That equation concedes the Hayek principle that restraint (or coercion) must, if it is to be regarded as a denial of freedom, be the product of one man's power over another. In the absence of such coercion, a man is free to follow whatever course of action Z denotes. But it is the *opportunity* to perform the task that Z denotes which gives reality to the concept of freedom. It is the opportunity to do or become Z which makes the absence of constraint by Y have any real value. The opportunity may be impaired by others exercising a similar right; and only the state can resolve the conflict. Even if

> as a routine consequence of my exercising my freedom . . . some persons are put in the position of lacking effective agency (the power to act in their own best interest) then I am by my action, although not my intention, supporting a system which lowers the value of liberty for others and this is coercive.'[25]

That is a highly charitable interpretation of the intention (or lack of intention) of the powerful.

For the socialist concept of freedom takes the 'negative' view of liberty as its starting point. Like Hayek, Nozek and Berlin, socialists are opposed – in principle – to coercion by the state or the coercion of one individual by another. Socialists do not argue with the obvious view, expressed by some new liberals as if it possessed an intellectual novelty, that the extreme case of being 'unfree' is being physically prevented from performing an act which would otherwise be performed. However, socialists (in common with the neo liberals) have to decide in what circumstances coercion is justified. The Defence of the Realm Act made Britain less free. It was, rightly, justified by its necessity in the face of the threat from Nazi Germany. In less dramatic circumstances, the processes of democracy have to determine where the boundaries of 'negative liberty' are drawn,

[25] R. Plant, 'Welfare State and Welfare Society', *Government and Opposition*, **Journal of Comparative Politics**, Vol. 20, No. 3, Summer 1985, p. 311.

for 'unfettered' freedom for one citizen may conflict with the 'unfettered' freedom of another. The only acceptable rule about the limitation of liberty, by which democrats can be guided, is John Stuart Mill's rule. Liberty may have to be curtailed when its unrestricted existence damages the interests of others. But even that conventionally acceptable response creates almost as many problems as it resolves. Who is to define 'the interests of others' and decide when it is reasonable to protect them? And what agency is to enforce the protection? It is easy enough to agree that the sale of narcotics should be illegal. But it is less obvious that the Sabbatarians should be accommodated by the prohibition of the sale of anything on Sundays. The socialist answer is that freedom for one group may be curtailed, when its exercise would limit the freedom of another. For socialists are interested in the sum of freedom. And since they understand the relationship between freedom and equality, they do not believe in the freedom to rack-rent, the freedom to pauperise by imposing starvation wages or the freedom to deny access to essential resources.

The philosophers of negative freedom – Hayek, Nozek and Berlin – will go on to argue that liberty has nothing to do with the possession of goods and the consequent enjoyment of powers and opportunities. Their criticism of the concept of 'agency' – the possession of the power to exercise rights – includes the *reductio ad absurdum* that by such a definition, a man or woman is only 'free' when he or she possesses sufficient resources to perform every task that may seem attractive or appealing. Negative freedom, they argue, is much more determinate. It exists when unjustifiable and intentional coercion is removed – a point which can be easily recognised and precisely defined. With the positive definition, there is, the argument runs, no stopping point when it is possible to announce the achievement of complete freedom.

The convenience of a definition is not its most important attribute. Even with the negative view of liberty there are some complicated questions to be answered about acceptable derogations from the perfect state. But the real objection to the critics' view of positive liberty is not the accusation that their theory is equally inadequate. The connection between negative liberty and the power to exercise it is obvious; and that connection takes the argument half-way towards the acceptance of the positive definition. The absence of coercion has little value, if actions, which free men and women are theoretically allowed to perform, cannot in practice be performed because of economic weakness. There must be a connection between 'being free to' and 'being able to'. Unless we are able to act, the right to act loses its value. The relation between liberties and resources can be extended into the assertion that the greater the resources an individual possesses the greater the freedom he or she enjoys – as the lifestyle of many millionaires demonstrates. Not everybody can be a millionaire, so it may be that not everybody can possess the resources which wholly make them free. But more people can be made more free by the provision of the extra opportunities and resources that make liberty a reality.

Indeed, without the possession of basic resources, the removal of coercion makes no discernible change to the real ability to behave in the way which the absence of coercion makes theoretically possible. Freedom involves the possession of 'agency', the power as well as the right to act.

> From this it follows that I cannot rationally respect persons and value their capacity as rational agents while at the same time being indifferent to whether they have the general resources to make agency effective. In this sense, therefore, basic needs, or the necessary conditions of action, are the primary goods – goods which have to be obtained whatever else I might want.[26]

These essential goods are a 'basic class of welfare needs which all citizens have in common' – housing, education, health provision, a level of income that sustains more than bare existence. Without the possession of these primary goods, it is impossible to exercise the rights bestowed by the existence of negative liberty. Without the general availability of those primary goods and the accommodation of those basic needs a society cannot be called free. A democratic society has to decide whether it wants to extend real freedom by consciously extending the general distribution of those resources which make freedom a reality. The definition of true liberty allows no hedging or fudging. The political process must decide how much liberty society proposes to provide. The decision is not funda-

[26] R. Plant, 'The Defence of Welfare' (*The Very Idea of the Welfare State*, Eds Bean, Ferns and Whynter, Tavistock, London, 1983), p. 22.

mentally different from that taken by democracies in the pursuit of other aims which cannot be wholly realised.

> The question of degree suggests even more clearly the importance of political choice . . . Needs are not only elusive, they are expansive . . . But it would be wrong to suggest that therefore need cannot be a distributive principle. It is, rather, a principle subject to political limitation . . . Consider the case of physical security in a modern American city. We could provide absolute security, eliminate every source of violence except domestic violence, if we put street lights at every ten yards and stationed a policeman every thirty yards throughout the city. But that would be very expensive and so we settle for something less. How much less can only be decided politically.[27]

And it cannot be distinguished from the power to act as a free man and woman. Yet:

> It is still consistently assumed by the privileged classes that when the state holds its hand, what remains as a result of its inaction is liberty. In reality, as far as the mass of mankind is concerned is not liberty but tyranny.[28]

In fact, the state can be an instrument for either the suppression or the extension of freedom. 'The British version of socialism involves not the curtailment of liberties but their more general extension and is, for that reason, denounced as tyrannical by those whose authority is likely, as a consequence, to suffer diminition.'[29] They have justified their denunciation by defining freedom in a way which maintains the authority of the rich and the powerful. The duty of socialists is to organise the state – which is no more and no less than the common will which we must mobilise – in a way which demonstrably increases the *sum* of liberty.

[27] M. Walzer, *Spheres of Justice* (Robertson, Oxford, 1983), 'Welfare, Membership and Need'.
[28] R. H. Tawney, *The Radical Tradition* (Penguin, London, 1964), Ch. 10, p. 166.
[29] *ibid.*, p. 166.

Chapter Five

Liberty and the State

The notion that freedom amounts to no more than the absence of restraint boasts illustrious origins. 'A free man,' wrote Hobbes, 'is he who is not hindered to do what he has the will to do'[1]; and Helvetius insisted that 'the free man is the man who is not in irons, not imprisoned in gaol, not terrorised like a slave'.[2] He then went on to set out the principles which have been taken up by modern libertarian philosophers – the absence of ability to perform tasks or enjoy pleasures is not, in itself, an absence of freedom. To Helvetius and his like the complaint that liberty has been denied has meaning only if the act which the complainant was not allowed to perform was within his or her immediate capability. To these philosophical forebears of Hayek and the new liberals, liberty is only denied to one individual by the deliberate coercive act of another. 'It is not,' Helvetius said, 'a lack of freedom not to fly like an eagle or swim like a whale.' Genetics, medical science, climate and the market all act upon men and women in ways which prevent them from doing what they would choose to do. But to describe these deprivations as denials of liberty is – according to subscribers to the 'personal coercion' school of philosophy – wholly meaningless. The school has distinguished modern members, including Sir Isaiah Berlin, who contends that 'if I am prevented by others from doing what I would otherwise do, to that extent I am unfree. But if I say . . . that I cannot read because I am blind . . . it would be eccentricity to say that I am to that degree enslaved or unfree.'[3]

To Sir Isaiah Berlin, it is an 'eccentricity' to argue that a blind man is enslaved because he cannot see. Similarly, Helvetius

---

[1] T. Hobbes, *Leviathan* (Everyman, London, 1976), Ch. 21, 'Of the Liberty of Subjects', p. 110.
[2] Helvetius in I. Berlin, *Inaugural Lecture as Professor of Social and Political Theory* (Clarendon Press, Oxford, 1958), p. 7.
[3] *ibid.*

explains that man's inability to fly cannot be an infraction of his natural rights, since flight is not natural to the human species. Caged skylarks, hooded falcons, eagles with clipped wings are – we must presume from the Helvetian analysis – slaves. Hayek would agree, for they are earthbound by the wilful act of their captors. On the other hand, at least according to Berlin, birds born with a congenital deficiency have nothing to complain about; they are the victims of genetic misadventure. Such handicaps are unrelated to rights or the denial of rights, for they are not the intentional results of the acts of other human beings. Or is there a confusion of prepositions? Should the statement not read that handicaps are unrelated to rights and the denial of rights *when* they are not the intentional result of the acts of other human beings? For blind men and earthbound birds may suffer their disabilities as the result of a variety of different causes. It becomes necessary to examine some examples of how handicaps – indeed, how the handicaps which Isaiah Berlin chooses for his illustration – actually come about. It is also necessary to apply conscious and wilful semantic precision to other parts of the formula. For if the essential requirements of coercion are 'deliberate acts', it is necessary to know what is meant (in the context of state action) by 'deliberate' and what constitutes an 'act'.

The coercion theory can be clarified by an examination of those brutal societies where the penal code includes the punishment of blinding. The convicted criminal who is blinded by the decision of the courts is, by the Berlin theory of coercion, denied the right to see in a way which is an undoubted infraction of his liberties – since sight is his natural condition in the way that flight is natural to birds. In his case, the conscious act is not in doubt. The decision to put out his eyes was taken with judicial deliberation. But what of the blind man who once could see but who has lost his sight through *deliberate* negligence – the result of machinery that an employer would not shield with suitable protection, a chemical cure adulterated by cheap substitutes, or the failure of a parent to provide proper food? Certainly, the courts would adjudge each of those examples as instances in which the blind man's handicap was the direct result of the wilful act of another human being. If Isaiah Berlin's blindness analogy has any meaning at all, it must apply to them. Like the caged bird, by the behaviour of another human being they were denied the right which it is natural for them to enjoy. The behaviour amounts, in each case, to a failure to act rather than the positive act of poking and gouging. But to say that liberty is only denied by acts of commission is to accept (reverting to the example of a previous chapter) that throwing a child in a river is wrong, but acting in a way which is certain to result in its being drowned is not morally reprehensible. The acts of omission, in the context of the hypothesised blindness, need to be clearly understood. The unguarded machinery, the adulterated chemical, and the abandoned child are only the victims of chance in a very limited sense of that idea. The poverty which results from the unrestricted operation of the free market is not pure chance. The consequences of unguarded machinery, adulterated chemical, abandoned children and low levels of public expenditure can be foreseen. When potential consequences can be foreseen, they can be remedied or avoided. Those who fail to provide the proper protection usually do so in the knowledge – or, indeed, the certainty – that they are putting others at risk. Indeed, whilst the risk is not an object in itself, it is *intentionally* created, because it is profitable or convenient to take the chance with other people's well-being. It is, after all, barely more than a hundred years since we prohibited the practice of sending little boys up chimneys in the certainty that they would contract cancer of the scrotum and palate. The prohibition of the practice was fiercely contested by chimney sweeps who resented a restriction placed on their rights to hire (and fire in a special sense of the word) whoever they chose. If the models supplied us by Helvetius and Isaiah Berlin have any intellectual force, it is impossible to argue that those little boys were not denied their natural rights to health and life.

The blindness hypothesis may, at first, seem a highly over-dramatised illustration which is only accepted as a legitimate model because it is employed by a philosopher of Isaiah Berlin's distinction. But when we examine an extension of the notion against the criteria laid down by the neo liberals for the rules which should govern the truly libertarian state, the example takes on increasing reality. Recall the progression. The 'naturally' blind are wrong to complain of liberty denied. The intentionally blinded can, presumably, make that complaint with justification. Those blinded because of another human being's belief that their sight was less important than profit or convenience are similarly entitled to feel aggrieved. In each case, a natural right has been denied. That leaves little room for doubt about what moral judgment is appropriate for a state or society which knows that by organising itself in one way blindness will be increased, and that by organising itself in a different fashion blindness will be reduced, but consciously and wilfully chooses the alternative which produces the larger amount of blindness. That society is not – even by minimalist standards – free. But such a society is not inconceivable, no matter how improbable it may sound when described in the stark language of its cold reality. Practical examples of how Britain discharges parallel moral duties are barely less extraordinary when set down as part of the process of known cause and wilful effect. In Britain today, the rich survive many forms of diagnosable and curable disease which prove fatal to the lower-income groups who can afford neither the tests nor treatment which are not readily available on the National Health Service. It would be foolish to argue that society can meet all the demands made – or likely to be made – upon it by, say, the health service. That is not because, in the cliché of Enoch Powell, if needs are supposed to be satisfied at no cost to the individual at the point of receipt, the demand is infinite. The health service is apparently insatiable because medical science constantly discovers new (and expensive) ways of keeping patients alive and making the sick healthy again. So both the cost of care and the demand for care escalate. The argument that society will never be able to provide complete health care for everybody is not an argument for abdication from any view about how limited resources should be distributed. Quite the opposite: it is the most potent argument for producing a theory of distribution which is consistent with social justice.

Failure to finance the necessary equipment and staff is not because we cannot afford it in the way that the pre-war poor were unable to pay a doctor's bill. It is because either consciously or unconsciously society chooses to spend less on health care and more on something else. It is increasingly difficult to take refuge in the excuse that the decision is unconscious. Doctors announce on television that they must make agonising decisions about which patients to save and which to let die. Those who die do so as the result of the state's collective judgment that other items of national expenditure are more important than the reduction of death from containable disease. Before the cry goes up that, wicked as such a decision may be, it has no connection with liberty, it is worth remembering that at least one philosopher sees a relationship between purchasing power and freedom. That philosopher is F. A. Hayek.

We do not provide all the dialysis equipment that we need – or organise effective cervical cancer screening, or provide the services which would reduce pre-, peri- and post-natal deaths, or replace the hip joints that agonise elderly arthritics, or finance hundreds of other essential medical services – because we will not raise the taxes necessary to finance such improvements or will not switch public expenditure from other less essential services. The limitation on taxes is justified by 'the right of working men and women to keep what they earn' – not the wish or the political necessity, but the right. To increase income tax by a penny on the standard rate with the specific intention of improving the quality of public medicine amounts to what Hayek derided as providing 'that different treatment which is necessary in order to place people who are very different into the same material position'. That is to say, the poor would receive the medical care which, if the laws of the market were allowed to prevail, would be the preserve of the rich. Since they could only be so elevated by redistributing wealth, the healing process would also involve 'agreement by the majority on sharing the booty gained by overwhelming a minority of fellow citizens or deciding how much is taken from them'. That, Hayek tells us, 'is not democracy' but 'the kind of immorality towards which unlimited democracy is moving'.[4] Never underestimate the passion with which the rich demand protection of their right to let other people live and die in poverty – or the excesses of false logic to which they go to justify their selfishness.

Hayek's refreshing insistence that liberty is about purchasing power puts the modern libertarian argument in realistic perspective. For Hayek is right to say that choosing any system other than that which results from market forces is imposing a system of social justice upon society. His mistake is to pretend that accepting market allocation does not involve a choice of system. Markets happen to be the system of social justice which the rich

[4] F. A. Hayek, *Studies in Philosophy, Politics and Economics* (Routledge & Kegan Paul, London, 1967), p. 170.

and powerful in general prefer. Working on the false premise that what he regards as the model of the good society is the 'natural society', Hayek argues that any other (socialists would argue *any*) system of social justice lacks legitimacy because it would not be generally accepted by members of the society on which it was imposed. Clearly, Berlin (who does not believe in quietism) insists that the 'notion of economic freedom depends on particular social and economic theory about the cause of poverty and weakness'[5]. Rawls asserts that 'a theory of justice depends on a theory of society'[6]. And it is certainly not for socialists to argue that there is no ideological basis either to their vision of the good life or to the definitions of the virtuous community in which that life can be led. The socialist view of society is based on the belief in the equal value of all human beings and the consequent obligation to provide them with as equal a share of society's benefits as it is possible to distribute. That is an assertion which socialists must insist is self-evident. It is no more possible to justify that belief with evidence and explanation than it is to justify in logic the Sermon on the Mount. The extension of freedom is an essential element within the philosophy of socialism. The belief in freedom and equality stands on the intrinsic merits of the ideal. Only the connection between them can be empirically demonstrated. Similarly, the relationship between the various forms of freedom – social, political, legal and economic – can, to a degree, be tested on the evidence of the way in which increasing any one of them enhances or diminishes the other. That is a first principle, an article of belief. But it is important to defend that ideological precept at least against the criticism of its application – the fear that an extension of positive freedoms in their economic form will reduce the legal and political freedoms which are available. The crude criticism alleges that the policies which allow everyone to have decent medical treatment are also those which forbid anyone from having different medical treatment and that to provide a house and holiday for every family may result in some being denied the houses which their individuality demands and the holidays which their talents deserve.

That allegation is – in some extreme cases – true. If the ability

[5] I. Berlin, *Inaugural Lecture as Professor of Social and Political Theory* (Clarendon Press, Oxford, 1958), p. 8.
[6] J. Rawls, *A Theory of Justice* (Oxford University Press, Oxford, 1972).

of a landlord to live in a castle and spend a third of the year in the south of France were dependent on his ability to finance those pleasures by charging unreasonable rents for inhabitable hovels, a civilised society would deny the landlord such freedoms. There is no advantage to be gained from denying the difficult choices which the promotion of real freedom requires, for it is clear that to increase the freedom of some may be to diminish the freedom of others. Freedom is not a finite commodity which has to be distributed on the understanding that if some get more others get less, but its overall increase may involve the reduction of unrestrained freedom enjoyed by a small minority. The extension of freedom involves some difficult decisions about distribution. That is one of the reasons why we have run away from it for so long.

Since the prohibition of fee-paying public schools and private medicine would immensely improve the quality of health care and education available to all the community, it would produce an equally immense increase in social and economic freedom at the expense of a small reduction in liberty as traditionally defined. To direct labour as a way of securing full employment or to prohibit home-ownership and allow the state to allocate 'housing accommodation' would produce an unacceptable reduction in freedom, even if it brought an end to the dole queues and to homelessness and overcrowding. Libertarians will argue that such a choice of policies is wholly subjective and that whilst one government may draw the line at the direction of labour, the prohibition of private medicine will establish the acceptability of state intervention in such matters and bring the day nearer when direction of labour is introduced. It is not possible to rest on the comforting reassurance of our characters and personalities to demonstrate that no such thing will happen. Critics are more likely to be confounded by the careful description of the rules by which it is possible to balance the limitations placed on one group against the additional advantages created for another.

The problems – as is so often the case with problems for politicians as distinct from theologians – concern where to draw the line. Socialists – not to mention members of the moderate right – will not find much difficulty in taxing millionaires in order to provide a better health service; nor will either of these groups resent or resist the undoubted 'coercion' involved in a whole range of prohibitions which prevent power from being misused and the possession of wealth from being exploited to the detriment of the poor. But socialists will not, or should not, approve of a whole range of other coercive acts which might on the application of the same principle be said to increase the total *sum* of freedom but do so by such a marginal amount that it is wrong to risk the danger which such policies imply. The danger is that the enthusiasm for (indeed, the belief in) the state's ability to increase equality and extend freedom will simply get out of hand – and what began as a genuine attempt to improve the liberties as well as to increase the material comforts of the whole community ends in intolerable levels of government bureaucracy and the suppression of those forms of individualism and personal expression which are essential to civilisation as well as liberty.

The obvious example is the Soviet Union, from which many democratic socialists have returned with the grudging admission that 'at least there is no unemployment'. The simple fact is the price that the system pays – in terms of personal freedom as well as efficiency – is too high to be justified, even by the remarkable achievement of being able to offer every citizen a job. It is necessary to look at the liberties enjoyed by a society as a whole. A country where legal coercion is virtually non-existent but within which millions of men and women are prevented from exercising the effective rights of citizenship because of their poverty would not, by any decent definition, be called a free society; but neither would a country in which an adequate level of subsistence was guaranteed by a wholly tyrannical system of law and regulation. Socialists who regard each sort of freedom as equally important are handicapped by their inability to lay down an iron law which determines the dividing line between the promotion and protection of each definition. Too little equality results in too little freedom. But the active promotion of *total* equality may actually inhibit the freedom that greater equality is intended to make possible. The problem is knowing where to draw the dividing line.

Rawls has constructed a formula to determine the acceptable level of inequality. Hirsch has suggested that there are physical and psychological limits to the extension of equality as well as the extent of growth. Only the new libertarian right has developed a theory on the interaction of liberty and equality that attempts precisely to relate the consequences of pursuing each objective. The theory is wrong, but that makes it no less compelling – indeed, its misguided simplicity is part of its appeal. The libertarian case is that every extension of equality is likely to be an infraction of liberty. The socialist case is that the relationship of the two conditions have to be envisaged as a curve. Freedom is increased with the promotion of equality until the pursuit of equality begins to have exactly the opposite effect. Then the additional equality actually reduces liberty. The problem is to decide when the top of the curve has been reached. We are clearly well below it in the United Kingdom. But there is clearly no algebraic formulation which enables us to judge the moment, for a whole society, when bonus turns into liability. We have to judge items of policy on their individual outcome. That, says the libertarian right, is the primrose path to tyranny. For once a state begins to 'create' greater equality, it does not know when or where to stop. That is why Hayek and company say that the process should not be allowed to start. That view is clearly unacceptable to socialists, but socialists have to pay proper regard to the fear that once we begin the promotion of equality we have started off down the road to serfdom. For, nonsensical though that view is, versions of it possess an intellectual respectability.

Isaiah Berlin made the point exactly in his *Inaugural Lecture*. It is, he says, 'the positive conception of liberty – not freedom from, but freedom to – which the adherents of the negative notion represent as, at times, no better than a specious disguise for brutal tyranny'.[7] The brutal tyranny begins – if it begins at all – when governments decide not that they are liberating men and women in order that the largest number of them can act as free agents in their own interests, but when the state decides what the citizens' best interests are – whether the individuals who make up the nation realise it or not. The idea of the state knowing best – rightly opposed and denounced by John Stuart Mill – is not a notion that can be attributed to any single political ideology. Islamic Fundamentalists believe it; so do Marxists – at least for the years before the state withers away. The problem of that idea is not its political associations but its naïvety. Sometimes the imposition of collective will is obviously necessary. But there must never be an attempt to justify

[7] I. Berlin, *Inaugural Lecture as Professor of Social and Political Theory* (Clarendon Press, Oxford, 1958), p. 7.

coercion on the grounds that it produces social or economic results which those who impose it assert to be desirable. Its justification is that, in the end, it enhances freedom not limits it. That has always to be the test. Without it, even the most distinguished disciples of liberty find themselves arguing strange cases in peculiar company.

Bentham stands at the top of authoritarianism's slippery slope by progressing from the assertion that all laws are infractions of liberty to an analysis of when such infractions are tolerable. 'Is it not liberty to do evil? If not, what is? Do we not say that it is necessary to take liberty from idiots and "bad men" because they abuse it?'[8] We can agree with his judgment on bad men, if their behaviour is accepted as evil by rational society and proved by the processes of law. But what of the idiots? The confinement of the criminally insane is generally accepted. But is that the sort of idiot whom Bentham had in mind? In the Soviet Union, they define idiocy differently and confine those who are embraced by their definitions in institutions for the politically deviant. Spinoza elaborated upon the point with an alarming analogy which compared coercion of the state's enemies with restraints on children. 'Children, although they are coerced, are not slaves' because 'they obey orders given in their own interests'. That impeccable statement of state paternalism is a product of classical élitism. 'No one,' says Fitche, 'has rights against reason', and he goes on to insist that 'to compel men to adopt the right form of government, to impose right on them by force, is not only the right but the sacred duty of every man who has both the insight and the power to do so'.[9] Thus paternalism mates with élitism and produces authoritarianism. The philosopher kings may be Old Etonians, members of the Central Soviet, property-owners with sufficiently valuable properties to entitle them to vote, first-class honours graduates, members of hereditarily powerful families, but the theory still applies. It involves a deep contempt of 'ordinary people' – whether it is the vanguard socialism of the modern Trotskyite or the patent disregard of the depressed 20 per cent which is exhibited by Thatcherite Conservatives.

Socialists must draw a sharp distinction between creating the conditions within which the maximum number of men and

[8] J. Bentham, quoted in *ibid.*, p. 33.
[9] Fitche, quoted in *ibid.*, p. 36.

women can exercise the greatest amount of effective freedom and the regulation of society according to some external view of what is best for them. Socialists attempt to organise society in a way which allows increasing numbers of men and women to make those choices for themselves. The creation of the conditions which allow the greatest sum of liberty almost certainly requires a curtailment of the rights presently enjoyed by the privileged minority. But the totality of rights is increased. Regulation – instruction by authority on the way in which individuals must behave – according to some preconceived notion of the good life may just possibly extend the sum of real freedom. But the most likely outcome is a net reduction in the total liberty available within society. It is not the duty of socialist governments to tell men and women how they should behave – except when a course of conduct might prejudice or damage the interests of others. It is the duty of socialist governments to prevent one group of men and women – acting as individuals, corporations or institutions – from coercing their fellow citizens by the use of political influence or economic power. Socialists should not confuse the first course of action with the second, because each involves the infraction of some rights. In the second case (despite and because of a limited infraction of the liberties of the powerful minorities) the sum total of freedom is increased. In the first, it is almost certainly reduced – in some cases, grossly so.

The line between the two conditions is not one which can be drawn exactly. It is the political strength – though the intellectual weakness – of the neo liberals to possess iron laws which they believe can be applied to every complex human situation. To distribute any commodity by means other than the mechanism of the free market is *automatically* to deny justice – for some individuals will be denied benefits which the markets would provide. For the government to restrict or constrain the behaviour of any of its citizens for any reason other than the preservation of the state is *automatically* an infraction of liberties which ought to be inalienable. And even the constraints which are imposed to maintain the autonomous integrity of the state must do no more than provide the framework of its existence. Laws which prohibit the misappropriation of private property – as well as police to enforce those prohibitions – are necessary. But tax-financed spending on projects which are believed to reduce theft and burglary – the alleviation of poverty and rehabilitation of offenders – is, however, outside a universally accepted concept of social justice and is, therefore, outside the proper area of state involvement. To apply the neo liberals' theories to the realities of real life is to expose at once the fundamental silliness of their arbitrary dictates. With such absolute rules, based on such arbitrary, first principles, the neo liberals can make instant judgments about the propriety of any proposed law or item of public expenditure. They therefore enjoy the consolation of certainty which is denied to those who hold a more sophisticated view of the proper organisation of society.

Socialists should not be embarrassed because they are not guided by intellectual tyrannies, for the world cannot be decently governed by such simplicities. They should be guided by the general principles of Rawls, who says that inequality is 'justifiable only if the difference in expectation is to the advantage of the representative man who is worse-off'[10], and Hirsch, who accepts that, to the extent that some inequalities may add to the wealth available to all, a measure of inequality could operate to the benefit of all.[11] There is, then, in principle, an optimum degree of inequality. But that assertion does not tell us how to deal with specific cases. For, as Hirsch wryly admits, if there is in practice an optimum degree of inequality, 'the problem is to find it'. The importance of the approach exemplified by Rawls and Hirsch is that it rejects formulae that demand either the total abdication of the state or the state domination of its citizens' lives. But there is an indispensable rule which has to be applied when the essentially subjective decisions about new laws and regulations are made. When we are not *certain* that the reduction in the liberties of one group results in extensions of liberties for another which produce a net increase in the sum of freedom, we should not impose the new regulations or impose the new laws. John Stuart Mill points the way. The state cannot 'constrain' a man for what it regards (against his judgment) as 'his own good'. And a good deal of administrative and bureaucratic 'inconvenience' can be borne 'for the sake of greater human freedom'.

Those general rules are much more important guides to our

[10] J. Rawls, *A Theory of Justice* (Oxford University Press, Oxford, 1972).
[11] F. S. Hirsch, *Social Limits to Growth* (Routledge & Kegan Paul, London, 1978).

legislative conduct than the strained and strangulated models of conduct which the neo liberals examine as a guide to public policy. Though it may be at least diverting to examine our principles against the sort of measurements which they regard as important. Working on the precedent of Isaiah Berlin's macabre example of blindness as a condition against which freedom (or its absence) can be measured, we may be able to examine with profit a subject which is presently exciting the far right in America: the propriety of a free market in human blood, organs and tissue. Free markets in these commodities – like all free markets – are defended by those who trade in them as essential to the preservation of essential liberties. P. Carlinger, the general manager of Pioneer Blood Services Inc., insists that if 'competition for blood were eliminated it would be the entering wedge for the destruction of our entire anti-monopoly structure'.[12] And the simple fact that the demand for organs exceeds their supply raises the market question of a higher price – or, in British terms, a price which changes a gift into a sale – bringing forward the extra supply of goods which will create the essential equilibrium. We can take the blindness analogy a step further. 'Natural' blindness is not an infraction of liberty – unless the condition could have been avoided but was either imposed by a brutal state or allowed by a callous society. What are we to think about blindness willingly accepted for payment? Is a state which prohibits it 'free'? The absurdity of the question illustrates the absurdity of new liberal philosophy, for some of its adherents insist that the prohibition of tissue and organ sales is in itself an 'infraction of liberty'. In *The Gift Relationship*, Richard Titmuss describes the potential market for eyes in Britain.

> At one such bank, the South Eastern Regional Eye Bank, 448 eyes were donated in 1965 – a number that had been steadily rising. Because the supply of donated eyes is much less in other countries without a National Health Service than it is in Britain 73 of these 448 corneas were exported as free gifts to India, Jamaica, South Africa, Singapore, Turkey, Hong Kong and other countries. Should human eyes, bequeathed by donors, or given by relatives to unknown strangers be treated as consumption goods and sold to the highest bidder? These are not just

[12] R. M. Titmuss, *The Gift Relationship* (Allen & Unwin, London, 1970), p. 158.

99

idle theoretical questions as experience in the United States and other countries has shown in recent years in the expanding area of organ transplantation.[13]

We already know that poor Indian donors have sold kidneys to rich Western recipients, that women are prepared to bear children for money, and that agencies have been set up to organise surrogate parenthood and that there is, in the United States, a body of opinion that demands a free market in adoption. Each of these potential areas for sale and profit is regarded by the libertarian right as a challenge to the equalitarian left. Could not the sum of freedom – in its most positive sense the ability to do what we want to do – be enhanced by healthy citizens being obliged to share their eyes and kidneys with their sick contemporaries who would be liberated from their incapacities by a process which would only partly disable the donors? We react against such a suggestion with disgust and disbelief, and we are right to do so. But we are then asked by the new right why, if it is acceptable to remove part of a man's wealth and distribute it for the benefit of his fellow citizens, it is not right to do the same with his body – particularly if he values a kidney less than he values his bank balance and would rather lose an eye than sacrifice a fortune. The neo liberals are explicit.

> Since society is willing to pay people to put their lives and health at risk in hazardous occupations, it is difficult to see why it should be thought objectionable to risk impairment by the sale of tissue . . . Justice Candozo said that each had property rights in his own body, but a conspiracy of physicists has greatly reduced the value of those rights . . . Decision-making by doctors therefore means that aggregate utility is less than maximised.[14]

The aesthetic answer, that a state should not pursue policies which are instinctively repulsive to a majority, is important. But it is not conclusive. The same can be said for the supplementary objection which Titmuss offers as a result of his researches into the collection and distribution of human blood.

[13] *ibid.*, Ch. 13, 'Who is My Stranger?', p. 219.
[14] S. Rottenburg, *The Production and Exchange of Used Body Parts.*

From our study of the private market in blood in the United States we have concluded that the commercialisation of blood and donor relationship represses the expression of altruism, erodes the sense of community, lowers scientific standards, limits both personal and professional freedoms, sanctions the making of profits in hospitals and clinical laboratories, legalises hostility between doctor and patient, subjects critical areas of medicine to the laws of the market place, places immense social cost on those lease able to bear them . . .[15]

The list of detriments makes up a whole paragraph. And it is reasonable to support the point that most – though not all – of the problems which beset the commercial collection and distribution of blood and body tissues would also prejudice any system of allocation which was based on any other principle than the freely made gift. But that is a pragmatic objection. We instinctively, and rightly, feel the need for a coherent objection in principle.

The objection in principle can be simply, if imprecisely, stated. Even liberty and equality are not ends in themselves. They are intermediate objectives which, having been achieved or more nearly approached, enable the achievement of the real aim: the full flowering of the individual human spirit. The ultimate ideal cannot be achieved – indeed it cannot even be approached – by policies which dehumanise the individuals whose lives pursuit of the ideal claims to enhance. It is for that reason that society is, or should be, repelled by the advocacy of a free market in organs, blood, tissue. The idea of transplants, adoptions or surrogacies being enforced by the state is no less repulsive – whether or not (on the basis of some mechanical equation) such state-imposed obligations would increase the sum of human happiness, increase the totality of freedom or reduce inequalities within society. The fashionable neo liberal debates about how organs and tissue provide a dramatic example of an area where the state should do no more than set the tone and hold the ring.

But there are other parts of life – conscientious and intellectual, as well as physical – where the same rules must apply. How many children would be removed from their parents if *all* that we wanted was a more equal distribution of those early

[15] R. M. Titmuss, *The Gift Relationship* (Allen & Unwin, London, 1970), Ch. 14, 'The Right to Give', p. 245.

benefits which prejudice the prospects of later prosperity? About 5 per cent of the population is psychologically incapable of organising family life which benefits rather than handicaps the children within the family. If *all* we wanted was the maximum amount of personal freedom, would we allow the Islamic Church to preach a gospel which results in an essentially second-class status for Muslim women or the Christian Church to promote inter-communal distrust by insisting in Northern Ireland on separate and specific denominational education? There are some areas of life where the state must hold back. The inability to draw the exact boundary line will be seized upon by the libertarians of the new right as proof that once the state begins to interfere, the enthusiasm for intervention which interference stimulates will promote escalating excesses of intrusion and direction.

The best defence against that accusation is the demonstration (in deeds as well as words) that socialists take freedom seriously. Socialists must become far more conscious than in the past of the need for active promotion of the greater freedom which comes from extended democracy, the positive promotion of choice and organisation of public affairs in units small enough to make the extended democracy effective and the prospect of increased choice meaningful. Opposition to authoritarianism, wherever it is to be found, must be open and obvious. Soviet tyranny is no more acceptable than South American tyranny. Indeed, in a personal sense, it is a good deal more offensive, because it hides behind a noble ideological title to which it is not entitled. Nor is it possible to distinguish between black freedom and white. It is probably inevitable that as emergent Africa struggles towards national identity, some liberty is sacrificed. But that does not make the sacrifice right. There are very little thanks likely to be offered to those who say that the new sovereign states are compressing into half a century of their history excesses which Western European countries spread over a thousand years. To the new nations, it will sound patronising, and to their enemies, it will sound like an excuse. *But whatever is said, it is necessary to be clear that the extension of the sum of freedom – real freedom – is the ultimate and fundamental object of government, and that the idea endures over time and space.* It is in the pursuit of that aim – and that aim alone – that state intervention is justified. And, in addition to those noble principles, we must be adding the practical rule which is worth repeating to bureaucrats and administrators, as well as politicians: when in doubt as to whether government action will or will not increase the sum of effective freedom, *do* nothing.

That rule has to apply in local as well as in national government, trades unions as well as political parties. Convincing advocates of the new liberties and extended freedom must be clear opponents of the old autocracies. It is impossible to defend the denial of local authority appointments to dissenters from the true faith of socialism or the refusal to allow the formal democratic process – either by trades unions which refuse to ballot their members or groups of protestors who break up local council meetings – and still maintain a reputation for protecting freedom and struggling for a wider diffusion of liberty. If positive action is to be introduced (as it must be introduced), to ensure that the minority groups receive the fair share of respect and resources which they are now denied, we must ensure that affirmative action does not become an excuse for denying the proper rights of the less articulate members of the majority population. True libertarians cannot afford to be identified with the fashionable view of liberty espoused by small-circulation magazines and middle-class dinner parties – protection from the petty bureaucrats of state and local government – and, at the same time, appear careless about the traditional liberties that many millions of men and women recognise. To establish the moral legitimacy which is necessary for the new freedoms to be accepted as naturally as the old liberties, it is essential that their advocates ensure that old liberties go hand in hand. Democratic socialism is the natural progress of John Stuart Mill's central precept on government conduct:

> This conduct consists, first, in not injuring the interests of one another, or rather certain interest which, either by express legal provision or tacit understanding, ought to be considered as rights; and secondly, in each person's bearing his share (to be fixed on some equitable principle) of the labours and sacrifices incurred by defending the society or its members from injury or molestation.[16]

Those who deny socialism's right to claim that statement as part of its ideological history face as difficult a task in justifying

---

[16] J. S. Mill, *On Liberty* (Parker & Son, London, 1859), IV, 'Of the Limits to the Authority of Society over the Individual', pp. 134–5.

their assertion as do those who claim that Mill is the prophet of agnostic government concerned with the framework, not the nature, of society. Is there not now a 'tacit understanding' that civilised governments have a duty to organise adequate health care for all their citizens? And do not the 'labours and sacrifices' of 'defending the society and all its members from injury' include paying for that health care? At its most minimal, the answer is that the freedom of the rich to maintain their riches to a point where adequate medical services cannot be adequately funded is a freedom which should not be accepted by a civilised society. The bolder answer to the question is that the generality of men and women have a right to receive the best medical services which the combined resources of the state can provide – and to deny the generality of men and women that right is an infraction of their liberties. It is, however, cheap, and it absolves the rich from an undoubted infraction which lies at the heart of all their highfalutin objections to increasing the sum of freedom – 'ever-increasing taxation, ever-increasing public expenditures'.[17]

The writings of F. A. Hayek on liberty – and the actions of politicians who have been guided by him – demonstrate that noble aspirations to freedom have, in modern times, been interpreted in the language of class interests. Those who want to maintain and enhance their wealth and power have advocated a form of freedom which enables them to do so. Sir Isaiah Berlin describes the urge for representative government in less than idealistic language.

> It seems unlikely that this demand for liberty has even been made by any but a small minority of highly civilised and self-conscious human beings. The bulk of humanity has certainly at most times been prepared to sacrifice this for other goals: security, status, prosperity, power, virtue, rewards in the next world; or justice, equality, fraternity and many other values which appear wholly, or in part, incompatible with the attainment of the greater degree of individual liberty and certainly do not need it as a precondition of our recognition . . . men who have fought for freedom have commonly fought for the right to be governed by themselves or their representatives.[18]

[17] I. Gilmour, *Inside Right* (Hutchinson, London, 1977), p. 179.
[18] I. Berlin, *Inaugural Lecture as Professor of Social and Political Theory* (Clarendon Press, Oxford, 1958), p. 158.

If, as socialists should believe, equality and liberty are indivisible, it first seems extraordinary that the extension of democracy has not produced a simultaneous increase in both conditions. Society remains unequal and unfree largely because the privileged have held on to their privileges by exploiting their entrenched position. Liberty has not been diffused from the 'highly civilised and self conscious human being' to the whole population because of the barriers – political and intellectual – which those groups have placed on the path to progress. For much of the argument about equality is the product of the simple fact which Sir Isaiah Berlin has described. Democracy has largely evolved as the right of small, élite groups to be 'governed by themselves or their representatives'. And government by the élite has turned out to be government for the élite. Nothing demonstrates that more clearly than the fatuous argument that equality impairs economic performance.

Chapter Six

When Everybody
is Somebody

The 'small minority of highly civilised and self-conscious human beings'[1], who were identified by Sir Isaiah Berlin as the true begetters of our constitutional liberty, fought for more than the right to be governed by themselves or their representatives. They fought for the world to be judged by their standards and in their interests, and the concept of freedom which they assiduously insinuated into our thinking – as if it were the only, the best or the most objective definition – was balanced by arguments against equality which were similarly calculated to preserve the power and prosperity of the establishment. The success of their campaign is beyond dispute. It has been fought with great sophistication. The establishment has always been ready to bend a little rather than risk the complete breakdown of their system. The franchise has been gradually extended; economic concessions have been granted. The hierarchies may have changed in composition, but not in shape or character. A ruling élite have remained in charge, partly as a result of their subtlety, partly because they have blended small changes with the constant repetition that big changes would be bad for us all. The fear of greater equality has infected millions of men and women who would undoubtedly benefit from the more even distribution of resources and has encouraged the patently false assumption that a system which does not favour the élite must be against the interests of the whole community.

An examination of the theory that improvements in the conditions of the rich automatically and inevitably help to improve the conditions of the poor has already shown the

[1] I. Berlin, *Inaugural Lecture as Professor of Social and Political Theory* (Clarendon Press, Oxford, 1958), pp. 46–7.

trickle-down theory to be short of supporting evidence but well endowed with sentimental humbug. Of course, nobody argues that *nothing* trickles down. It is not surprising – nor particularly admirable – that a society which increases the earnings and the resources of the most favoured members' classes also (as a by-product of that process) alleviates the suffering of the most disadvantaged groups within it. The extraordinary fact is that the bottom deciles in society have progressed so slowly whilst the top deciles have moved with such speed. The question we have to answer is not whether the slowest ship in the fleet has moved slightly more quickly because of the pace of the speed-boats at the front of the flotilla. Our real enquiry concerns whether or not the boats at the back would have moved forward at a faster rate had the whole fleet been organised in order to encourage their progress. Socialists argue that the positive promotion of equality would improve both the relative and absolute position of the least-advantaged members of society. Indeed, far from holding back the progress of society as a whole and impairing its economic efficiency, equality will actually improve the performance of the whole economy and increase its productive potential. Once again, it is important not to fall into the absolutist trap which is set by equality's opponents. Perhaps a system of arithmetic equality, arbitrarily imposed by an authoritarian bureaucracy, would produce all sorts of economic catastrophes – the sort of catastrophes which we have witnessed in Eastern Europe *without* any real equality. But that is not the sort of society which socialists hope to build. The egalitarian society encourages the talents and energies of all its members – not just the advantaged minority. Indeed, the whole argument for greater economic equality has been persuasively argued in the language of marginal utility.[2] The human happiness or pattern of economic actions of a millionaire is unlikely to be changed if his annual tax bill is increased by £5,000; but many of the 20 pensioners who, in consequence, could receive a weekly increase of £5 would feel that the world had dramatically improved.

The notion that extensions of equality must result in unaccept-able losses of output and efficiency is essentially based on the conviction that progress is dependent upon the performance of a

[2] See Douglas Jay, *The Socialist Case* (Faber, London, 1937).

small minority of society's members – the talented and industrious élite – and that it is their needs around which society must be organised. The obvious example of the theory is to be found in the whole philosophy of differentials in both primary and secondary incomes. It is assumed that advantaged groups must have their advantages – both absolute and relative – guaranteed and, indeed, whenever possible enhanced. For it is claimed that if either advantage is eroded, the vital élite will either emigrate to less egalitarian countries or choose sullenly not to work to their full capabilities. The emigration option is clearly not available to the generality of workers, but sullen withdrawal certainly is. Yet it is never suggested that they need the incentive of constantly increasing living standards.

'We have,' wrote Adam Smith, 'no Acts of Parliament against combining to lower the price of work, but many against combining to raise it.'[3] Since his day, a number of Acts have been passed, both to facilitate 'combination' and to prohibit starvation wages. But during the 1970s and 1980s the national mood and government policy changed. The Thatcher government – whilst proclaiming the need for financial incentives – has removed trades union immunities and abolished or emasculated the Wages Councils. The egalitarian argument is that the full human resources of society have to be liberated by incentives which apply to the whole population – the incentive of continually improving material standards for each of the social groups and the less tangible but equally important incentive of being regarded as equal (in society's concern and esteem) to any and every other member. The incentives which are associated with concern and respect are easy to deride as the product of moral sentimentality, but they are highly regarded by the upper echelons of wealth and privilege. Senior civil servants are said to be spurred on by the recognition provided by the honours system. White-collar workers regard the escape from the indignity of 'clocking-on' as more than a convenience. Managers resist the idea of eating in the same restaurant as that which is used by those whom they manage; indeed, they expect the two different places to be separated by different names – dining-room and canteen. Often, the recipients of the highest salaries insist that additions to their earnings are necessary not to

---

[3] A. Smith, *The Wealth of Nations* (Methuen & Co., London, 1930), Vol. 1, p. 68.

increase their purchasing power but to demonstrate the esteem in which they are held. What is intangible when applied to the lowest paid is material when related to those who earn top salaries. This chapter is concerned with employing society's resources to the full. That involves the organisation of our affairs to ensure that outcome. It also requires us to put incentives into their proper perspective. Incentives are important; they are important to everybody, yet not as important to the very rich (at least in terms of improving their performance) as the very rich make out.

The analysis of what makes a man or woman perform, at work, to the utmost levels of ability and energy is a complicated and controversial study. According to Professor Frederick Herzberg of the University of Utah it contains two distinct elements: the Adam Factor, which, since it is concerned with the avoidance of suffering and deprivation, translates itself into the desire for pay, and the Abraham Factor which impels a worker to seek the feeling of achievement, the confidence of recognition, responsibility and the prospects of advancement. Herzberg did his work on satisfaction and dissatisfaction in employment amongst the engineers and accountants of Pittsburgh. But there is absolutely no reason to assume that the blastfurnacemen and steelworkers of that town were so different from their professional contemporaries that they were motivated by totally different stimuli. To ensure the best economic performance from workers of any sort, society must both pay them enough and convince them that they have the respect of both their employers and the community.[4]

An examination of the practical applications of equality must be preceded by a parenthesis in which another allegation about its economic consequence is considered: the allegation that equality is incompatible with the existence of competition and the market distribution of resources, and that those who seek equality wish to create a Soviet-command economy in which nationalised monopolies regulate their output and prices according to a central plan. The rôle of markets in a democratic society is the subject of a subsequent chapter. Here, three things have to be said about them in order that we avoid even temporary confusion. Certainly markets allocate resources in a

[4] For comparisons of the rival theories of efficiency and motivation see Pugh, Hickson and Hinings, *Writers on Organisations* (Penguin, London, 1971).

way which accentuates inequalities and cannot, therefore, be left to operate in every sector without either direction or control. However, leaving a large part of the economy to be governed and guided by the market distribution is essential to liberty as well as efficiency. But that substantial market sector need not be privately owned. Once we begin properly to define social ownership (a task attempted in Chapter 10) in terms at once more accurate and more imaginative than the nationalised corporation, we begin to understand that competition and capitalism are not synonymous. Indeed, since capitalism breeds monopoly and monopoly (not socialism) is the true antithesis of competition, capitalism and competition are incompatible. A fourth point on the subject of markets hardly needs to be made. They do not possess the moral significance or the power to promote efficiency which is attributed to them by F. A. Hayek and his disciples. They are another example of the way in which bar-room opinions – dressed up in ponderous language – acquire a spurious authority.

Market distribution means many different things to different people. If it means a system which allows production to be determined by demand, socialists should – as a general rule – support such a system. But that does not mean that socialists should support a market distribution of income – either primary or secondary. Evan Durbin, the author of *The Politics of Democratic Socialism* and a major force in the Labour Party's pre-war economic thinking, insisted that

> apart from a limited number of social services, the production of no final commodity should be subsidised out of general funds; if people are not willing to pay what it costs to produce goods, they must really prefer to buy and consume something else.[5]

It is difficult to imagine a more robust statement of support for the market system – though the 'general fund' qualification does allow room for subsidies intended to promote employment and other aims desirable to the community as a whole. But whilst democratic socialists support demand-led production, the level and pattern of that demand cannot be left for the market alone to determine. The overall total will be determined by

[5] Quoted by Elizabeth Durbin, *New Jerusalems* (Routledge & Kegan Paul, London, 1985), Ch. 8, 'The New Fabians' Plan for Socialism', p. 177.

macro-economic considerations. The *pattern* will depend partly on the way in which the general level of economic activity is to be regulated and upon the nature of the society by which the demand is generated. It is essential to influence the distribution of the incomes which produce aggregate purchasing power; and an understanding of demand management, as well as of the problems associated with velocity of circulation and the propensity to consume, allows governments to arrange change in the pattern of consumption without creating insuperable economic problems. A reduction in the demand for champagne, fur coats and pearl necklaces will not, in itself, inhibit economic progress, particularly if it is matched by an increase in the demand for consumer durables from those families who still do their washing by hand, keep their food in unhygienic cupboards and are isolated in old age because they cannot afford a telephone. Socialists are not opposed to the market allocation of most goods and services. Socialists are opposed to the so-called market allocation of income, though – thanks to inheritance – the market on purchasing power is, even now, hideously imperfect. The question that a sensible egalitarian policy thus provokes is not, therefore, about allocative efficiency. It concerns social justice in one form or another. In one of its manifestations, that concept is said to be constantly on the lips of upwardly mobile, able and ambitious young executives and technologists. 'Why,' they are thought to ask, 'should I support a system which would pay me less than I would receive if the market allocated my earnings?' or (in the slightly less elevated version) 'if I lived in America?' The related questions are, 'Why should I contribute to the cost of services for others whose earning capacity does not allow them to provide for themselves?' and 'Why should I accept limitations on the way in which I spend my earnings in order to co-operate with an organisation of society which is intended to meet the needs of others?'

There are, of course, moral answers to all those questions – answers which challenge the implied assumption that earning power is somehow related to intrinsic worth and ultimate potential. But such arguments are not certain to appeal to the potential tax exile or the instinctive devotee of unrestricted enterprise. Such people, if they are to be convinced at all, have to be persuaded that there are practical and material arguments for equality. For them, we have to provide answers to the sort of

111

rhetorical question asked by Sir Woodrow Wyatt in his little book *What's Left of Labour*? It is the typical enquiry of a bewildered bourgeois father.

> What is a higher earner to do about the education of his children? . . . Until the top earner sees the state schools providing an education and attitude to life as that provided by the public schools, why should he subject his children to them if he can avoid it?[6]

Such questions will not be convincingly answered by priggish expressions of moral outrage. Simply striking moral poses (or even taking up intellectually acceptable moral positions) about the antisocial habits of parents who ask such questions is an unproductive, as well as unattractive way to behave. Opponents of private health schemes and private schools do their cause no service by sanctimonious disapproval of the father who is anxious to do the best for his daughter and the mother who makes sacrifices for the future of her son. Our complaint is not against them individually; it is against the society and the philosophy of society which encourages them to break ranks with their fellow citizens in the hope of competitive advantage.

The whole argument in favour of breaking ranks is concerned with the élitist view of society – not the desirability but the necessity of some individuals making special progress and receiving special incentives. The case for private education is based on one of two possible assertions. The first is that in a free society, a family has the right to spend its legitimate earnings in whatever way it chooses. Its vulgar form is the question: 'Why is it right to spend our money on beer, cigarettes and continental holidays, but wrong to spend it on school fees?' The answer has already been provided by Mill. There cannot be freedom to behave in a way which damages the interests of others thus confounded. In the second assertion the public-school apologists switch tack and develop their own version of the trickle-down theory. An exclusive form of education – which is different from and superior to the state system – is *necessary for society* as a whole. First, such a system improves general educational standards by setting the educational pace. Second, according to its proponents, it is necessary for the progress and expansion of

[6] W. Wyatt, *What's Left of Labour?* (Sidgwick & Jackson, London, 1977), Ch. 10, p. 135.

society. For the education provided for the generality of men and women is not good enough for future leaders of society.

The special needs argument (like the incentive argument) is about people who are different from, and better than, the rest of society. Sir Woodrow's implication is clear. State schools are inferior to those attended by the children of high earners, and therefore not good enough for those parents who can afford anything better. But his reaction less concerns the improvement of the state sector than the right of a fortunate few to do the best for themselves whilst leaving the second best for everyone else. The Woodrow Wyatt position, although it takes refuge behind a vague inchoate idea of general improvement, is essentially the advocacy of different levels of provision. For anyone who argues the case for the high-income earner with such passion is unlikely to advocate 'equality of outcome' in education, by which the high-income parent is encouraged to choose the general system of education for their children. It is not the academic quality which counts, but the difference.

Indeed, the whole incentive argument – the need for a special group to be offered special advantages and encouragement – depends on the preservation of the inequalities that give some people the chance to rise above their previous peers. For much of the impetus to make progress in modern society is not the hope of doing better in itself, but the hope of doing better than others. Whatever effect that dynamic has on the economic progress of society, it certainly undermines the liberal hope that 'the official distinction between working men and gentlemen' would be replaced by the recognition that 'by employment at least, every man *is* a gentleman'[7]; for when working men become gentlemen, gentlemen want to become something else. The liberal theory of advance begins with the individual progress of a limited number of talented individuals; then the initial relative advantage of the vanguard turns into the general progress of the lower-income groups within society. The potential results of such a process are, if the theory holds good, immense.

> This growth process has the statistical property that a relatively short period of compounding would raise the consumption of

---

[7] Quoted in A. C. Pigou (ed.), *Memorials of Alfred Marshall* (Macmillan, London, 1925), pp. 101–118.

the mass of lower-income groups to levels higher than would result from redistribution of all the excess resources currently accruing to top-income groups. This is the crude but classical case for giving priority to growth rather than to redistribution, a case that is regularly revived in popular discussion with an undiminished air of breathtaking novelty.[8]

However, growth may not be a choice which is open to us – partly because the world economy can either not organise or not sustain the continual output which we once believed to be a normal feature of modern existence or because growth has 'limits' which we once did conceive. Hirsch, of course, argues that growth and equality are simply different sorts of chimera, both of which end with disappointment for both rich and poor: 'economic growth in advanced societies carries some element of built-in frustration: the growth process, when sustained and generalised, fails to deliver its full promise. The growth process runs into social scarcity.'[9] Hirsch's position – 'that there is no such thing as levelling up . . . One's reward is set by one's position on the slope and the slope itself prevents a levelling from below as well as from above'[10] – does not help us to determine the relationship between efficiency and equality, growth and redistribution. The underlying assumption that 'too much equality' holds back economic advance is deeply ingrained in the common subconscious of industrial society, but it does not withstand objective examination. The theory is dependent on the view that the enthusiasm of the talented few is more important to the material well-being of all society than is the full involvement of the whole of that society's members. The rich are said to need immediate material incentives. The poor – whilst being careful not to price themselves out of jobs – must survive and participate on no greater encouragement than the hope that *if* they move up a social class or two, then they will be thought to need material incentives. The futility of that argument is easily demonstrated by a brief examination of the performance of those sectors of the economy in which the effects of inequality can be most easily measured. The first is the education system in Britain.

---

[8] F. A. Hirsch, *The Social Limits to Growth* (Routledge & Kegan Paul, London, 1960), Pt 4, 'Prospective and Conclusions', p. 175.
[9] *ibid.*
[10] *ibid.*, p. 176.

Education is the paradigm of positional goods, the commodity which many parents want for their children, not simply in adequate quantity and quality, but in a form which clearly distinguishes it as better than the supply obtained by their competitors. The special features about which parents are concerned may be a knowledge of Greek, a familiarity with the New Testament, the ability to win an open scholarship to Oxford or a clearly recognisable school uniform. The ability of the school to provide most of these advantages will be manifest by the size of the classes in which the pupils are taught, the qualifications of the staff and past results. Sometimes the special and superior characteristics which fathers seek and mothers desire will be social rather than academic. Schools which inculcate certain values – military at Wellington, pacifist at Acomb – will command high fees. Even schools which simply demonstrate their difference by insisting on blazers for boys and boaters for girls will be able to fill their classrooms with paying pupils. That such schools are in demand is not open to dispute; and that part of their attraction is the fact of being different – whatever the nature of the difference – is equally certain. What is in popular doubt is the effect, on the whole education system, of segregated education. In determining the answer, prejudice competes with evidence to provide the conclusion.

Education has always been a positional good. One hundred and fifty years before Fred Hirsch coined the phrase, Matthew Arnold – the prophet and apostle of equality – quoted a leader from the nineteenth-century *Times*:

> The whole system of this country, like the constitution we boast to inherit and are glad to uphold, is made up of established facts, prescriptive authorities, existing usages, powers that be, persons in possession and communities and classes that have won domination for themselves and will hold it against all comers.[11]

That was an argument about the desirability – perhaps even the possibiity – of providing a national system of education. The arguments of 1870 were reproduced 100 years later when comprehensive education was being extended throughout Great Britain. As a result of the ignorance and misunderstanding,

[11] M. Arnold, *Culture and Anarchy*, Ch. 3 'Barbarians, Philistines, Populace', p. 313.

115

these arguments were espoused for years by parents who advocated them to the disadvantage of their own children. In the twenty years between 1945 and 1965, thousands of families, whose sons and daughters had no real choice about obtaining a place at a grammar school, fought for the retention of selective education – because they preferred the chance (no matter how remote) of achieving something different to the certainty of a better education than that which, in reality, the system would provide. The propaganda and the prejudice had an extraordinary effect. The old selective grammar schools were revered as centres of excellence, not because they were excellent but because they were selective. In many cases, their academic records were appalling. In September of each year, a fourth-form-entry school received 120 new pupils – each one chosen because of intellectual potential and most of them the products of ambitious and supportive families. The new entrants were then taught by highly qualified teachers in small classes. Money was spent on them which, had they been registered in other schools, they would have been denied. Yet, in most cases, the sum total of this school's academic achievements was places in provincial universities, polytechnics and colleges of education for 15 out of the original 120 pupils.

Looking back, it seems extraordinary that so many parents accepted the inadequacies of the old grammar schools with good grace. It was even more incredible that the parents of the grammar-school rejects should have tolerated for any period of time a system which formally and officially designated their children as 'failures' and therefore made them recipients of a type of education which was known to be inferior to the best which society could offer – with no other refuge or consolation than technical arguments about the selection methods. They tolerated it so long for four reasons:

1. A peculiar combination of arithmetic incompetence and psychological irrationality gave parents of children below the age of eleven the idea that their sons and daughters were being 'given a chance'. Perhaps the British middle classes realised that 85 per cent of any age group *could not* qualify for grammar-school places, that there were just not enough glittering prizes to go round. But seriously, as most of them were concerned about the educational prospects of

their sons and daughters, they felt the attraction of a lottery determining their children's future prospects. The likelihood is that they would win nothing; but there was a chance of winning a lot.

2. There was a fear that to deny privilege to a fortunate few would somehow upset the proper order of society. The idea that Waterloo was won on the playing fields of Eton has joined with the notion that the Battle of Britain would have been lost had it not been for the direct grant schools. Thanks to our history, the generality of British citizens did not have the confidence to resist and resent an education system which favoured a few and penalised many.

3. There was assiduous cultivation of the nonsense that the cost of adequate education for all is so prohibitive that society has to make a choice: either educate a small proportion of its citizens adequately or spread the education budget so thinly across the whole academic spectrum that no one is properly educated. The majority are thus required to make a sacrifice in order to provide a high quality education for their future masters.

4. Philistine Britain was reluctant to adopt what it believed to be the 'theory' of the non-selective education as distinct from the established practice of secondary segregation. Comprehensive education was not simply a theory. It was a new theory and, therefore, all the more suspect. Thirty years after its introduction, the comprehensive system was still dismissed as an 'experiment'.

It is not possible here to recite the whole theory of non-selective education – the encouragement that comes from the declaration of belief in a child's potential as compared with the disincentive of being publicly labelled as an 'eleven-plus failure'; the chance of improvement which it offers late development; and the improved use of resources which flow from an even distribution of teaching talent and physical equipment, which comes from insisting on parity of provision instead of pretending that there can be parity of esteem as the end product of a system which is designed to demonstrate and entrench differences in perceived worth. But it is possible to demonstrate the outcome of the introduction of the non-selective system – at least in terms

of the hard facts of examination results. Critics of the compre-
hensives will argue that the improvement in academic achievement is coincidental; though before the statistics were available,
they argued (during the so-called Great Debate and within the
strangely named Black Papers) that the end of selection would
depress overall standards, even according to the criteria which
the élitists once embraced but now deride. About 'results', they
were simply wrong. The figures for the decade in which non-
selective education was established are indisputable. In the
school year 1974–5, 12.4 per cent of pupils in the maintained
sector ended their education with one or more A-level passes.
By 1983–4, the percentage had risen to 14.3 per cent. Over the
same period, leavers with five or more O-levels (Grades A–C)
or CSE passes at Grade 1 increased from 7.8 per cent to 10.5 per
cent. Leavers with no CSE or GCE qualifications fell from 29.8
per cent to 9.9 per cent.[12]

That evidence is uncontravertible. But it does not demonstrate
that our schools are doing as well for the nation's children (and
in consequence for the nation's prospects) as is necessary.
Indeed, the education system hovers on the brink of catastrophe.
But that is not because it is based on too much equality. The
problem with British schools is that they are part of a society
which has turned its back on equality and created whole
generations of pupils who are wholly and understandably
alienated from society. In an age when inner-city school leavers
have a one in twenty chance of getting a job, it is not surprising
if inner-city truancy is rife and inner-city academic motivation
notably absent. At a time when inner-city careers teachers are
retrained to help prepare young people for long-term unemployment, it would be unreasonable to expect either William
Shakespeare or Isaac Newton to be the dominant classroom
influences. The miracle is that, under present conditions, our
schools have done so well.

Despite the evidence, it is depressingly probable that if the
system of selection had been organised in a way which only
worked to the disadvantage of the working classes, we would
probably still suffer the damaging effects of segregated secondary
schools. The bias of the system against the interests of the
working class prolonged its active life. But, in the end, the

[12] Statistics of Education, *School Leavers CSE and GCE 1984*, DoES.

118

articulate and thinking members of the upwardly mobile classes also rebelled – going together (not without some embarrassment) with the enlightened opinion that had always argued that greater equality would promote a higher, not lower, level of national performance. Had the proponents of the 'comprehensive experiment' not won the argument we would, today, be a less well educated society. In education, equality and overall efficiency go hand in hand.

That proposition is equally true in hundreds of other fields of economic activity, but we are prevented from acknowledging the truth by the centuries of prejudice which have taught us to believe that human progress is dependent upon individual endeavour. In one sense, it is. But it is not always dependent on individual action or upon individual action alone. Progress is actually held back by individual action by or on behalf of the rich and the powerful when the promotion of their individual interest inhibits movement towards the common economic good. The prejudice in favour of unqualified individualism is buttressed by two other related items of conventional wisdom and accepted truth. The first is that money spent privately is more likely to benefit the commercial economy than money spent by a public institution. Thus, it is beneficial to build a new factory but profligate to invest in the roads and sewers on which its viability depends. That arithmetical idiocy is even built into public sector accounting. Investment in British Telecom, made the day after its privatisation, is regarded as productive capital formation. The day before privatisation, exactly the same investment was adjudged to be a profligate addition to the Public Sector Borrowing Requirement.

Indeed, the conventions of Treasury accounting provide the second wave of reinforcements for the theories which assert, without offering proof, that efficiency comes from private spending alone. For Treasury accounting assumes that costs which cannot be calculated and entered into the columns of the Blue Book of public expenditure do not exist. Yet most of us know that such costs are real because we have, to our detriment and disadvantage, paid them. The problem is that in a progressive tax system (even one like that which currently operates in Great Britain and is only mildly progressive) the equation of income to expenditure gets hopelessly confused by class interests. Taxes are paid by the articulate well-to-do who

119

can calculate the size of the bill they pay for services which, whilst available to them, they probably ignore in favour of superior private provision. The services, on the other hand, are either enjoyed by the inarticulate poor or by such a wide spectrum of the population that it is impossible to calculate the benefit which they provide with any like precision. We can only calculate in the most impressionistic terms the cost saving of clean air; the financial benefit of reducing the total hospital bill for patients suffering with respiratory diseases; the price paid for the erosion and dilapidation of our buildings. The costs of these invisible detriments were never calculated, but they are real enough, nevertheless. They fall, equally, on rich and poor. Indeed, in terms of the reductions which they make in competitive efficiency, the damage which they do to the economy is probably greatest when such costs are levied on the well-to-do. Let us take a simple example which embraces three damaging prejudices in a single episode of maladministration.

It is assumed that reductions in rates are, by definition, likely to improve the economic prospects of the area in which the rates are levied, for the reductions will reduce the overheads of companies within that town or county. Clearly, that may be the case. Aesthetic and social considerations (which are not the concern of this chapter) aside, to end a local authority subsidy to a repertory theatre or a battered wives' refuge might reduce the rates and cut industrial costs. But the pressure to switch from public to private expenditure inevitably results in a reduction in services with a direct economic importance. One obvious example is road building and mending, where money is now regularly 'saved', either by leaving the work undone or by employing 'cheaper' private contractors. Very often the private contractors are cheaper because they do the work more slowly or less well. The egalitarian resists such privatisation because of the hardship it causes the less well-off who are peculiarly dependent on public services. The damage done to their interests is most dramatically illustrated by privatisation in the health service, where the standards of cleaning, laundering and cooking have all, on occasion, been reduced by privatisation. But in road repairs and maintenance, the same rule applies. Broken paving stones and blocked gutters are a greater problem to pensioners living on supplementary benefit than they are to the company directors who want to keep the rates down, for pensioners use the pavements more frequently than company directors. But a second result needs to be considered. All over the country, there are company directors who ought to be hustling for export orders, supervising the quality control of their product, or raising new investment funds but who are sitting in traffic jams because the hole in the road has not been mended. Many more are sitting in stationary railway trains because British Rail cannot afford the cost of either new stock or adequate maintenance. The cost to their companies cannot be shown in a balance sheet. So we pretend that it does not exist. The price of reducing that cost is more public expenditure. So we do not even consider which is the best bargain. Thanks to the cult of individualism, we often deny ourselves the greater efficiency that comes from collective effort.

The proposition that collective activity is likely to be inefficient and unproductive whilst individual enterprise is certain to promote prosperity and growth is, in part, based on a fatuous over-confidence in the market and invariable merits of competition. It is also based on the proposition that progress is dependent on the existence of a society divided by hierarchies of wealth and power – ladders up which the elect and ordained can climb. But such a theory wholly neglects the psychology of those who are not the chosen few with a genetic make-up and family background which makes them capable of rising above their fellow men. The alienation of the generality of British workers has held back our economic progress to a degree which is probably unequalled either by our tradition of low investment or reluctance to innovate and our nineteenth-century reliance on invisible earnings from the empire. The morale of working men and women – enthusiasm for employment which goes beyond the need to earn a weekly wage – is a vital but often forgotten element in every industrial equation. Britain – neither mobile nor equal – has ignored that vital element, with desperate consequences for our national prosperity.

The four arguments by which selective schools were for so long defended are still applied to other aspects of our society – even by individuals who suffer from the acceptance of such spurious logic. Their constant repetition shows how unconcerned we remain about social cohesion. Everybody should have a chance to rise above the general level of society, even though

121

(by definition) that 'chance' can have no real meaning for most of the population. A disturbance of the traditional order of society would damage the interests of even those individuals in the lower echelons of society, even though they have precious little to lose. The cost of providing a decent life for the least advantaged families would be prohibitive – even though vast amounts of natural income could be diverted from less essential objectives. Equality is a theory, an aspiration, an ideal, and therefore highly dangerous, even though inequality is a philosophical prejudice masquerading as a social and biological inevitability. In no area of life do those arguments do more damage than when they are applied to the 'incentives' which are necessary for the successful progress of the economy.

The incentive argument is crucially dependent on the theory that society's progress requires an élite minority. No one denies that encouragement – in terms of material reward, recognition or the esteem of peers – is important. But the incentive argument says more than that: it insists that the progress of society is dependent not on the prospect of doing better – but on the prospect of doing better than other people. It is based on the theory of individual advance – or the hope of individual advance – not the prospect of general improvement. It depends, in part, on the dark side of the limits to growth theory. For if a whole class could advance into the position once occupied by their social superiors, the prospect of superior individuals being encouraged by the hope of greater rewards for their special talents would be eroded. If Hirsch is right, the prospects of most members of society climbing very far up the incentive ladder are about as good as the chance of most children being allocated grammar school places under the old eleven-plus examination system. But the intelligent tadpoles in Tawney's pond reconcile themselves to inferior status and inferior wages, because a few of their number will one day receive the respect and salary due to frogs. Or at least they once did. Perhaps they would again if there was in Britain any tradition of social and economic mobility. The dynamic of the United States was partly dependent on the little black boy in Watts or Harlem really believing that only failures of intellect and industry would prevent him from becoming President. When he stopped believing that, he began to burn the ghettos down.

In Britain, we have never believed in redemption through

mobility, so there has been no sudden, head-on collision with reality and consequent outbursts of rebellion and resentment. But the damage done to our society – particularly its economic prospects – has probably been more damaging. Today, Britain is appreciably less prosperous than many of the countries about which Victorian music-hall comedians sang their contemptuous songs. And our relative decline accelerates. We can, if we choose, attribute our failures to debilitating national character-istics – neither a popular nor a plausible explanation of why the success which characterised our economy before 1870 dis-appeared thereafter. We can blame it on the destabilising influence of government intervention or the debilitating effects of welfare. But the decline began four decades before Beveridge and Keynes began to exert their insidious influence, and many of our more successful competitors run far more interventionist policies and provide far higher levels of welfare than we have ever experienced in Britain. We can curse our bad luck or our bad timing and complain that we have the wrong relationship of land mass to population; or that we sacrificed our assets to win two world wars to which America made only a belated contribution, Sweden and Austria no contribution at all, and during which Japan and Germany cunningly managed to have all their obsolete industry destroyed. We could add that we abandoned a century of overseas investment and a century of invisible exports in order to give independence to what were once our colonies. And part of each explanation is undoubtedly true. But the explanations concern the past. They are of proper interest to historians of our industrial decline. They are not, however, particularly valuable to politicians whose primary interest should be changing and improving the future. We cannot recreate the Raj, prohibit Eastern Europe textile production or resuscitate the habit of travelling long distances by sea. We need – if we are to revive our chronically flagging economy and boost our persistently low national morale, as well as national income – to find a remedy which is about 'now', not 'then'.

One is readily to hand. It concerns an aspect of the British economy on which both socialists and conservatives agree – though there is a widening divergence about the proper remedy. We need to change the nature of British society. It is the most fundamental of all the supply-side proposals. Those limited reforms – extensions and new forms of public ownership, for example – will be related to the primary objective. But they will succeed in giving the British economy the boost which it needs not only insofar as they contribute to the conviction that British industry belongs to the people who work within it. Today, too many British workers feel alienated from the system within which they earn their livings.

No one who has watched British society since the war can honestly doubt that both its organisation and the mores which it has encouraged have a massively adverse effect on our economic performance, natural cohesion and collective self-confidence. Britain is the one society in the western world which has simultaneously rejected mobility and equality. In Britain, the class system is more entrenched and more respected, more complicated, more formally recognised and officially accepted than in any other industrialised democracy. Spared the trauma of revolution (we escaped completely in 1789 and virtually in 1848, and we were on the wrong side in 1776) we never sloughed off the trappings of hierarchy and deference. We added to them other complex tests of social acceptability – accent, type of education as distinct from educational attainment, social origins and even place of birth. The dominant class sometimes appeared to liberalise the organisation and apparatus of the state. But the changes always preserved the existence of a distinct officer class. In British society, there has never been smooth progress from warrant officer to second lieutenant. The classes are stratified; movement between them is *intentionally* restricted. We have turned our backs on real equality. When we should have chosen a conscious attempt to distribute resources more equally, we have not even provided some of our citizens with sufficient resources to make them truly free.

Equality of income is not an attempt to make everyone identical or a hope that we can be cajoled or coerced into behaving in the same way. It is the organisation of society with the conscious intention of minimising inequalities. That principle can be applied, with enormous material benefit, to the organisation of the economy. Socialists are, by definition, what is fashionably called 'supply-siders'. We believe in economic progress – as well as social advance – by changing the structure of the economy in a way which promotes our goals of general freedom and increased equality. We believe, too, in the

124

promotion of these ethical values which in a democracy are essential if freedom and equality are to be extended. To achieve that aim, we must demonstrate that equality and the freedom it brings will produce benefits in which the whole community can share.

THE PRACTICE

Chapter Seven

Choose Equality

That in the past the pursuit of liberty through equality has sometimes failed is not in dispute. But the pursuit of liberty through the unregulated economy and the promotion of freedom by the state simply abandoning restraint over weak and powerful alike have failed continually and conspicuously. Socialists take it for granted that a society in which monopolies are allowed to flourish and where wealth is allowed to extend its power without restraint cannot be a genuinely free society. In the second half of this book the conditions of economic equality are set out. Much of the first half was devoted to criticism of the arbitrary – indeed artificial – distinction which is made between social freedom, political liberty and economic equality: the three conditions are inseparable and the aim of all three is individual emancipation. And it is worth spending a moment considering why, in the past, the pursuit of that aim has sometimes been side-tracked into policies which actually reduce the liberties which they are supposed to enhance.

Part of the problem is the paradox of the relationship between our overriding principle and the practice by which that principle is applied. *Socialism requires the use of collective power to increase individual rights and to extend individual freedom.*

Until power and wealth are evenly distributed, the only way in which the weak and poor can pursue their aims is by concerted action for a common goal. But the collective action is not an end in itself. Once the victorious army has liberated the oppressed people, the temptation to worship both the military ethic and the military technique becomes almost irresistible. The confusion of means and ends is often more sentimental than sinister. Surely, the rhetorical question runs, we can do more together? And so we can. But what we can do by common action ought to be directed to the extension of individual freedom. There is no reason, apart from linguistic confusion, to believe that collective action should result in a collectivist society. Power, once attained, is certainly difficult to relinquish. But – to extend the military analogy – socialists rarely retain power like liberating armies which forget, once the tyrant is defeated, that one tyranny is very much like another. When socialists retain for the government rights which should be passed out to the people, there is usually a genuine belief that the suffocating hand of state bureaucracy will provide the greatest good for the greatest number. That may be because some socialists do not understand that the greatest good is the greatest freedom and that the only argument of consequence is how it can be extended to the greatest number. It may be the product of misplaced paternalism and the presumptuous notion that those who are elected always can judge what is best for those by whom they are elected. Those, comparatively common, errors need closer examination. But much of the problem stems from the willingness to argue the case within the terms set down by our opponents. When freedom is defined as the absence of restraint, socialists know that it does little or nothing to liberate the generality of men and women. If socialists insisted on defining freedom in a way which is related to the reality of making people free, two benefits would result. First, at least one side of the political argument would have taken up an intellectually defensible position. Second, democratic socialism would be seen as primarily concerned with freedom – and democratic socialists would take greater care both to observe that article of faith and to avoid a reputation for heretical disregard for that cannon of belief.

The intellectual confusion about the meaning of freedom (and the abduction of the word by the political right) is undoubtedly the principal reason why it is popularly supposed that socialists do not care about liberty. There is something in our nature which encourages the British to believe that denial of the rich's right to send their sons to the private school of their choice is an infringement of liberty whilst the denial of the poor's ability to send their children to a decent school of any sort is not. But socialists in Britain, and radicals before them, must take some of the blame for not tackling the freedom argument head on. That has been attempted in the previous six chapters. The other major social failing has been either weak-minded belief or meek acceptance of the propaganda that socialism involves a directed economy, governed by state monopolies through the bureaucratic allocation of resources. That is the subject of the next six chapters. Two minor obstacles to the understanding of freedom's inalienable connection with socialism are worth a moment's examination before we discuss that particular liability; for by examining them it is possible to illustrate avoidable confusions and help construct a description of what a society committed to the freedom that equality of outcome brings is like. The two detriments are a popular misunderstanding about the rôle and responsibility of trades unions and a widely held misconception about the record of local government. In both cases it would be disingenuous not to admit that socialists, operating in both areas, have from time to time seemed hell-bent on proving their critics right.

The argument about the place of trades unions in society illustrates the confusion which has beset both the opponents and advocates of collective industrial action. It was mirrored in the discussion which occupied the trades unions during 1985 and 1986: the argument about whether their conduct should, in future, be circumscribed by the imposition of legislative constraint upon their actions or by the establishment of positive legal rights. The choice is, of course, artificial and only made by those who have fallen into the trap of talking about the unions as if they act against the interests of their members and must be stopped by the power of the state from doing so. From time to time trades unions will, because of ignorance or malice, damage their own members' cause. They will sometimes damage the national interest – though that is quite a different matter and deserves closer examination. But that is no reason why socialists should regard trades unions as vehicles for anything other than the pursuit of individual emancipation. The dichotomy between 'trades unionism' and 'individualism' is wholly false. When the behaviour of a trades union seeks to make the distinction defensible, the trades unions have failed in their purpose.

The trades unions exist to protect, by collective action, the individual rights of their members. The basic purpose of trades union association is the achievement, for individuals who could not obtain them on their own, of rights which their richer and more powerful contemporaries are able to acquire by their personal strength. The highest level of remuneration consistent

131

with the success of the employing company, protection against unfair or arbitrary dismissal, decent working conditions, severance pay and pension are all rights which the highly skilled and the very prosperous negotiate and secure individually. The fact that the less skilled and the less well-off negotiate them collectively does not make them any the less individual rights. Of course, a wage negotiation carried out on behalf of a whole group of workers may pay some of them more than they are worth and pay others less. But we should be neither surprised or horrified by that. It is an inadequate way to decide pay levels, but it is no less adequate than other methods. We have not yet decided even how to define, even less how to measure, a fair wage. None of the theories makes sense. Tool-room fitters and stockyard labourers (or for that matter Queen's Counsels and stockbrokers) are no more paid according to their marginal revenue product than they are according to a calculation of how their labours compare with the effort needed to catch a beaver. In an unplanned economy, the powerful individuals get what they reasonably can. The trades unions attempt the same for their individual members; and the disciples of individualism ought not to complain. They will soon begin to use their power to obtain for their members privileges which have previously been thought of as the exclusive preserve of workers who occupy a higher place on the social scale; and they will soon begin to demand that their members enjoy the rights of share ownership. That is, of course, a manifestation of personal rather than collective ambition. It represents the ambition of an individual rather than the hopes of a class. They will advance their claims with more conviction, and therefore more success, if they remember and explain that the union exists as a collective vehicle for individual aspirations. The unions must not act as if they believe unions to be an object in themselves.

The trades unionists' demand for greater control over the conduct of the trades unions is now irresistible. The spread of balloting – postal balloting in particular – is only one manifestation of the growing insistence that the trades unions only exist to represent the views and protect the interests of their members. There remains, however, occasion when a damaging distinction may be made between the interests of the workers in an industry and the interests of the union. It was, for example, intolerable that, during the time when industrial democracy was last seriously considered, some of the union leaders who wished to see its establishment thought of the unions as the exclusive representatives of the workers within the democratised companies. It is easy to understand – and right to endorse – the argument that since unions are a power for good, they must be retained in that condition by protection from the erosion of their importance which would follow the easy distribution of benefit to unionists and non-unionists alike. If we have to choose between the risk of a union losing some of its power (and therefore some of its appeal) and workers being denied rights which in a wholly socialist society they would be granted, it is not difficult to decide where the lot should fall. A socialist belief in freedom requires us to choose the more general, and more equal, distribution of rights.

The subject of primary incomes – and therefore the contentious clichés about 'incomes policy' and 'free collective bargaining' – is dealt with at length in the final chapter. But it is worth observing here that whatever the arguments may be against some form of income planning (and those arguments are formidable) we should dismiss, with at best embarrassment, the complaint that it leaves too many trades unionists unoccupied and too many branch agendas deprived of any interesting items of business. The trades unions do not exist in order to exist; they are there to do their best for their members. Were it to be proved that the members did better under some other system of wage determination, it would be the clear duty of the trades unions to step aside.

In much the same way, it is imperative for local authorities – particularly socialist local authorities – constantly to recall that their existence is not an end in itself. The contribution made by town and county councils to the achievement of a more civilised and more compassionate society is immense. They have certainly moved Britain further along the road to democratic socialism than anything which national government can boast. And those general encomia are appropriate to many – though not all – of the much maligned labour councils of the 1980s. The GLC, for example, although indulging in all sorts of trivial absurdities, principally concerned itself with the provision of major benefits. The problems of local government – at least in terms of their rôle as agencies for promoting individual rights – most frequently occurred under a previous generation of

133

councillors and aldermen. It was they who sometimes fell into the error of believing, or acting as if they believed, that municipal government was an end in itself. It would be easy to offer the resistance to council-home sales as the prime example of recent attempts to elevate the importance of the corporation over the desires and interests of its ratepayers. No doubt there were some housing-committee chairmen whose objection to the 'right to buy' was based on their reluctance to see a reduction in the size of the corporate estate which they managed and felt they owned. But most of the resistance to the sale of municipal property was a product of the principle with which this book attempts to deal. Socialist councillors saw the right of one family to buy cheaply the house in which they lived as the denial of another family's right to live in a decent house at all. General opposition to council-house sales was misconceived, but it was misconceived for honourable reasons. The consideration which prompted the rejection of one set of rights was an attempt to protect another. At least the councillors were asking the right questions, even though they gave the answer which – on any considered view – was likely to reduce rather than increase the sum of liberty. The same defence cannot be advanced for those councillors who insist on regulations which, whilst masquerading as protection for the whole community, are really no more than the preservation of municipal uniformity or bureaucratic con- venience. There was a time when pigeon-keeping was prohibited on Sheffield council estates and when, in the same city, it was an offence (punishable with eviction) to paint a front door in anything except the stipulated colour, to fence in pieces of garden which were adjacent to individual houses but designated collective property, or to make structural changes inside or outside which, in private property, would have been unhesi- tatingly designated as improvements. Even today – in many great cities – allocation policy, repair procedures and rent- collection schedules are more to the convenience of housing officers than of help to their tenants. They are perhaps minor sins, but they are sins to be avoided, and they help us to draw up the operating rules of the socialist society. The operating rules which should govern its social and bureaucratic organisation are those which produce the freedom that comes from real equality. That requires those who pursue that end constantly to measure their policy decisions against the fundamental question: does it increase equality, and in doing so does it increase the sum of human freedom?

Some of the policies which provide an affirmative answer to that question can easily be described. A socialist government committed to real equality will clearly embark on a massive programme of redistribution, confident that it is more likely to improve overall economic performance than to depress it and certain that it will produce a more efficient rather than a less effective use of resources. Equality of outcome is a close relation of utilitarianism. To distribute the Duke of Westminster's millions amongst the tenants of the Peabody Trust flats which stand on his land would clearly increase the prospect of human happiness. It is difficult to imagine what it is that the Duke does with his countless millions since they amount to more than a man can count – let alone spend – in a single lifetime. It is not, however, difficult to conceive how the fortune would be spent if it were spread between several thousands of comparatively poor families. Of course, some of it would go on beer and tobacco. But we ought not to be too sanctimonious about that – particularly if we are supporters of the view that a real extension in individual choice is the object of policy. But much of it would clearly be used for purposes which were undeniably desirable, even by the most sanctimonious standards. More important, it would offer the economic basis for emancipation: the material ability to make more of the choices which society theoretically provides. Were the Duke of Westminster's fortune to be reduced by draconian action to a minimal part of what it is today – leaving him, let us say, with no more than £5–£10 million – the deprivation would not, in the real meaning of the term, reduce his ability to make the choices which determine the pattern and quality of life. However, were the money distributed amongst the poor, there would be a major increase in their freedom. New opportunities would open up before them – material, aesthetic, even spiritual. Freedom is closely related to purchasing power. If you doubt it, ask the Duke of Westminster. By a conscious policy of redistribution we increase the purchasing power and the freedom of those to whom the resources are given without a corresponding reduction in the purchasing power and freedom of those from whom it is taken away. *Equality of outcome is really an extension of marginal utility.*

The fundamental question – much more difficult to answer than the so-called dilemma of redistribution itself – is the form which the redistribution should take. For those who believe in freedom, it is clearly better to redistribute in cash rather than kind, income (primary and secondary) rather than the social wage. For a redistribution which takes the form of goods and services provided by the state inevitably imposes consumption patterns on those who receive it. Often the consumption patterns are wholly desirable and uncontentiously beneficial. Often it is necessary to ensure that those patterns are repeated in order to avoid the social consequences which would flow from their abandonment. There are no circumstances in which we could leave participation in the health service to voluntary decision. The health service is an instrument of collective protection. Socialists will profoundly disagree with those neo liberals who defend the right of men and women to neglect medical care for themselves and to die of whatever diseases they choose to neglect. But only idiots will support a collapse in general medical provision and the consequent contamination of society as a whole. The necessity for generalised medical cover has been accepted since the introduction of compulsory vaccination. And the health service is, in part, a continuation and extension of that principle. In part it was intended to provide – by redistribution – an essential service which the poor had been unable to afford. But the intention was not to offer them choices which they had previously been denied. Medicine was free at the point of use so that patients should take it, not take it or leave it. The subsidy was intended to influence, perhaps even determine, conduct.

The government was deciding the nature of the good, and healthy, life. And in this particular, the government was quite right. In other areas, government subsidy is not so much concerned with setting a pattern of national conduct as providing individuals on low income with the chance to enjoy services and opportunities which more prosperous citizens are able to finance out of their own resources. The subsidised bus fares of the metropolitan counties were meant to encourage travel by public transport and thereby reduce road congestion. Pensioners' bus passes are intended to help pensioners with their travel costs. General subsidies are not intended to supplement income so much as to change behaviour. Specific subsidies are meant to increase purchasing power. But they *may* do it in a way which, given a free choice, would not be the first priority of the recipient. Thus pensioners may choose to travel (free) to the park when, if they were given the cost of their bus fare, they would choose to buy a newspaper and read it at home. Of course, the cost of buying the *Guardian* may be, in real terms, higher than allowing the occupation of a seat which would otherwise be empty. But the principle is clearly demonstrated. Until there is a far greater equality of income, personal subsidies are essential. But one crucial advantage of moving towards a more equal income level is the opportunity which it provides to allow more citizens to make their own choices.

For those choices to be effective, the men and women who make them have to be provided with a maximum amount of information about the alternatives from which they may choose. That, of course, includes information about government – not simply accounts of what the government has done, offered for retrospective examination and possible criticism, but descriptions of the current options open to government and explanations of why the chosen path was followed. Britain remains the most secretive society in Western Europe. Indeed, Professor Ralf Dahrendorf suggested in his Reith Lectures that it was by preserving the monopoly on information that the British establishment maintained its authority. That authority will not be eroded by House of Commons select committees which examine departmental ministers and senior civil servants but do not possess the power to push and probe, which is the hallmark of the Congressional Committees which they so unsuccessfully attempt to imitate. The select committee system is simply a recent example of the establishment allowing the system to bend a little in order that it should not break. Faced with a specific decision to reveal or not to reveal, it is the instinct of British government, and the reflex response of British civil servants, to keep the information within a magic circle. That passionate prejudice will be overcome only by the creation of a legislative obligation to make *everything* public – only compelling reasons of uncontestable national interest justify an exemption to the statutory rôle. British history is littered with examples, from the invasion of Suez to the attempted sale of British Leyland, of policy which the government endeavoured to pursue in private because they knew that its decisions would not command public support. Such conduct has little to do with democracy and is only obliquely related to the governance of truly free people.

But socialists believe that the people must be protected against private as well as public tyranny, and the power that comes from knowledge must be given to consumers in their inevitable battles against manufacturers and retailers and to workers in their long struggle for fair wages, decent conditions and proper representation. It is preposterous that a car manufacturer can sell a customer £10,000 worth of complicated equipment without being explicit about the durability of its parts and the opportunities, which the design engineers ignored, to increase the working life of expensive components. It is unreasonable to expect trades unions to strike reasonable bargains unless they possess the knowledge on which reason can be based. And if, as will be argued in future chapters, socialists should aim to make the economy more efficient (as well as make society more equal and more free) by extending workers' management rights over the companies which employ them, it is essential that the new 'owners' and 'managers' be supplied with the information which enables them to discharge their new responsibilities with judgment based on knowledge. To make Britain a truly free and equal society, we have to break down the barriers of secrecy which divide society into complicated hierarchies of ignorance and knowledge.

The wider dissemination of information is the part of the freedom and equality argument which it is easiest to advance. Though there are, no doubt, some members of the new libertarian right who believe that the knowledge that their product was 'unsafe at any speed' was the exclusive possession of American motor-car manufacturers and could not be removed from their ownership without an infraction of natural rights. And it is comparatively easy to explain the case for extending material equality by redistribution, even in the language of the new liberals. A high level of taxation levied on the capital and income of the rich clearly is an infraction of their rights to spend their money as they choose. But if it sustains a level of child benefit which liberates inner-city children from sickness and deprivation, the totality of freedom has clearly been increased. For those children – healthier, better educated and more self-confident – are clearly enabled to enjoy theoretical rights which were previously beyond their practical attainment.

'Taxing people is wrong,' said S. E. Finer, the Gladstone Professor of Government in the University of Oxford. But he did not go on to explain whether or not in his view it was equally immoral to deny people the basic necessities of a decent house, an adequate school, the prospects of permanent employment – all aspects of the civilised society which taxes provide. Every increase in public expenditure is, according to the neo liberal definition, a denial of freedom to the subscribing taxpayer. But what it provides for the recipient of government expenditure is very often a greater freedom than that denied by the taxation. There are, however, more difficult questions to be answered about more complicated issues. They involve the organisation of society and the socialist belief that inevitable natural differences should not be extended by the structure of the state into gross inequalities. It is easy to say that such a situation is avoided by a combination of progressive taxation and high levels of welfare, education and social security provision. That is certainly the beginning of the process, for it allows the concentration of compensating resources on the areas of greatest need. The best (and the most easily accessible) pre-school provision should be in the areas where children of nursery-school age live in circumstances which reduce their educational prospects. At present, quite the opposite is likely to happen, and medical treatment is more easily available to the congenitally healthy middle classes than to the sickness-prone children of first-generation immigrants. The case for helping them can be advanced in terms of pure compassion – adding the socialists' ideological commitment to equality (or not) according to circumstances and according to taste.

The argument for changing the structure of society so as to make it work, in favour rather than against its less privileged members, is more difficult to popularise. That is, in very large part, because the state would have to set the new rules and the state is neither popular nor trusted. For many people it is difficult to imagine the state working for individuals rather than against individualism. There is in the public mind an instinctive suspicion that the state must be an instrument of authority rather than of liberation. It is the agency of regulation, and regulations are thought to be, by definition, the negation of rights. Some regulation – determined, monitored and enforced by democratic will – is essential to the protection of individual rights. Indeed, it is necessary for a well ordered society. It is Margaret Thatcher who, in advocating extensions of police powers, says that she is protecting the right not to be burgled, the freedom not to be assaulted and the liberty to avoid sexual abuse. Even the neo liberals of the far right believe in the state's duty to protect itself from external aggression and internal disorder. That requires coercive organisation. Milton Friedman did not, to my knowledge, demonstrate against conscription during the war in Vietnam; nor does he audibly complain against the constant increase in his tax bill which results from the escalating arms budget. Nor do many neo liberals feel an irresistible liberal urge to oppose extensions of those authoritarian ordinances which preserve the privileges of the prosperous and the advantages of the financially secure. The new right does not oppose zoning regulations which prevent desirable residences from being overlooked. It only opposes extensions of public-sector housing which protect the poor from being overcrowded. We all believe in the power of the state when the state acts to protect our interests. There is no difference in principle between the state levying extra taxes and imposing new laws in order to defeat the menace of invasion and the state behaving in exactly the same way in order to combat the threat of poverty, sickness and civil commotion. We may argue that in 1940 invasion was more of a real and tangible prospect than was social disintegration in 1979; and we may go on to insist that the state could defeat Nazi Germany but cannot beat poverty. But, in both cases, the argument is about something other than the *propriety* of state action. In the first argument the reservation concerned *necessity*. In the second, the doubts related to the likelihood of success. But in both cases the same underlying principle applies. If the crisis is sufficiently desperate, and if collective action will solve it, then we are neither so nihilistic nor so self-sacrificial as to oppose the powers of the state being employed. To embrace state action to solve the security crisis of 1940 but to reject it as a solution to the potential poverty crisis of 1945 is merely to put our crises in order of personal importance.

Few people are opposed to the state power which achieves their chosen aims and when (for the purpose of our present examination a more important qualification) its exercise seems likely to achieve the stated object rather than becoming defused into a miasma of pointless bureaucratic regulation. To the followers of Friedman and Hayek who say, in effect, that the state must be employed rigidly to hold the ring within which the roughest and best-trained boxers thrash their opponents, there is little to be said except that it is possible to construct a nobler description of the state's duties. A more difficult argument to answer comes from the well-intentioned and compassionate who claim that whilst the state may initially be employed for purposes which are desirable in themselves and achieved by actions which are within the state's competence, the process, so honourably begun, always ends with bureaucratic interference in matters best left to the individual. From that has developed the notion that any development of state power is, by its nature, certain to limit the sum of individual freedom. It is as if there is a total amount of power within any community and when the state extends its authority the power available to individuals is automatically diminished. But power is not finite; it is capable of extension. The rule of the state ought to include the taking of those powers which enable it to increase the power of the individuals within it. The state can perform that rôle. The cynics who insist that it may intend to make men and women free, but by interference only further enslaves them, are wrong. The error has been encouraged by the mistakes and misconceptions of individual politicians both national and local.

It is no good for socialists simply to argue that next time round they can be trusted, that given another chance they will always use the apparatus of the state to enhance freedom and never to limit it: more persuasive proof is needed of such good intentions. The importance of making our intention clear, though bearing witness will not, in itself, be enough, should not be underrated. It is not surprising that British socialists are thought to undervalue liberty; they do not talk about it sufficiently to give a credible impression of concern. But more tangible proof is also needed; sureties have to be given. One is the increasing liberalisation of socialism's own institutions, the Labour Party and the trades unions. But something more certain than that will be needed too. The best and surest way of demonstrating that the state will not exploit the people is to pass the state's power into the people's hands. Socialists – suffering from the paternalistic legacy of Burke's doctrine on representative government – are inclined to argue that if they do what the people want, they may be forced into doing the wrong things. It

141

therefore follows that extending the opportunities for direct democracy will lead to all manner of legislative and administrative tragedies.

Hayek judged the people better. He said (see Chapter 3) that democracy led inevitably to equality – since it benefited the masses against the classes and the masses have most votes. That judgment was confirmed by the British experience of educational reorganisation – once the truth about the selective system was revealed. It is certainly endorsed by the desire to defend the health service and reduce unemployment – if necessary at the cost of postponing tax cuts. That does not mean that every vote in every forum will always and invariably be a choice of the equality and freedom alternative. The likelihood is that the smaller the unit of choice, the more likely are the participants to vote for their own rather than the general interest; and there will be some areas in which it is necessary to take special precautions to protect minorities against the tyranny that majorities would impose. If – as we should – we give municipal tenants power over the management of their estates, it will be necessary to retain allocation policy within the responsibility of a central authority – or to lay down national guidelines which prohibit by law discrimination against ethnic minorities, religious or racial groups. Similar precautions will have to be taken in areas where elected local authorities are now free to exploit sections of their communities in the interest of more powerful groups. It is, for example, intolerable that the distribution of pre-school places should be determined by the activities of pressure groups which – being largely made up of middle-class activists – argue most strongly for extra facilities in their own middle-class areas. The imposition by national government of minimum standards of provision or an obligation to operate policies which do not discriminate against women or minority groups does not, in itself, prohibit the extension of democratic control. Democratic socialists do not pretend that the state will or should wither away, but they do believe that it should be kept in its proper place. Opposition to the intrusive state does not require the withdrawal of the state from those functions which are necessary for it to perform in the interests of greater equality and freedom. We could not allow tenant management committees to prohibit the allocation of houses within their areas to black or Asian families or to set up the segregated ghettos for designated

problem families which have been demanded on some corporation estates. But that does not mean that the tenants' committees
cannot take responsibility for the organisation of repairs or the
specification of management rules governing the use of open
spaces, the care and maintenance of communal property and the
designation of traffic-free roads and parking areas. If national
and local government simply retained the powers which were
necessary for the economies of scale to be enjoyed and the
objects of greater equality and freedom to be pursued, the
corporation tenant would enjoy far greater freedom and
responsibility than he does today.

The same rule applies to the government and management of
schools. If 'parent power' – currently espoused by the social
democrats – is a concept which has any real meaning, it is a
notion which needs careful examination by both the real
libertarian and the genuine egalitarian. For, whilst in one of its
manifestations it can diffuse and devolve power towards the
recipients and away from the providers of education, in other
forms it can become no more than a vehicle for middle-class
hegemony over secondary schools. 'Parent power' is, by its
nature, bound to favour the articulate, self-confident, success-
orientated middle classes. If those talents and energies are
harnessed to improve the education system in part or in whole
the result is obviously to be welcomed. But what appears to be
an extension of choice can easily become a system by which the
strongest groups are able to acquire a disproportionate share of
available resources. The 'voucher scheme' (designated unworkable rather than undesirable by Sir Keith Joseph in 1985)
illustrates the problem exactly; though, since vouchers are
'parent power' at its most dangerous extreme, it naturally
over-emphasises the dangers inherent in less divisive
schemes.

Supposing that in a segment of a great city parents were issued
with pieces of paper which acted as passports to places in the
school of their choice, the result can be easily described. A
league table of schools would be created. The middle classes
would be the first to know which the 'good schools' were and
would become the most determined campaigners in the battle to
obtain places within them. The 'good schools' – attracting the
most highly motivated pupils and the most qualified teachers –
would improve. The 'worst schools' would deteriorate, suffer

public excoriation and become populated only by pupils who could not find places in superior establishments. If, in addition to taking complete control over allocation policy, parents were able to decide the curriculum and distribute resources within the education region, the distinctions and divisions would be emphasised. The 'sink schools' would be regarded as unworthy of investment. The school which topped the table would be rewarded by special allowances and posts of special responsibility – a situation not fundamentally different from the way in which funds were allocated between the old grammar schools and the secondary moderns which were said to enjoy 'parity of esteem'. What began as an attempt to increase the power of consumers over producers – always a desirable object for those who believe in equality and freedom – ends as the concentration of power in the hands of one small powerful group. But opposition to schemes which have the appearance of extending choice whilst, in reality, only entrenching privilege should not prejudice education administrators against extensions of parents' rights and parental choice in areas where one group of parents cannot, by their superior negotiating power, prejudice the interests of another. Parents should dominate governing bodies. The representatives elected in those circumstances are more likely to be the upwardly mobile than the socially depressed. But in the management of a single school their energy and self-interest will be an indispensable engine of improvement for the whole institution. Parents, governors or not, must be given real and continuous access to teachers and the right to comment on, if not to determine, the curriculum. Their close and continuous involvement may be both an inconvenience and embarrassment to the staff of the schools where the governance is changed, but extensions of democracy invariably have that effect on the centres of power which they assault.

The duty of national and local government to pass on to its voter many of the powers which once were kept within Parliament and town halls is only half of the obligation to greater freedom. The state must play a positive rôle in organising equality: in preventing the abrogation of rights to a single select group, in prohibiting an unreasonable distribution of resources and in encouraging the greater liberty that such a process provides. The obvious examples are the most contentious. That is why they have those characteristics. The passion

144

aroused by discussing them is increased by the inevitable resentment generated by the intrusion of politics into such intimate family matters as health and education. It is worth repeating that it is both wrong and unattractive to moralise about the iniquity of mothers going out to work in order to pay for their sons' education or fathers who abandon smoking and drinking in order to provide their daughters with private medical care. There is no unitary morality which insists that what is right for the community as a whole must be right for every individual family within it. To excoriate the family that pays for private health or education is an error of logic comparable only with the most common justification for allowing the continued existence of the private sector. When challenged with all the sophistries about reducing pressure on public resources and setting higher standards for the state services to follow, the apologists for independent schools and pay beds always take refuge in the ultimate absurdity. Why, they ask, do we object to individuals spending their own hard-earned money on medicine and education when we take no exception to them squandering their pay on continental holidays, exotic consumer goods and flashy clothes? The answer is, of course, that such tawdry demonstrations of material success do not harm the rest of the community to any significant (or irremediable) extent. They may proclaim a difference in wealth and remuneration; but they do not entrench and accentuate those differences in the way in which they are entrenched and accentuated by dividing education and medicine between the private haves and the public have-nots. Nor do the fripperies of conspicuous consumption produce the damaging result which is undoubtedly the consequence of the existence of private education and private medicine. The socialist complaint about their existence does not concern the personal morality of those who take advantage of them. It concerns their effect on the public at large.

The existence of private sectors in both health and education has four indisputable effects.

1. Private sectors are in themselves a declaration of the divisions in society and a manifestation of the social acceptability of those decisions. They are an endorsement of the idea that even in the provision of life's basic services, a superior level of provision is available for those who can

afford its extra expense. The demonstration that society allows such discrepancies between the quality of help which it makes available to different classes of citizens encourages the belief that differences between the classes are natural and different levels of life chances are inevitable and right.

2. They provide a conduit through which the favoured minority can keep in constant touch with opportunities to increase their good fortune. Private medical schemes, having treated a specific condition, offer a general level of health assessment and concern which is not possible on the public service. The private sector of education offers opportunities for employment which are only obliquely related to merit and which are not available on similar terms to products of the state system. It is the antithesis of the double detriment which operates against the poor by preventing them from buying cheaply in bulk or obtaining cheap credit. It is a double privilege which perpetuates itself and grows upon itself.

3. They absorb a disproportionate share of scarce resources which, if they were spread more evenly, could distribute health care and education according to need and merit rather than against the criteria of the greatest ability to pay.

4. They isolate the influential from the failings and inadequacies of the public system and therefore deny that system the benefits which it would enjoy were its interests to be espoused by those who control public spending and investment. The public health and education services would undoubtedly improve if children of senior civil servants attended state schools and the wives of stock-brokers and newspaper editors were forced to wait for medical care in overcrowded and dilapidated outpatients' departments.

By any reasonable analysis, the existence of a private system in both education and medicine does more than offer the recipients of private provision a superior service. It depresses the service provided in the public sector. The generality of men and women are not simply relatively disadvantaged. There is an absolute reduction in the standard of provision which they would receive from a unified system. There is no echelon or

146

trickle-down effect. The level of provision generally available (and the chance, *in reality*, to choose better education and health care) would, for a majority of men and women, be improved. The abolition of private medicine and private education would, by any sensible analysis, increase the *sum* of liberties. It would reduce the freedom of prospective Old Etonians; but for those children who, in truth, have not even a distant prospect of Eton College, new horizons would be created as their educational opportunities improved. To shrink from the assault on private medicine and private education is either to lack courage or to neglect a real chance to extend the totality of freedom.

To neglect that chance is to debilitate society as well as to penalise a majority of men and women within it. For the alienation that comes from class differences has done chronic damage to the material as well as the moral prospects of Great Britain. In Britain, wrote Matthew Arnold, 'inequality is a religion'. It is a religion which must bear much of the responsibility for a century of decline. 'On one side,' Arnold explained, 'inequality harms by pampering; on the other by vulgarising and depression. A system founded on it is against nature, and, in the long run, breaks down.' It was for that reason that he urged the readers of *Culture and Anarchy* to 'choose quality and flee greed'. We should do the same. For to choose equality is to choose freedom as well.

Chapter Eight

There Must Be Markets

The first half of this book argued that socialism is about the pursuit of equality that makes an extension of true liberty possible. The object of socialism is the real – as distinct from the theoretical – emancipation of previously powerless citizens; a condition which can only be approached if society is organised with the conscious intention of achieving that aim. That is a strand of the democratic socialist thinking – which flows from Bernstein, through Strachey and Durbin, and was most recently expounded by Crosland – which argues that to create socialism, we must organise society with that specific intention. That does not mean that a specific form of industrial or economic organisation is socialism, but that a form of organisaion is a necessity to socialism's achievement. Those who define socialism as the pursuit of equality and freedom need to organise the economy to achieve those ends.

Those ends cannot be achieved through the operation of unregulated markets, through what has come to be called 'free enterprise', but is rarely the free competition (and never the perfect competition) for which the theorists of the new right pine. Nor is it the 'planned economy' of the Soviet centralised state which allocates resources according to the bureaucratic judgment of government functionaries. Neither system provides the equal share of resources or the conditions of economic liberty which socialists demand. Nor does any other form of economic organisation which can be described in a single paragraph and offered as a prescription suitable to every circumstance.

The strength of the neo liberals' philosophy – discussed in previous chapters – is that they answer questions about resource allocation with glib certainty. First they attribute to markets a philosophical importance which markets do not possess, then

148

they insist that the theory of markets on which they base their philosophy is universally applicable. The socialist conclusion must be more rational. If socialism is about the emancipation of the individual, socialists must support a theory of economic organisation that provides the best possible prospect for the largest number of people to achieve that emancipation. The neo liberals will assure us that such an objective requires the automatic and invariable support of market allocation. The world is more complex than they understand or admit. There are, in a complicated economy, complicated problems about the allocation of resources. It is preposterous to argue that all the doubts and dilemmas can be overcome by the application of the same formula. Sometimes planning will – by popular agreement – best meet our aims. R. H. Tawney points out that even in 1914 nobody suggested that the defence budget should be distributed between the individual members of the British Expeditionary Force and the most efficient warriors amongst them allowed to make the quickest progress to Berlin. On other occasions market forces will be the proper instrument of allocation. Socialists have not always been certain where markets 'should end' and 'planning' begin.

Most Labour Party members understand and accept that, for a large proportion of the economy, markets must determine price and the allocation of resources. The markets may have to be regulated – by price control, by the prohibition of monopoly, by subsidy, by tax incentive or by regulations protecting the workers, the consumer and the environment. However, when asked about the theory by which such a necessity is justified, most party members will describe the operation of 'market forces' in wholly pejorative terms. Market forces are said to respond to demand as measured by purchasing power when in a decent (that is to say socialist) economy production would be planned to meet 'needs' or 'wants' rather than left to respond to the stimulus of bank account and cheque book. Often markets, being associated with competition, are dismissed as a clear manifestation of the capitalist system, ignoring the fact that most businessmen 'rarely meet together even for merriment and diversion, but the conversation ends in conspiring against the public on some contrivance to raise prices'[1] – markets are

[1] A. Smith, *The Wealth of Nations* (Methuen & Co., London, 1930), Vol. II, Ch. 10, p. 130.

not a natural condition in the sense that they occur without actively being encouraged. The alternative to the active encouragement of competition – and the markets which allow it to determine prices and allocate resources – is not socialist planning. It is monopoly, oligopoly or cartels. It may be state monopoly, but it will be monopoly nevertheless and could, therefore, create all the problems of inefficient organisation and potential consumer exploitation which are the monopoly's hallmark.

In sentimental socialist circles, it is common to juxtapose not competition and monopoly but competition and co-operation. Competition is represented as the ethos of individual greed, whilst co-operation is described as the manifestation of the noble desire to work together. Socialists certainly believe in co-operation, but the repetition of its virtues does not solve any of the problems concerning the way in which we allocate resources. In the market system, given the necessary purchasing power, the consumers purchase the goods of their choice. In a Soviet economy, they receive the goods which they are allocated. Neither system is acceptable to socialists. The alternative has to be something more practical than a slogan.

The fact is that sometimes market allocation will suit socialism's purposes and sometimes it will not. In deciding when it is desirable, when the markets should be regulated and when the system must be replaced with some other form of allocation, it is essential not to be trapped into believing that the existence of markets determines the form of ownership possible within them. If the Labour Party abandons the confusion that social ownership and nationalisation are one and the same, there is no insurmountable reason why a socialist economy should not contain a large number of autonomous companies which, whilst owned by the workers within them, the consumers who buy from them, or the municipalities in which they operate, are nevertheless in healthy competition with each other. They would, like the privately owned autonomous firms with which they also compete, need to be subject to some national guidelines. Those are set out in Chapter 11. For the socialist 'owners' and the professional managers which they employed would, like their counterparts in the private sector, often wish to pursue policies which were to their sectional advantage but against the best interest of the economy as a whole. If it is better

150

for the economy as a whole to create extra jobs in Newcastle, but private information technology companies prefer to expand in Staines, there is no reason to believe that an information technology co-operative will pursue the national (rather than its own sectional) interest with any more socialist purity than is to be found within the average public limited company. The 'ground rules of the mixed economy', which a socialist government would lay down, would apply to socially owned as much as to private companies. One section of those ground rules (described in Chapter 11) will be intended to deter the creation of undesirable monopolies or – when monopoly is either inevitable or, because of the nature of the industry, positively desirable – prevent dominant firms from exercising the exploitive powers that concentration provides. But the idea that markets and socialism are mutually exclusive is clearly nonsense – unless socialism is defined as *state* ownership rather than *social* ownership. *State* ownership does not, if it is extended to the whole economy, conform to the essential socialist rule that the organisation of society must be as much concerned with freedom as with equality.

However, to argue that the operation of a substantial market sector is essential both to the promotion of efficiency and to the maintenance of a free society is not to invest markets with the moral significance which the messianic wing of the neo liberal movement proclaims that they possess. To describe the extreme position taken up by reputable neo liberals is not simply to create straw men who can be demolished by a single match or a gentle push. Of course, the extreme statement of the market position is simultaneously threatening and ridiculous.

> The right of free speech and the right to vote and the other political freedoms which we normally hold in such high regard are important to me only to the extent that they influence our abilities to protect the freedom of choice granted to us in the private sector of the economy.[2]

But some practising politicians openly subscribe to a view of markets' metaphysical importance that is different from that nonsense only in degree.

---

[2] M. Jenson, *The Banker*, October 1978.

The free enterprise economy is the true counterpart of democracy: it is the only system which gives everyone a say. Everyone who goes into a shop and chooses one article rather than another is casting a vote in the economic ballot box: with thousands or millions of others. That choice is signalled to production and investment and helps to mould the world just a tiny fraction nearer to people's desire. In this great and continuous general election of the free economy nobody, not even the poorest, is disenfranchised: we are voting all the time.[3]

The recognition that Enoch Powell's effusions – and its second-rate imitation in David Owen's call for 'an endorsement of the market mechanism which is in a sense a continuous referendum'[4] – is metaphysical claptrap and ought not to result in the espousal of diametrically opposed nonsense. Markets cannot in themselves guarantee either the optimum distribution of resources or the maximum satisfaction of individual desires and needs. But, in some sectors of the economy, they can *contribute* to both ends. In other areas of the economy, the efficiency will best be served by managed investment, output and prices. And the two should not be thought of as mutually exclusive. Markets will be influenced by government policy. Since Gladstone's time, the price of gin has been partly decided by competition and production costs, but mostly determined by the level of excise duty. The planned sector will be influenced by competition. There is a managed market in milk, but schoolboys remain free to buy lemonade instead. The problem for democratic socialists is deciding when regulated markets ought to be encouraged and where managed markets are best accepted or created. Such judgments cannot be made rationally by those who regard either the competitive or managed economy as an institution which possesses spiritual significance.

If David Owen had chosen to paraphrase and précis Milton Friedman instead of Enoch Powell, he would have endorsed the view that markets not so much stand side by side with universal suffrage but are, in terms of popular representation, superior to it. 'In the economic market . . . each person gets what he pays for. There is a $ for a $ relationship. Therefore you have an incentive proportionate to the cost to examine what you are

[3] J. E. Powell, *Freedom and Reality* (Batsford, London, 1969), p. 33.
[4] D. Owen, 'Agenda for Competition and Compassion', *Economic Affairs*, Vol. 4, No. 1, 1983.

getting.'[5] Milton Friedman holds democracy in contempt – regarding it as an institution which encourages ignorant voters to cast their ballots for what they (often mistakenly) believe to be their sectoral interest without any concern for the cost or effect on others of the mandate which they have endorsed. Those same individuals, when forced to pay a dime or a dollar are, on the Friedman analysis, changed into cognisant human beings who are both prudent and knowledgeable; or, at least, they are sufficiently prudent, and knowledgeable enough, to 'examine' what they are paying good money to acquire. Of course, for markets to operate in the way that Friedman suggests – creating a self-equilibrating economy in which they 'clear' so as to produce the most efficient balance of employment, investment and output – those who operate within them have to do a good deal better than 'examine' the price and value of their purchases. They have to know what alternatives are available and to what other potential uses the funds employed to purchase them might be put. Markets require knowledge that many – in some cases most, in a few cases all – consumers do not possess. The neo liberals will expostulate that they have never hypo-thesised 'perfect competition' and are not, therefore, obliged to assume the 'perfect knowledge' that Alfred Marshall said was that condition's basic requirement. Indeed, they will protest that they are only too aware of the imperfections within the market and that although they argue and struggle for their removal they are too realistic even to hope that the distortions will all, one day, be removed. Quite so. But that requires them to adopt a consistent position about what markets can achieve. In some circumstances, markets – with all their imperfections – are by far the best way of determining price and allocating resources. In others, they are an arbitrary, socially insensitive and highly inefficient instrument of price and distribution; though even then it is necessary to find a system which – for the sector in question – replaces markets without intensifying the problems which they create. That is the rational view, not the view of the new libertarian right, who have an *absolute* faith in markets under all conditions. To sanctify them by favourable comparison to the democratic process – as if they are *always* the form of organisation for which society should strive – is to downgrade

[5] M. Friedman, 'The Line We Do Not Cross', *Encounter*, November 1976.

either democracy or the intellectual apparatus of the people who make such claims. For markets often do not behave in a way which is remotely consistent with the claims made on their behalf; and in other areas, it is impossible (if even the most minimal standard of general well-being and overall efficiency is to be respected) to allow market criteria to determine decisions concerning price, location, investment and the availability of goods and services.

Putting aside even minimal social considerations is necessary in order to argue in favour of the virtues of market allocation in every particular sector and to demonstrate that it is *possible* to create a genuine market within it. J. K. Galbraith explains that the whole notion of consumer sovereignty is flawed, in that it assumes a dynamic rôle for the purchasers of goods and services but a passive one for producers who are assumed to do no more than respond to the demands which tastes dictate. Producers too have an independent life and are therefore busily engaged in influencing the choices which their customers make. That may be an activity which is, socially, wholly desirable. Improved forms of sanitary protection were popularised by the discreet but determined advertising campaign of the monopoly which developed them. But often advertising simply teaches people to want what the producers have judged to be a potentially profitable new line of output. The junk food industry – and the consequent decline in children's dietary habits – is a perfect example. Either way, they actually create wants for their products rather than meeting endogenous demands – undermining the consumer sovereignty argument upon which markets depend. Galbraith goes on to argue that the market, being another term for the random operation of rules which may serve no desirable end, is not a method of allocation and price determination which always appeals to sensible entrepreneurs. Large companies plan markets out of existence – either by assuming monopoly control or by determining the demand which they go on to meet. And the exponents of that system should not complain when socialist economic planning does the same. But our planning – unlike that of the giant companies – must be accountable and democratic.

> The genius of the industrial system lies in its organised use of capital and technology. This is made possible . . . by extensively

replacing the market with planning. The notable accomplishments of the industrial system are all the results of such planning: there would be no flights to the moon (and not many to Los Angeles) were market incentives relied upon to bring into existence the required vehicles. The same is true of other services, amenities and artifacts of the industrial system . . . In all cases there are careful projections of output, careful control of prices, careful steps to see that the projections of output are validated in the greatest possible measure by consumer response. To leave these matters to the market would be regarded by those principally involved as the equivalent of leaving them to chance.[6]

The Austrian school of economics of which Hayek was such a distinguished member (with von Mises, Menger, Hutt and Rothbard) will argue that 'in the course of human events there is no stability and consequently no safety.'[7] But their supporters in the real world of the real economy struggle to create both conditions, as Galbraith explains. Market apologists will argue that Galbraith underestimates the effects of the market, that he describes no more than market imperfection and that 'efficiency' – as they themselves define it – would be even better served if the market were allowed to operate unhindered and the entrepreneurs described above employed their talent maximising their results according to its unpredictable rules. The same apologists might add (for public transport is the constant example over which market philosophers argue) that we would at least have been spared the cost of Concorde had those who made it and raised the funds to pay for it first anticipated its performance in the passenger-carrying airline market and then discovered that the rigorous application of such criteria disqualified the plane for anything other than fantasy status. Such discussions – particularly the circular and self-fulfilling contention that the market produces the best results when they are defined in a way which confirms the importance of market forces – were all very well in the days when the unspoken truth about markets was that they are sometimes the best instrument of allocation and sometimes are not. In those successfully cynical days Galbraith could write:

[6] J. K. Galbraith, *The New Industrial State* (Hamish Hamilton, London, 1967), Ch. 22, p. 256.
[7] L. von Mises, in T. Mischel, *Human Action* (Yale University Press, London, 1949), p. 113.

> Since all the relevant groups affirm the importance of free markets in principle, while needing control in practice, the solution has been to impose control in practice while affirming the commitment to force markets in principle. This semantic triumph has been aided by long-standing recognition that what is not permissible in principle is often necessary in practice.[8]

But now in Britain, the Conservative government has begun to treat the idea of markets as if that system is innately superior to any other forms of organisation and should be imposed on as much of the economy as is possible. They then conclude that when markets cannot be created, the public service which remains should be looked upon as inferior – wasteful, expensive, incompetent, authoritarian and insensitive. That is, in part, the product of an error which mirrors the mistake made by some socialists. For the government seems to assume that market organisation and private ownership are synonymous. The effects of that confusion combined with the belief in the universal superiority of market organisation result in the privatisation programmes (which are doing so much damage to health and local authority services) and the sale of public utilities in the apparent belief that once in private hands, all monopolies will begin to respond to market forces.

In one sense the privatisation programme has worked. By farming out hospital cleaning and laundry and by inviting private tenders for the removal of refuse previously collected by council workers, the markets have been cleared at a new point of equilibrium – the jobs are being done less adequately but at a lower cost. But that is not quite what Professor Friedman promised us. About the sale of public utilities – concerns which by any sensible analysis must remain as monopolies either public or private – the most distinguished market philosophers are more cautious. But it is argued by their political apologists that even a private monopoly is better than a publicly owned one, since it must perform in a way which avoids bankruptcy and liquidation. That is simply untrue. British Leyland in Britain and Chrysler in the USA have been saved from their own private folly because of the unacceptable consequences of their collapse. It is hard to imagine the government allowing privatised gas or telephones to go out of business. Indeed, the

---

[8] J. K. Galbraith, *The New Industrial State* (Hamish Hamilton, London, 1967), Ch. 26, 'The Industrial System and the State'.

only economic argument for privatising such monopolies or near monopolies is the certainty that they will – as limited companies – be able to provide a lower level of public service than was possible when they operated as state corporations. Rural telephone boxes will actually disappear after they have been classified as 'uneconomic'; harsher rules will govern disconnection policy. Such greater 'efficiencies' only appear on a scale of values created by the market theorists themselves. Of course, cynics will argue that the privatisation of the public utilities had little to do with economic theory, as distinct from fiscal necessity and ideological prejudice. Perhaps so; but no Chancellor could have boldly announced that he was selling North Sea Oil to finance a cut in the unearned income surcharge; nor could a prime minister simply assert that she preferred private ownership as a matter of primitive prejudice. A superficially convincing reason had, therefore, to be created: it was called 'the greater efficiency of the markets' and Labour can only counteract it with an answer which offers a rational definition of the market's value. That begins with the assertion that where markets – because of the size of the industrial sector or the nature of the product – do not exist, then the consequent monopoly should be publicly rather than privately owned: or, until that is possible, subject to the scrutiny and regulation which prevents it from abusing its monopoly status.

Accepting that view liberates us from the error that publicly owned or socially planned sectors of the economy have to behave like the poor cousins of private enterprise concerns, apologetically aping them when they can. The result of such imitation is hybrid institutions uncertain of their rôle, increasingly incompetent in the performance of their proper duties and pathetically incapable of pleasing those critics who want them to behave like textbook private enterprise companies. The whole operation of the public-sector pricing and profit policy illustrates the confusion. External financing requirements impose on the gas and electricity generating industries an obligation to obtain a short-term return on invested capital which is calculated with the primary intention of acting as a fuel tax and reducing the Public Sector Borrowing Requirement. Then public enterprise is criticised for maintaining high prices. State monopolies 'usually find it impossible to fulfil plans (where they are expressed in terms of profit rate, in quantity or in value of turnover) at the customers' expense'[9]. That is not how public enterprise should operate, nor should it be subsidised in the financing of wasteful expenditures, or allowed to incur unnecessary cost by managerial inefficiency. The first step towards ensuring that such a proper balance is struck is the understanding that some sectors should be susceptible to market pressures and others should not. The two categories will not be easily labelled as 'private' and 'public', for in the primarily private sector, social ownership of many sorts will be encouraged, and the public sector will not be wholly without private investment. The divide will be between those industries which are expected to operate within markets and those which are not; and the place at which the line is drawn will not even help us to answer any of the simplistic questions about whether or not and to what degree the economy can be described as 'socialist'. The boundary which divides the market from the non-market sector is normally constructed by reference to technical not ideological considerations.

We can, without fear of being thought unnecessarily contentious, insist as a matter of fact that market forces will not have their full beneficial effects on those sectors of the economy where there is no competitive market. We have already insisted that it is unreasonable to hope or fear to find the perfect textbook market. But for markets to work at all, there need to be customers with sufficient knowledge to make a cognisant choice and the economic capability of bargaining about price and quality. The consumers do not have to possess equal power to influence the market; that would only be necessary when trying to make some sort of reality out of the Friedman–Hayek, Powell–Owen fantasy of competition as an essential counterpart to democracy. But even when there is a market, where there are enough competing commodities to make a choice possible, the consumer is often in no real position first to make a judgment and second to use it in order to influence the economic behaviour of the firms from whose products the choice was made.

Hugh Gaitskell – making his maiden speech on 24 August 1945 – offered the negative, though important judgment that 'if you are going to have private enterprise, it is better to have it

[9] A. Nove, *The Economics of Feasible Socialism* (Allen & Unwin, London, 1985), pt 4, p. 167.

competitive'. That phrase encapsulated the opinions that he had formed during five years working as a civil servant in the Board of Trade. The departmental paper which concluded and summarised his work on the subject contained two passages which remain crucially relevant to the socialist management of the economy.

> This country must restore adaptability and enterprise to its industries and must break through the net of trade restrictions, if it is to succeed in raising industrial efficiency, in maintaining employment at a high level, and so in improving the standard of life . . .

> An attack on monopoly is not to be confused with an attack on private enterprise. On the contrary, private enterprise and private monopoly are ultimately incompatible. In a democratic country, the public must be the master of industry. This condition is sufficiently satisfied in trades in which the competition is maintained: but where free competition does not exist, it can only be satisfied by the introduction of adequate measures of Government control or supervision over monopolies, or by actual State ownership. Thus the larger the sphere of monopoly, the smaller must ultimately become the sphere of private enterprise.[10]

The clear implication of Gaitskell's judgment is that sectors which were either 'natural' monopolies or which had been intentionally monopolised for the convenience of their owners should, as a general rule, be taken into public ownership. Lenin, perhaps surprisingly, took a more market-orientated view, suggesting not so much that monopoly should be the preserve of the state as that the state should mobilise the market.

> Capitalism long ago abolished small independent commodity production, under which competition could develop enterprise, energy and bold initiative to any considerable extent, and substituted for it . . . joint companies, syndicates and other monopolies . . . Now that a socialist government is in power our task is to organise competition.[11]

Some parts of the economy are – by their nature – not likely to feel the pull of market forces. The firms within them are of such

[10] H. Gaitskell, Dept Paper.
[11] Lenin, *Collected Works* (Lawrence & Wishart, London, 1979), Vol. 2, p. 256).

a size – or the activities which they perform are of such a nature – that a simple concern dominates the whole sector and to break it up would destroy economies of scale which contribute to rather than diminish its efficiency. Where such dominant firms exist, they should be subject to controls which, in a sense, act as a market surrogate by prohibiting the artificially high prices and general consumer exploitation which monopoly status allows. This chapter simply asserts the existence of such dominant companies, some public and some private. The ways in which they should be prevented from using their market domination to exploit their customers are discussed later. Many of the dominant firms are what have come to be called public utilities, but whatever their form of ownership, such giant concerns share a similar relationship with markets.

All such companies benefit from (and are protected against the entry of new competition by) the economies of scale. Whether or not the production of gas and electricity is controlled by a statutory monopoly, no thrusting entrepreneur is going to lay an alternative pipe-line system or build a second national grid. British Telecom, although privatised and obliged (like Bell Telephones) to allow the connection of other suppliers' equipment, is still a monopoly. Theorists may argue that it is possible to choose letter post, citizen band radio or jungle drums, or even that we are free to choose to send no messages at all and spend the money that we save on outdated textbooks. But in the real world British Telecom and British Gas, both before and after privatisation, retain the same economic status. They were changed from public to private monopolies and, in both conditions, they were barely susceptible to market forces. Further, it is unlikely that their consumer sensitivity – the hallmark of the market – has been increased by their transformation. The influence of Parliament, although woefully inadequate, exerted a pressure in favour of a level of service, a structure of prices and a respect for employees which the privatised companies no longer feel.

What is more, there are other economic conditions which must be taken into account if we are to secure the form of commercial and industrial organisation which is best for society as a whole. Even if we accept the hard-faced standards of those neo liberals who will not acknowledge the moral obligation to ensure that the economy supports some ethical aims, three facts of economic life ought to influence attitudes towards the existence and operation of markets.

First, there are external costs which need to be held down in the interest of the efficiency of the whole economy but which can only be reduced by individual companies taking decisions which are not purely related to the pursuit of their own profit maximisation. The decision to send large quantities of bulky goods by road rather than by rail may benefit an individual manufacturer, but the resulting congestion will involve other road users in increased expenditure. Second, there are external benefits which, having been made and paid for, may bring no advantage to the specific firm, but nevertheless increase the overall efficiency of the economies in which that firm operates. The branch railway line which is kept open despite running at an operating loss provides both amenity and convenience for the villages *en route*. It also may make it possible for the inhabitants of those villages to find profitable work and for business to develop and expand within the villages themselves. The contribution which that branch line makes to national wealth will not be recorded in the British Rail balance sheet, but it will be real. Third, the diseconomy of allowing more and more of both the public and private sector to operate according to crude and highly limited short-term market criteria can be measured in the ever-increasing financial burden of unemployment – a cost which is rarely calculated when a coal mine is closed or a government grant withdrawn. One of the curses of public accounting is the system's failure to record all the adverse effects of lower spending. The burdens on the health service imposed through extended life in decaying slums and the talent lost because sixteen-year-olds cannot afford to stay at school cannot be quantified and entered in the columns of the autumn financial statement. It is, however, no less real for that. The fantasists are those people who believe either that such costs do not exist or that they can be ignored because they are not quantified and written down in an abstract of statistics.

In many ways, the behaviour of monopolies will be identical, whether they are in public or in private ownership. They assess the demand for their output not plant by plant but centrally, and decisions on investment are based on an information which is only available at the centre to the headquarters bureaucracy. Market prices and market data are not decisive determinants of

161

planning decisions which are related to a longer term perspective than a response to immediate competitive pressures would allow. Decisions are taken by a technical bureaucracy, which is headed by professional directors whose connection with the ownership of the company is probably little more than the legal minimum shareholding. For all these reasons, a large number of private companies are not and cannot be part of the process which Milton Friedman described as the economic protection against coercion.

> So long as effective freedom of exchange is monitored, the central feature of market organisation of economic activity is that of preventing one person from interfering with another in respect of most of his activities. The consumer is protected from the coercion by the seller because of the presence of other sellers with whom he can deal. The seller is protected from coercion by the consumer because of other consumers to whom he can sell. The employed is protected from coercion by the employer because of other employees for whom he can work and so on. And the market does this impersonally and without centralised authority.[12]

It is difficult to believe that anyone who could offer such an opinion has not just arrived from Mars rather than the University of Chicago. In fact we are again being subjected to the intellectual sleight of hand which so disfigures the claims to unique integrity so often made by the neo liberal movement and its followers. Professor Friedman is describing what would happen in a wholly theoretical world of his own creation, but when politically convenient he pretends that such a world exists around us. When we remind him that it does not, that in reality the consumer is often exploited not protected by the imperfect workings of the market, his apologists say that such assertions are simply illustrative examples. They ought to be reminded of the lesson James Mill taught his six-year-old son – who became one of Professor Friedman's heroes: 'If theory and practice do not coincide then the theory is false or the practice is faulty.'

There are – without doubt – some sectors of the economy which are not, whatever world we might wish to live in, directly responsive to the price competition. In almost every economy in the world, whether or not the coal, oil, steel, chemical or

---

[12] M. Friedman, *Capitalism and Freedom* (Phoenix, London, 1982), p. 141.

computer industries are in public or private ownership they are protected from the market by monopoly or oligopoly organisation. Socialists will argue that the public utilities – which by their nature are likely to dominate the sectors in which they operate – cannot operate within the market sector. Gas and electricity concerns ought to operate according to qualitative as well as quantitative criteria – avoiding power cuts, providing services for outlying (and therefore uneconomic) areas, maintaining fuel supplies to families who are temporarily unable to pay their bill. The public utilities – according to socialist criteria – also have a part to play in general economic management. They can be used (by expanding their investment programmes at times of recession) to smooth out cyclical fluctuations; and they can help to combat mass unemployment, to assist in encouragement of good employment practices and to promote improved training techniques. A public sector, properly organised, can make a major contribution to planning. But it must be made plain now that it will be a framework within which both publicly owned enterprises as well as monopolised sectors can work. Planning has come to be derided by its opponents as the suppression of individual enterprise. It is no such thing. It is – or ought to be – an institutional framework within which enterprises (of all sorts) can flourish. Indeed, so great are the advantages which such planning can offer that – combined with the substantial understanding that much of the economy will be dominated by firms of such a size that they are natural monopolies – many socialists will ask only one question about markets: *why, under socialism, should they be allowed to exist at all?* The answer, in part, concerns the liberty which is an essential feature of a truly socialist society. It also relates to the efficiency that has been so conspicuously lacking in some societies which, after calling themselves socialist, organised their economies on centralised bureaucratic principles which are the antithesis of true socialism. But it is not a total or absolute answer based on a single universal truth. Without some market influence the economy will be inefficient and unresponsive to consumers' needs; with nothing except the market deciding distribution, the result will be exactly the same.

Alec Nove, in *The Economics of Feasible Socialism*, describes the objection to the complete replacement of markets by some other system of resource allocation. In the Soviet system, he says, 'the economic mechanism fails to respond to user requirements and generates far too much unintended and avoidable waste. Its centralisation faithfully reflects and re-inforces political centralisation . . . Marketless socialism can only mean centralised planning in which a large and necessarily hierarchical and bureaucratic organisation issues instructions, organises and co-ordinates' and must have as its 'counterpart the hierarchical and bureaucratic organisation of politics'.[13]

For the great problem which has to be solved in a marketless economy is the way in which resources are allocated. Capitalism does not possess a morally defensible theory of distribution. It is that failure which socialists believe demonstrates capitalism's moral abdication and which free marketeers insist proves that socialism is unrelated to reality. The true marketeers accept that the market – free, imperfect or restricted by monopoly – cannot answer any of the ethical questions about needs and deserts. Production, as regulated by markets, responds to both those imperatives only obliquely. Distribution is the servant of demand – effective demand as measured by purchasing power; and purchasing power may be possessed in greater abundance by those who have the fewest needs. The market system, in unequal societies, ensures that petrol which might be used for transporting food to Ethiopia is used for every sort of frivolous – or positively undesirable – purpose. But market theorists challenge socialists to provide an adequate alternative. The answer is that the only thing to be said about the market mechanism is that, for large parts of the economy, it is – despite its manifest unfairness – the best way of allocating resources that we can conceive. It is the best way in two senses. It is the best protection against the bureaucratic inefficiencies, which characterise much production in Soviet command economies, and the bureaucratic intrusions into personal liberty which such a system creates; and just as we must not become so preoccupied with competitive efficiency that we forget the overriding duty to pursue greater equality, so we must not become so blinkered in our ideological pursuit that we are prepared to jeopardise the success of the economy and therefore hold back the growth and

[13] A. Nove, *The Economics of Feasible Socialism* (Allen & Unwin, London, 1985), Pt. 4, 'Transition', pp. 176, 179.

expansion which would make the realisation of an equal society more likely. This is, in a sense, the inversion of 'the Difference Principle' as laid down by John Rawls and explained by the question about disparities of wealth and income which he asks himself and then answers.

> What can possibly justify this kind of initial inequality in life prospect? According to the difference principle it is justified only if the difference in expectation is to the advantage of the representative who is worse off.[14]

In short, we cannot afford the scarcities, the misallocation and the failure of supply and distribution which would actually follow if we seriously asserted that either markets or planning should be an invariable rôle. For 'planning for human need' poses great problems. Who is to determine what those needs are, how they are to be most efficiently met and what priorities are to be employed if all human needs cannot be met at once? It is a question which cannot be answered by the application of a convincing socialist theory for the distribution of shirts and ties, tablecloths, Cup Final tickets, continental holidays, lawn-mowers, paper handkerchiefs or ballpoint pens. Some of those commodities may be judged as necessities, but for all or any of them to be allocated to consumers by some state bureaucracy would be to impose a drab uniformity (as well as an economic torpor) on the society which distributed its goods in that way. But none of those goods are the 'basic needs' which are necessary for any man or woman who is to possess sufficient resources to be regarded as a free citizen equipped with the physical ability to take advantage of the theoretical liberties which a democratic state provides. Health, education, housing and a decent level of income (with which the choices can be made about lawnmowers, paper handkerchiefs and Cup Final tickets) are 'basic needs'. If these things are allocated by the market, some men and women will be denied the 'agency' which makes them free. These are practical and immediate examples directly related to the analysis (in previous chapters) of freedom within a state which fails to use its power to eradicate disability or fatal illness.

In the Freeman Road Hospital in Newcastle, orthopaedic surgeons, responding to the demands for greater efficiency,

---

[14] J. Rawls, *A Theory of Justice* (Oxford University Press, Oxford, 1972), p. 64.

developed ways in which the resources at their disposal could be more effectively used in the replacement of arthritic hip joints. Their improvement in efficiency produced so many operations that they exceeded the hospital's budget for the purchase of the artificial joints with which arthritic hips were replaced; patients waiting for the operation were therefore told that for months no more operations could be performed. Meanwhile, private and health-insurance patients in other hospitals were having hip joints replaced. There must be a better way of allocating hip joints than limiting their availability to the comparatively poor – whatever their need – and making them easily available to those who can afford 'the market rate'. In the same hospital, the use of a new drug for the treatment of ovarian cancer has been abandoned – despite its clinical superiority over the alternatives – because the cost of £700 a course is too expensive for the hospital's financial pay. It is available to private patients. In both instances, the market has been slightly moderated. Without some interference in its operation many patients would have received no treatment at all. But in each case, since total resources are limited, the market ensures that wealth can still buy an advantage, which ought to be wholly unacceptable in a democracy.

It is impossible to believe that the 'abolition of scarcity' which Marx prophesied will ever come about for the provision of medical care. Science constantly discovers new ways of saving life and restoring health – most of them far more expensive than the old, inferior techniques which they replace. The cost of health care is also increased by the special health service dynamic. Every new development generates extra needs. For the achievements of research include the extended lives of patients who would previously have died and who, in life, are a continued call on health service resources. It is intolerable that scarce medical resources should be distributed by simple market allocation. There are two essential, and related, stages in an acceptable system of distribution. The state should allocate, to the finance of medical care, as large a total as society can afford – never saying that lower taxes will encourage extended private provision. That total should be distributed according to acceptable criteria of need. And once need becomes the accepted criterion, the global total would undoubtedly increase, as those who decide on its size consider the possibility that one day they may be just on the margin of whatever rules which determine whether or not a candidate for treatment qualifies for help. A consensus on need – part professional, part democratic – is the only civilised way in which to distribute limited medical resources. The same rule applies to the distribution of education. After the state has done its best, an individual who wants to buy violin lessons for a son ought to be free to do so.

However, in other, less morally sensitive areas, only the markets can adequately allocate scarce resources. We have no clear idea how we should allocate a second – or indeed a first – motor car to a normal family. If we begin to draw up rules which are unrelated to market criteria we risk two terrible catastrophes: too few motor cars and too many bureaucrats with unreasonable power of the allocation over both the motor cars which are built and 'sold' and the families which receive them. The experience of Soviet economies which have attempted to 'plan' current production and the material inputs into industry are not encouraging. The complexity of a plan which allocates resources for the production of the millions of goods which are bought and sold in a sophisticated society is clearly too great to be mastered by an army of civil servants, no matter how advanced the equipment with which they are armed. The collection of the information is probably literally impossible; its collation is even more difficult. Further, were it possible to perform such tasks someone would have to be given the power to decide who qualified for the receipt of scarce consumer durables and foods in short supply. The easy answer is: better the bureaucrat than the power of the purse. We do not have to make any such absolute choice. The market can be the first determinant of how goods are allocated and the bias against the poor can be not so much modified as negated, by limiting the vast discrepancies in purchasing power by a conscious policy of reducing the incomes of the rich and increasing the earnings of the poor.

In any case the allocation of the hundreds of separate items which go into the production of even simple goods is clearly beyond human capability. Nove refers to *Pravda* of 28 November 1979.

> If, in the end, there are insufficient toothbrushes, detergents, babies' diapers, needles and thread one can (as Brezhnev has done) deplore this, but, given that the failure to provide them is

a consequence of the overwhelming complexity of the central plan (and the fact that such 'minor items' are likely to be the responsibility of junior officials without much claim on scarce resources), what better solution is there than to allow groups of citizens (co-operatives perhaps) to set up workshops to make such things.[15]

Nove makes, in literal parenthesis, a point about markets which socialists ought to understand and accept. On the subject of ownership markets are neutral. There is absolutely no reason why autonomous socially owned firms should not exist within them, competing either with privately owned concerns or with each other. The idea that socialism and markets are incompatible is the product – if it is the result of anything remotely intellectual – of Marx's confusion over value. Markets depend on price – the amount paid in return for the purchase of goods and services. Yet Marx constructed a theory of intrinsic value (real worth) which related to the quantity of labour used in the production of goods and the preparation of services. He complicated – perhaps even contradicted – his theory with the concept of use value, which implied that the labour value within a commodity only had any existence if it gave that commodity a utility. Engels 'clarified' the position in *Anti-Duhring*. 'It will be the utilities of different products compared with one another and with the quantities of labour necessary for their production which will determine the plan.'[16] That judgment created an uneasy feeling amongst innocent Marxists that society should be liberated from the tyranny of price and the iniquities of markets without helping them to decide how it might be done. It pointed out the moral weakness of the free enterprise system and the failure of its theorists even to attempt the construction of a system of distribution which has anything like ethical foundation. But then neither does Marxism. It speculates vapidly about the day when all wants are met, but it does not suggest when that day will dawn. And, in his *Critique of the Gotha Programme*, Marx accepted that even when the means of production were publicly owned, the pattern of distribution would not necessarily

---

[15] A. Nove, *The Economics of Feasible Socialism* (Allen & Unwin, London, 1985), Pt 1, 'The Legacy of Marx', p. 45.
[16] Quoted in A. Nove, *The Economics of Feasible Socialism* (Allen & Unwin, London, 1985), p. 21.

correspond to the needs of the recipient. Sensible socialists will be more concerned with market power – a more equal distribution of the resources which make up aggregate demand.

A free market in non-essentials within which genuine choices are made by consumers with identical purchasing power is a utopian dream. But utopia is the promised land; even though we will never enter in, we can approach it. Approaching it by moving towards more equal incomes which are spent within free markets is an essential ingredient of freedom, for it avoids organising the economy according to a detailed central plan; and to distribute goods in that way is to place in the hands of state officials power which is bound to be reflected in the general political organisation of the state.

If a man or woman – the word commissar has acquired its pejorative association for this very reason – has power to decide this allocation of goods, the availability of services and the prospect of work, then those individuals will assume powers which are inconsistent with a libertarian state. Socialists understand that such a degree of personal power is undesirable when it is manifest by the tyranny of the private economy and the autocracy of wealth. We must not tolerate such an authoritarian system just because it goes by another name. It is not necessary to believe and accept Hayek's contention that since markets act without intention, there is no justification in complaining about their results. The preservation of a pluralistic political system is most likely if anonymous forces rather than nominated individuals determine the distribution of goods and services outside those sectors of the economy where markets are either impossible or undesirable. That does not, of course, always legitimise the influence of those markets. The monopolies – where they are not publicly owned – have to be regulated. The sectors where competition exists have to conform to ground rules concerning good employment practices, honest advertising, pollution control, location policy; and those rules have to apply to autonomous socially owned companies as well as to private undertakings. That is the only system which is conducive to freedom as well as to efficiency.

If there were exclusive state property in the socialist state, the proletariat would be left propertyless. With no direct economic power, with no economic base for its class rule. In this case, those that govern would have to be at the same time both the representatives of the ruling class. However such a situation would be absurd.[17]

It would be more than absurd. It would be totalitarian, for the state would not wither away. That is another example of sentimental nonsense. The state would be in total control, the single employer, the single supplier. In those circumstances, the operation of 'the plan' would require the apparatus of state power. It would exercise, unfettered even by economic reality, all the prerogatives of ownership, and under such a system, autonomous and independent socially owned enterprises could not exist; for if a steel plant is allocated a tunnage of billets and blooms by the central steel authority and told, by the same agency, what they should make and how much of it should be made, co-operative or municipal organisation would be wholly impossible. Indeed, outside the area of natural monopoly, public utility, and social service, markets are *essential* to any definition of socialism which includes the encouragement of diversity and individual liberty and the economic autonomy (public or private) which goes with those essential conditions.

Working on that undeniable precept we can draw up some principles concerning the existence of markets in a socialist society.

> 1. In the area of social provision – health, housing, education – simple market regulation is unacceptable. In housing, those potential consumers who cannot afford adequate housing have to be assisted by the state. In education and health, scarce resources must be distributed according to need, not purchasing power.

> 2. The public utilities – transport, energy and telephones – cannot be judged according to their own short-term market-related performance because of their effects on other industries and the community at large.

> 3. There are a number of sectors which – because of their size and the nature of their product – are likely to grow to a size where markets have only a marginal effect on their performance.

[17] R. Selucky, *Marxism, Socialism and Freedom* (Macmillan, London, 1979), p. 70.

4. In the rest of the economy, the market (consisting of socially owned, private and hybrid companies) is, with all of its imperfections, the best basis on which to base the distribution of available resources. But in most sectors it cannot be left to itself. A whole range of government policies – tax incentives, fair employment regulations, subsidised investment – will, in effect, ensure that social obligations and wider economic considerations, in part, deflect the full operation of the market.

From those points a number of conclusions about public policy follow. The health, social and education services should be part of the public provision and insulated from the damaging effects of market privatisation. The public utilities should be socially owned and remain as central corporations with a national plan for their overall performance. Natural monopolies should be regulated by their transfer into public ownership, subject to the detailed government control which is practised in the USA, or subject to a competition policy which exposes them to some of the beneficial rigours of competition – if necessary by acting as a market surrogate by imposing price limitation. To allow monopolies to operate unchecked is to allow, at the very least, the opportunity to exploit. The market sector itself must be subject to some influence from central government – and those influences must include not only the ground rules of the mixed economy. They must allow the government to induce in market-orientated firms a willingness to take part in national macro-economic strategy concerning the level of investment and profits, the location of industry and the encouragement of exports. The alternative forms of ownership and management are, for the market sector, an independent issue, as is the question of democratic control of those areas in which the market cannot or will not apply. A libertarian view of socialism of the sort which is advocated here will not absolve the state for the exercise of onerous duties. But that is another story.

Chapter Nine

Is Nationalisation Enough?

Labour Party activists feel instinctively that an extension of public ownership is essential to the pursuit of socialism. But too few of the passionate advocates of what is damagingly referred to as 'nationalisation' have a clear view of why it is necessary to the achievement of their aims. That is because the essentially unthinking attachment of socialists to public ownership has resulted in two major errors. First, not being clear why an extension of the socially owned sector is desirable, Labour has been handicapped in its attempts to persuade floating voters that an extension is desirable. The announcement of a 'shopping list' of industries selected for nationalisation was emotionally satisfying to party members, but floating voters found it either irrelevant to their view of the world or a menacing invasion of the state into their daily lives. Second, lacking intellectual (as distinct from emotional) conviction, and having sacrificed popular support for what the public regard as state ownership, Labour failed to extend the public sector as much as was economically and socially desirable simply because 'nationalisation' was often not possible and other forms of social ownership were not considered. Labour has failed hopelessly to examine the forms in which social ownership should be extended.

That failure is the inevitable result of the Labour Party's heterogeneous origins in Marxism, methodism, liberalism and Fabian gentle common sense. The most influential intellectual forces within the early Labour Party never supported what has become the vulgar view: the supposedly self-evident need for more state corporations. The need for the common ownership of the means of production, distribution and exchange was qualified even as Sidney Webb wrote the crucial Clause IV at Labour's constitution. For (see Chapter 1) he insisted that socialists were 'open to choose from time to time whatever forms of common ownership' seemed appropriate in specific circumstances, and his wife's diaries reveal that the apparent prophet of nationalisation held an even more gradualist view of political advance than those which he admitted at the time: 'In his heart of hearts, I think he still believes in Fabian permeation of other parties as a more rapid way than the advent of a distinctly socialist government.'[1]

R. H. Tawney could never be accused of such apostasy. But he, too, urged an essentially empirical approach to public ownership, its extension being decided on 'the merits of the case' rather than by 'resounding declarations' about the merits of socialism or capitalism. Proudhon's notion that 'property is theft' was not the sort of socialist theory that appealed to him: 'Precisely as it is important to preserve the property which a man has as a result of his own labour it is important to abolish that which he has as the result of the labour of someone else.'[2] That is the theory of surplus value translated into ethical language. It is also a confused aphorism which possesses more literary style than philosophic substance. But it confirms that since the earliest years of its existence the Labour Party – even as represented by its most eminent philosophers – has been uncertain about the reasons why public ownership ought to be extended. The uncertainty has been intensified by a semantic complication concerning the word 'nationalisation'. The term is sometimes used to describe social ownership in general and sometimes employed to define one particular form of public enterprise – the state monopoly owned by the government and managed by a board of ministerial nominees.

In the public mind, the two definitions have become confused. Social ownership – indeed socialism itself – has become identified with the remote and bureaucratic state corporation. In fact, the Labour Party constitution – in a phrase which is often quoted but rarely thought about – promises 'to secure for the workers by hand and brain the full fruits of their labours'. And that can clearly be done in a number of different ways. It *may* mean the creation of state corporations which provide centralised ownership and management of a public utility. It may mean the establishment of single publicly owned companies

[1] B. Webb, *Diaries*, Vol. 4, 1924–43 (Virago, London, 1985), 19.9.25.
[2] R. H. Tawney, *The Acquisitive Society* (Wheatsheaf, Sussex, 1982), Pt 5, 'Property and Creative Work'.

which compete with private-sector rivals. It may require the increased involvement of local authorities in the ownership and management of enterprises within their boundaries – a form of organisation which if it has to be called an '-isation' of some sort, is clearly 'localisation' not 'nationalisation'. But municipalisation, as local authority enterprise has come to be called, is only one of the many possible alternatives. Social ownership may mean the encouragement of worker or consumer co-operatives which are not the property of the general public or state at all. It may mean that workers' investment funds on the Swedish model will allow large, trades-union controlled, equity stakes in private companies. It may mean employee share-option schemes which allow workers both to buy shares and to acquire the power of share ownership. The alternative models are infinite in type and number.

The semantic problem of 'nationalisation' is largely the product of two conflicting forces – *dirigiste* socialists and Herbert Morrison. In the 1920s the Soviet Union was thought of more as the triumph of working men and women over feudalism than as the home of Stalinist liquidations, the suppression of minorities, the occupation of neighbouring countries and the sacrifice of the domestic economy to the needs of an ever expanding defence budget. The state and socialism seemed – *to a minority of Party members* – to be indivisible. They were naturally enough the most passionate enthusiasts for the form of public ownership which ironically was both advocated and implemented by one of their natural opponents within the Party. Herbert Morrison was instinctively sceptical about both the desirability and practicality of extensive public ownership. At the 1934 Party Conference he led the opposition to Stafford Cripps's *Socialist Labour League* proposals for nationalisation without compensation. But as part of his ministerial and party duties, Morrison became increasingly associated with public ownership by state corporation: first through the London Passenger Transport Board, and then, because of his responsibility for the preparation of the 1945 election programme, Morrison became increasingly committed to the form of public ownership which is now actually called 'Morrisonian nationalisation'. In Morrison's time it was regarded as the appropriate form for social ownership of the public utilities. But in the miasma of despair and sloppy thinking which followed the

174

defeat of 1951, it was all too often taken to be – and described as – the method of economic organisation which was essential to, indeed synonymous with, socialist advance. In Germany (where democratic socialists take ideas more seriously) the SPD formally shed its state-ownership aspirations and liabilities in the Bad Godesberg Declaration. In Sweden, there has been half a century of careful argument relating public ownership to national necessity. The 'Workers' Investment Fund' – proposed in 1983 – carefully linked the acquisition of share ownership with krone depreciation and wage stability. In Britain, the talk of 'nationalisation' – at various times embracing sugar, cement, chemicals, building and the 'top 200 monopolies' which are easier to abuse than to identify – has combined with the intrusive style adopted by some Labour local authorities to provide the ingredients of an authoritarian nightmare:

> It is indeed not so much the existence of the state (which we can scarcely expect to see pass out of existence in the immediate future) that is the problem. It is the total *monopolisation* by the state over the past century or so, of every shred of authority in every field of activity. The state has become in modern times, the all powerful, all purpose, omnicompetent organisation which totally rules men's lives. And yet it is, in the eyes of most men, a vast, impersonal, inhuman and almost abstract machine that is not only – except in the most theoretical sense – beyond their control, but corresponds in no way to what they feel to be their own, immediate, living community. *By equating socialism with state ownership, therefore, modern socialist thinking serves only to intensify the discrepancy between authority and community.*[3]

All that is wrong with that judgment is that it is historically incorrect. Modern socialist *'thinking'* equates no such things. Socialism is equated with state ownership in *Daily Express* editorials and in the speeches of the less cerebral members of the National Executive Committee, but not by Tony Crosland or by the dozens of other less famous but influential writers on the theory of modern socialism. Of course, the less cerebral members of the National Executive do provide ammunition for the *Daily Express* pop-gun; though whether we should expect the same superficiality from the scholar (and minister in the

---

[3] E. Luard, *Socialism Without the State* (Macmillan, London, 1979), Ch. 2, 'The Takeover of Socialism by the State', p. 29.

Callaghan government) who is quoted above is open to doubt. We can put his error down to the trauma which followed the abandonment of a Party which he had supported for two decades and a simple ignorance, not only of what Labour 'thinkers' write but also of what Labour governments do.

The Attlee government of 1945–51 'nationalised' one public utility for each of its six years in office. Other Labour governments nationalised aerospace and shipbuilding; took a stake in oil extraction by the creation of a state oil company; rescued British Leyland by buying out the ailing giant's assets and taking responsibility for its reorganisation; and saved Ferranti from collapse and liquidation by relieving that company's shareholders of the burden of its accumulated debt, and, when government action had put it back on its feet, gave it back to the directors who have presided over the near catastrophe. These various and varied 'extensions of public ownership' were seen and represented as individual acts – contested by the Tories in the House of Commons at the time, but, with the exception of steel, not thought of (until the arrival of the new Thatcherite ideologists) as candidates for immediate denationalisation. Indeed, the state acquisition of the aircraft-engine division of Rolls-Royce was, ideologically, a similar operation, designed to save a collapsing company. The decision was apparently offensive to Margaret Thatcher, who although she sat silent in the Cabinet of the time, later determined to sell Rolls-Royce back to private enterprise. But it was taken by a Tory government as a matter of uncontentious necessity. Between 1945 and 1951, railways, coal mines, gas and electricity undertakings, steel and the Bank of England moved into the public sector in what is now thought – within the romantic tendency of the Labour Party – to have been a fervour of doctrinal delight. What is more, they were all (with the exception of the Bank of England) 'nationalised' on the Morrisonian model. At least to the opponents of public ownership in the popular press they were instruments for the fusion of socialism and state. The truth is different and more dull. It demonstrates that Labour governments – and Labour Parties expecting to form governments – have always taken a prosaically practical view of public ownership, seeing it as a means to an end, not as an objective in itself.

176

The Attlee manifesto for the 1945 election promised the public ownership of all the public utilities. But it was not constructed without the usual conference dramas of rebellion and rejection, accusation of apostasy and protestation of the platform's good faith and better sense.

> For Labour's electoral future, the most important debate was the NEC's policy document, *Economic Controls, Public Ownership and Full Employment*. This reaffirmed the principle of public ownership and proposed taking control of the Bank of England but otherwise contained no specific commitments to nationalise particular industries. Delegates were unhappy with this caution and a resolution was passed from the floor calling for 'the transfer to public ownership of the land, large scale building, heavy industry and all forms of banking, transport and fuel and power'. Labour never did, in fact, nationalise land or building and would certainly have nationalised fuel, power and transport anyway.[4]

What appeared in the programme was what seemed *necessary* to its authors and was justified by them in practical language which made their opponents appear old-fashioned, prejudiced, doctrinaire and motivated by self-interest. The Labour Party argued that it was doing no more than continuing the inevitable process which had begun a hundred years before and could only be slowed down at the expense of industrial efficiency and social justice.

> Public regulation of industry during the nineteenth century arose mainly out of the need of way-leaves for some industries. In return for the grant of compulsory purchase powers, Parliament imposed obligations on those industries. Individual Acts were followed by general Acts, consolidating Acts and finally almost this whole group of industries, the public utilities – roads, railways, canals, telegraphs, telephones, tramways, gas and electricity – has been nationalised.[5]

Whether the Labour Party knew it or not, it was evolving a theory of public ownership for the public utilities. The case for their nationalisation – in the precise sense of that word – is over-

[4] B. Donoughue and G. W. Jones, *Herbert Morrison* (Weidenfeld & Nicolson, London, 1973), Ch. 24, 'Pot War Reconstruction and the 1945 General Election', pp. 330-31.
[5] Warswick and Ady, eds, *The British Economy 1945–50* (Clarendon Press, Oxford, 1952), Ch. 19 (H. Clegg on Nationalised Industries), pp. 426-7.

whelming. The 1945 manifesto described the public ownership proposals in language appropriate to an invincible practical case, and during the campaign, 'the argument was frequently made that such measures were essential to the interests of efficiency';[6] whilst the public ownership programme was 'justified in the terms of practical arguments for efficiency' in a way which was 'designed to draw in the uncommitted voters'.[7] Even then, the disadvantages of associating socialism and the state too closely were minimised. The public utilities had to be organised as centralised monopolies, and planned and managed by London-based boards, but

> It was a feature of *Let Us Face the Future*, the 1945 manifesto, that the term 'public ownership' was used more often than 'nationalisation'. The Bank of England was to be 'taken over' so as to ensure full employment. 'Public ownership of the fuel and power industries' would 'bring great economies in operation and make it possible to modernise production methods and raise safety standards in every colliery'. The same sort of advantage would flow from the 'public ownership of gas and electricity undertakings'; it 'will lower charges, prevent competitive waste, open the way for coordinated research and development and lead to the reforming of uneconomic areas of distribution'. The manifesto recommended 'public ownership of iron and steel' on similar grounds of increased efficiency.[8]

Those arguments could, indeed need to, be used in support of public utility 'nationalisation' more than forty years after they first appeared in Labour's post-war manifesto. But they are arguments which are special to those specific aspects of the economy. The failure of the last fifty years has been our failure first to differentiate between the forms of social ownership which are appropriate to different industrial sectors and then to justify each proposal on its individual merits. The price which has been paid for this intellectual neglect is not only political – although millions of votes have been lost by the failure to make the cogent case for nationalisation of the utilities. But there is a second problem: if it is not clear why they have been taken into

[6] *ibid.*, Introduction.
[7] H. Pelling, *The Labour Governments 1945–51* (Macmillan, London, 1984), Ch. I, 'The General Election', p. 26.
[8] *ibid.*, Ch. 5, 'Morrison and Nationalisation', p. 77.

public ownership in the first place, it is difficult to judge whether or not they are achieving the object of their change of status.

The case for public ownership of the basic utilities is closely related to the case for their *national* organisation and ownership:

1. Since the rest of the economy is dependent upon the organisation and performance of basic utilities it would be wrong to leave their operation to the vagaries of free competition and the demands of a profit-orientated market. It might be wholly right and reasonable for a private railway company to close down an unprofitable branch line; but the closure could have adverse consequences for companies served by the railway and, as a result, for the economy as a whole.

2. The utilities provide for individuals basic services which should be available to them as a matter of right. The provision of those services should not, therefore, be (solely) dependent on a consumer's ability to pay and the product of the utilities should be universally available at a roughly uniform price. The crofters of the Outer Hebrides have the same right to light and heat as the commuters of Clapham. Nationalisation, when it fails to provide such a service, fails in its purpose.

3. By their nature, the utilities are likely to be organised, or are best organised, as monopolies. It is essential that they should be under a form of control which prevents them from exploiting their monopoly status and outright nationalisation achieves that end most directly. It is not possible for the same crofters to telephone the mainland by any other system than the now privately owned British Telecom. The company's monopoly status should not be reflected in its tariff.

4. It is necessary for a socialist government to plan both the level of demand and the location of industry. Ownership of a number of major enterprises enables it to determine employment levels, prices and investment over a wide area of the economy. A government which owns the coal mines could subsidise coking coal and thus hold down the price of steel, and encourage employment in the steel-using industries.

Inevitably, those aims are occasionally and in part in conflict with each other. Keeping open an unprofitable branch line may require – in the absence of an acceptable level of government subsidy – a differential pricing policy which ensures a high and constant income from the captive customers on profitable routes. There is also a wider 'planning function' which, for profitable nationalised industries, raises another form of conflict. It is possible to argue that a nationalised corporation can make its greatest contribution to national welfare by making a profit which is used to finance spending which is more desirable than the cheap provision of the commodity marketed by the publicly owned concern. Thus it could, theoretically, be right to set external financing limits for the gas industry which, in effect, produces a profit for the government to use on an increased old-age pension – though the case is more difficult to argue when pensioners are dying from hypothermia and the pension is no longer automatically improved with increases in national earnings. However, the dilemma remains: should a nationalised corporation struggle for competitive efficiency and high levels of profit, just as if it were a private company? The answer lies at the heart of the dilemma which has prejudiced the progress of the public utilities since they were nationalised.

Alex Nove, in *The Economics of Feasible Socialism*,[9] having asserted with depressing accuracy that 'the British species' of nationalisation arouses little enthusiasm in either socialists or non-socialists, lists what he regards as its original intentions: the dispossession of the big capitalists, the diversion of profit appropriation from the private to the public purse and the service of public good rather than the profit motive. 'Original intentions' were, of course, the product of the days when the Public Sector Borrowing Requirement (even less the money supply) rarely disturbed the nation's economic thought. But putting aside the macro-economic considerations of planning and the construction of the chosen fiscal and monetary environment, the nationalised corporations are still thought of as potential contributors to the achievement of those three 'original' aims. Unfortunately, those aims often come into conflict with each other and the conflict is intensified when the

---

[9] A. Nove, *The Economics of Feasible Socialism* (Allen & Unwin, London, 1985, Pt 4, 'Transition', p. 167.

'new obligation' of contributing to the success of the government's general strategy is added. Usually it is the consumer of
the nationalised industry's product who suffers, for it is always
'possible to fulfil plans (whether these are expressed in terms of
profit rate, in quantity or in value of turnover) at the customer's
expense'[10].

But with the nationalised monopolies, it is difficult to know
how – except by measuring the profit rate – performance can be
adequately measured. Most recent governments have chosen to
construct sophistications of the same crude calculation and
called them return on capital invested and external financing
limits. Inadequate as those measurements are, the 'success' of
nationalised monopolies has to be measured in some way, but it
cannot be tested against the criteria of customer satisfaction
with the price and the comfortingly commercial test of whether
or not they take their business somewhere else. Market research
and the institutions of consumerism can make a judgment of
sorts, but these do not offer the tangible test that profit and loss
accounts provide. However, the difficulty in assessing the
'success' of publicly-owned industries is not that they are
nationalised but that they are monopolies. Private monopolies
are similarly insulated from the market, but since that is the
object of their monopolisation they are more inclined to glory in
their condition than to worry about it. Nationalised utilities are,
on the other hand, inclined to worry about their monopoly
status -- particularly when it is pointed out to them by the
Opposition in Parliament. Nevertheless they often fall for the
temptation to exploit it, and when they do not exploit it for
themselves, the government (which owns them) is inclined to
insist on its exploitation.

The notorious insistence, by the Thatcher governments of the
early and middle eighties, that the energy industries should
produce a profit in excess of that which was necessary for
continued output and a reasonable return on capital, is the most
blatant example of the monopoly status of nationalised industries
being used by the government to exploit consumers in order to
fulfil wider economic aims. But other governments have felt the
temptation. Indeed, the Labour government of 1974–9 was so
conscious of the dangers that it attempted to set out in its

---

[10] *ibid.*, p. 170.

Nationalised Industry White Paper[11] the criteria by which the performance of the state-owned utilities should be judged. The aim was to make as many of the nationalised industries as possible self-financing. But the notion of self-financing needed careful and detailed definition.

The concept of 'self-financing' was defined in two distinct, but related, ways. First, financial targets were set over periods of three to five years. They were related to the percentage rate of return (before interest repayments) on capital employed or, in labour-intensive industries, the percentage rate of return on turnover. The rate (when calculated on capital) was assessed on total capital employed rather than on the current year's investment and those two basic criteria were hedged about by a whole series of qualifications. The rate of return might have to be modified by considerations of market prospects, scope for improved productivity, the effect on the Public Sector Borrowing Requirement, the obligations to counter-inflation policy and the social consequences of the pricing policy needed to meet the targets. The White Paper was explicit that 'the nationalised industries will not be forced into deficits by restraints on their prices', but it was equally opposed to inflationary price increases. The need to be self-financing was, in fact, balanced against the duty to support, or at least not run counter to, government economic and social policy.

Second, the nationalised industries were enjoined to pursue a 'required rate of return' – a long-term judgment about how much the public utilities would pay back to the nation in return for the funds which they had received as investment. The calculation was made on the basis of 'opportunity costs' – the return which the investment would have enjoyed had it been placed elsewhere. The actual figure would be based on market assumptions concerning the performance of comparable industries. But it was agreed that there were sectors of all nationalised industries 'where social obligations imply continuing losses'.[11]

It is difficult to read those carefully constructed principles and the reservations which qualified them almost out of existence without developing firm convictions about the White Paper's contents. First, it was a determined, indeed a heroic, attempt to lay down general principles concerning the performance – and

[11] Cmd No. 7131 (1978).

the monitoring of the performance – of nationalised industries. Second, the attempt was bound to fail, because there is no general rule of performance which can be applied to all nationalised industries at all times. There will be times when it is rational to argue that a public utility should hold down its prices artificially to achieve wider economic obligations or specific social goals; but there are other occasions when the drive to hold down costs destroys the purpose of nationalisation. The removal of rural telephone boxes, like the abandonment of coin-operated equipment in inner cities and its replacement by cash cards, may reduce costs in the country and thefts in the towns, but it also lowers the level of service below that which is expected from a socially conscious public service. The same is true of disconnection policy in the energy industries. The moguls of gas and electricity may argue that the failure of poor families to pay their bills is no concern of the industry but the responsibility of politicians. They will be right; but that does not mean that the obligation should not be exercised through the pricing and operating policies of the nationalised industries. The obligation has to be clearly costed and identified so as to enable two aims to be achieved in parallel: competitive efficiency and fulfilment of duties wider than those accepted by private enterprise.

A similar duty exists to make public what the chairmen of nationalised companies regard as a liability even greater than a socialist government's inclination to keep public utility prices down: the tendency of Conservative governments to push public utility prices up. There are reasons of principle (with which we shall deal presently) for objecting to the way in which the Thatcher administration of the 1970s and 1980s chose to cream off nationalised industry profits in order to hide the true level of public borrowing, and it was quite the wrong economic policy for the time. But the idea that a government should abdicate its right to influence public utility prices (upwards or downwards) is clearly absurd. 'If the criteria of the operation of nationalised industries can be seen as no different from those of private enterprise, why nationalise them at all?'[12] The rule for national-ised industry pricing policy should not be that the government

[12] A. Nove, *The Economics of Feasible Socialism* (Allen & Unwin, London, 1985), Pt 4, 'Transition', p. 171.

should not interfere, but that when it does it should interfere openly and honestly.

The truth, as revealed by the Labour government's attempt to construct sophisticated criteria and the Conservatives' more simplistic enthusiasm for 'external financing limits' – which produce a 'proper' return on capital – is that no general rules for judging the performance of nationalised industries can be constructed. For different industries are required to do different things at different times. Not all the public utilities will have the same economic and social objects and obligations. We will want to make them all efficient, but we may not want to minimise loss or maximise profit of every division of every public utility. For in the calculation of success of the true utilities a great deal of subjective judgment is an unavoidable ingredient. *Because of that the aims of the public utilities will never be clearly defined – their performance will always be in genuine doubt and their reputation will always be depressed by arguments which seem to be about how well they are performing but are, in fact, about whether or not they are performing the right task. Since we cannot adequately judge their success it is clearly better to limit the operation of the state monopoly to those sectors where one form of monopoly or another is inevitable, and extend social ownership of other sorts in areas where success (whether it is improved marginal revenue, diffusion of power to employees or greater sensitivity to consumer needs) can be more easily defined, assessed and increased.*

Anyone who doubts the dilemma concerning the function and behaviour of nationalised industries should examine a letter sent in February 1986 from Mrs J. Colclough, the Customer Service Manager at the British Telecom area office in Derby, to a subscriber in Eastwood, Nottingham. It was in reply to the allegation that the cost of calls from Eastwood to London was more expensive than the cost of calls to London from nearby Nottingham. Mrs Colclough explained the operation of the 'low cost (bl) route between Nottingham and London'. Typically, the letter began with an apology for the 'inordinate delay' (three months) in 'responding' to the enquiry.

> The bl charge band was introduced . . . for calls over direct routes between centres which carry large volumes of traffic, in order to pass on to customers the lower cost resulting from the economies of scale which are made possible through the use of

high capacity transmission equipment. These reduced rates form part of an overall strategy of aligning prices for individual services as closely as possible to costs and thus removing cross subsidisation, as required by the licence granted to British Telecom by the Department of Trade and Industry.

To opponents of denationalisation, the judgments come easily. The privately owned British Telecom, instead of providing a universal service at universally applied prices, constructs profit centres and charges its customers on the basis of the costs within their defined areas. The socialist naturally asks questions about the old-age pensioners of Eastwood who cannot afford to telephone their children in Ealing. Why should the millionaires of Nottingham not be required to pay a higher price when phoning their City stockbrokers, so as to keep the Eastwood cost down? It is then that the devotee of public ownership discovers the date at which the bl charge band was introduced and the differential price system put into operation: it was May 1982, when British Telecom was still in public ownership. The devotee begins to wonder at once if there are not good reasons for what, at first, seemed exploitation – the need to hold down general price levels, justify individual items of capital investment and set criteria by which operating efficiency can be measured. The real answer to all the difficult questions is that there are no absolute rules about the operation of the public utilities. We can construct some guidelines, but they will have to be applied flexibly; and since – by definition – classic nationalisation cannot fulfil all the obligations which socialists heap on it, it is necessary for us to promote other forms of common ownership which can achieve specific aims and, in doing so, help to give socialism a good name.

A description of the method by which the public utilities should be assessed and controlled needs to be preceded by a reassertion of principle. *Public ownership, in the form of state corporations centrally owned, planned and administered, is essential for the public utilities.* Such corporations are, by their nature, monopolies, when such concentration of economic power is unavoidable, are better publicly owned than privately owned. All other things being equal, they should provide a common level of service throughout the economy and, since they are responsible for activities on which other industries depend, their activities cannot be left to the vagaries of the market. The rational case for nationalisation – in the Morrisonian form – of the public utilities is overwhelming. But that should not delude us into believing that the state corporation is the ideal form of social ownership, or that it should be the model which we choose for extension into other parts of the economy; for – crucially – it lacks two of the elements which socialists should hope to find *automatically* present in the new forms of organisation which they hope to create. First, because of the nature of monopolies, public and private, the state corporation is endemically insensitive to the needs of its consumers, and second, largely because of its size, it is equally insensitive to the needs of its employees. Colliers who remember the days of the private coal owners contrast the years before and after nationalisation as eras of slavery and freedom, but a newer generation of miners find the Coal Board less responsive to their wishes than many private companies are to the aspirations of their employees. In both cases – the failure to meet the hopes of consumers as well as workers – the shortcomings associated with the arrogance of size and monopoly power are compounded by two related conditions: the emergence of a bureaucratic management which appears to believe that the production and distribution of the product is an end in itself and the influence of government which is likely to make the strategic decisions of a nationalised industry additionally remote from the immediate interests of those whom it was designed to serve.

The existence of autonomous, socially owned concerns, operating within a market, absolves us from two of the duties we are required to perform for nationalised corporations. First, their efficiency will be tested by the market itself – a discipline which any independent concern must face whatever its form of ownership. Second, that same discipline will require them to pay proper respect to their consumers. If they are workers' co-operatives – or if their workers play a substantial part in their organisation – the need to respond to the needs of their workers will automatically be fulfilled. Of course, they will lack some of the advantages of nationalised monopolies. They will be unsuitable to use as instruments of indicative planning or as vehicles either for surreptitious revenue collection or subsidy. Their pricing policy will be influenced by whatever inducements, regulations and prohibitions the government applies to companies in general – public and private. The same pressures will apply to their location and investment policies, their merger decisions, their advertising ethics and (in the case of consumer co-operatives and municipal undertakings) their industrial relations. The ground rules of the mixed economy – which circumscribe the behaviour of privately and socially owned concerns alike – are the subject of Chapter 11. The rules are necessary because of the great *advantages* possessed by that part of the public sector which is independent of national government: its freedom to take decisions based on its judgment of the market rather than by bureaucratic allocation of resources and determination of price. We have argued in the previous chapter that freedom as well as efficiency requires us to ensure that a majority of the economy is organised in that way. That obliges us to limit old-style nationalisation to the public utilities.

There is a second reason for that obligation; and it carries with it a duty to do what we can to change, in particular, the constitution of the state monopolies. One of the objects of social ownership is, or ought to be, the greater involvement of workers in the management of their companies. To socialists that seems right in itself, for, as we have now agreed, the equality we seek concerns the more even distribution of power as well as of wealth. But there are pragmatic reasons as well as reasons of principle for extending the involvement of employees in the decisions that govern their working lives. It is in no way to diminish the importance of market pressures to argue that the most successful concerns are those which simultaneously meet the requirement of their consumers and the aspirations of their workforce. The least successful companies – indeed the least successful economies, as Britain sadly proves – satisfy neither those who buy from them nor those who work within them. For a state-owned monopoly, partly because of its size, partly because of its constitution, the feeling of worker involvement is hard to establish. The purpose of nationalisation makes it impossible for policy decisions to be determined by the workers. Systems of consultation and notification have been set up – and ought to be extended. But it is not possible for miners to decide the price of coal or the total level of output; nor can the workers in the energy industries make the choice between coal-fired and nuclear power stations, the railwaymen decide which lines to electrify or the postmen decide on the cost of a first-class stamp.

Strategic decisions, about investment, location and price, will be taken by the owners and the directors who work on the owners' behalf at the owners' invitation; that means the government and the nationalised boards. To change that rule would destroy part of the objective of nationalisation. In autonomous, socially owned concerns, workers can become increasingly involved. The companies' performance would improve, and we would have taken a further step towards the more free, as well as more equal, society which socialists hope to create. For

> it is idle for a nation to blazon Liberty, Equality and Fraternity, or other resounding affirmations on the façades of public buildings, if to display the same motto on factories and mines would arouse only the cynical laughter that greets a reminder of idealisms turned sour and hopes unfulfilled.[13]

If we believe that socialism is about an extension of freedom brought about by a more equal distribution of resources we have to encourage that extension in every part of society. State monopolies are not the most fertile ground for the diffusion of power. We can, of course, argue sentimentally that as they are owned by a democratically elected government they are subject to absolute democratic control. The academic answer to that contention is that the distance between those who take the decisions and those whose lives are influenced by them is so great that there is no perceived (and perhaps no effective) connection between the whole electorate that exercises power over the masters of the nationalised industries and that part of the electorate which (by working in those industries) serves those masters. The practical answer is that any argument that suggests that the nationalised industry managements are anything other than remote from their employees is palpable nonsense. They are institutionally remote, forced, by the size of their industries, the bureaucracy of their organisation, the professional hierarchy in which they exist and the lowering presence of their owners in Whitehall, to take the national decisions on which both their name is based and their special form of organisation is justified.

It is as unreasonable to expect state monopolies to respond to the demands of real worker control as it would be to demand

---

[13] R. H. Tawney, *The Radical Tradition* (Allen & Unwin, London, 1966), Ch. 10, 'Social Democracy in Britain', p. 147.

such a system be adopted by the armed forces of the Crown. That is not to argue against state ownership any more than it is to argue against a disciplined army, navy and airforce. State ownership is the essential form of organisation for the essentially monopolistic public utilities. As in the case of British Leyland, it may be necessary (as a temporary expedient) to prop up an ailing but essential company by running its affairs in theory through the National Enterprise Board, but in practice by the Department of Industry. But even then such companies should be returned to their autonomous state – not by what has come, inelegantly, to be called privatisation but by a socialisation which allows workers, consumers and municipalities to own and govern them. We should not be put off from that course by the fear that independent social ownership is only suitable for small concerns. Foreign experience confirms that, properly organised, it is suitable for major companies. What is certain is that state monopolies are not, and in themselves cannot be, the path to socialism. They are a necessary framework within which socialism can be constructed. To understand them as anything else risks the failure to build socialism around and upon them – either by taking too little into public ownership or by taking too much into public ownership in the wrong way.

Chapter Ten

The Case for Clause IV

The narrow obsession with extending public ownership by Acts of Parliament, which specify complete state acquisition of whole industries and their management by government nominees, has limited the extent of public ownership in Britain. Acceptance of a wider definition would have produced a larger socially owned sector and set free forces which would have generated social ownership without every extension becoming an act of political controversy and which would have almost certainly gone on generating co-operatives, employee buy-outs, employee share-option plans and municipal enterprises – even during periods of Conservative government. The Labour Party now needs to develop and encourage diversity within the public sector – different patterns of ownership, influence and control which complement and overlap each other. The pluralistic economy should not be divided by rigid lines which determine where public ownership begins and private ownership ends. It should be made up of companies with a variety of owners, neither wholly public nor wholly private.

The achievement of that desirable objective will require the abandonment of some venerable shibboleths. The line which divides private and social ownership is neither exact nor immovable, and Labour should have accepted a blurring of the boundaries between the private and public sectors years ago. The Labour Party accepts it now. The change is largely the result of work done within local councils where, during the seventies, the nature of Labour local government changed. Into the town and county halls there came a new generation of socialists, who believed that the ideas of their predecessors had atrophied some time during the fifties and that the desire for municipal respectability had turned too many Labour councillors into a local government establishment. The new passion for ideological integrity was encouraged both by the assaults of the Thatcher government on local authority spending and autonomy and by the sudden increase in unemployment within many Labour-controlled municipal areas. From the front line, the new councillors looked for new opportunities both to help their communities and to demonstrate their creative commitment. The result was a variety of employment initiatives – most of which demonstrated, sooner or later, that for municipal enterprise to succeed it has both to work in partnership with local private interests and attract private capital from outside its own region.

The development of local enterprise agencies has begun to convince socialists that a complicated economy, the object of democratic socialism, may well best be achieved by public and private capital working together to create jobs. That lesson has been learned by hard experience. A by-product of the new understanding is the acceptance that when we consider the make-up of the mixed economy, we should begin to penetrate the entire system instead of selecting a whole sector of private enterprise for head-on assault and capture. The real aims of socialism – emancipation through the promotion of equality and the enhanced freedom which those changes in society bring – are at least as likely to be achieved by the alternative forms of public ownership as they are by outright nationalisation.

That view will, of course, be regarded as heresy by some traditional socialists. Before they condemn it as Fabian gradualism or a willingness to compromise with capitalism, they ought to pause and think of both the operation and the implications of a scheme recently proposed by the socialist government of Sweden. The scheme is an extreme example of the alternative methods of extending social ownership, but it is extreme in two distinct ways. First, if properly applied, it could produce a massive extension of the power of working men and women to influence both the conduct of the companies which employ them and the performance of the whole economy. Second, it remains so controversial, even by Swedish standards, that it was combated by Swedish employers with a campaign of unprecedented ferocity. Yet some sections of the Labour Party would not regard it as an extension of social ownership at all. For, instead of the total acquisition of a limited number of companies, it involves the gradual extension of influence and

191

control over a wide spectrum of private industry. It can, perhaps, best be described as a horizontal extension of social ownership, for it extends ownership widely across the whole economy rather than deeply into one company. The 'vertical' method takes outright control of one company (Rolls-Royce or British Leyland) or of one whole industry (gas or coal) but leaves the rest of the economy untouched. The 'horizontal' method – at least as developed in Sweden – is wholly dependent upon the extension of employee control, as distinct from state control. It invariably passes power to individual men and women (and the institutions which represent them) rather than to the state. That, in itself, is a contribution to the creation of a socialist society. It will also produce a whole series of subsidiary social, economic and industrial advantages. Production is not simply a mechanical process in which modern industrial workers can be encouraged to maximum performance by incentives and penalties. Efficiency is certainly raised by incentives and by pressure of markets, but not by those forces alone. There is overwhelming evidence that increased worker participation reduces work alienation and raises productivity. The average producer co-operatives have (for example) a superior record to private firms of similar size. The Swedish scheme shows how those industrially underrated commodities together with the altruism and common sense of workers can be employed to improve the general performance of the economy.

The scheme was the product of necessity – though it is worth noting that economic pressure produces in the Swedish socialist party a socialist, rather than a conventional, reaction. The immediate need for a new initiative in economic policy sprang from the depreciation of the krona. That process had two results: first, a substantial increase in profit for those Swedish companies which were major exporters and could exploit their new competitive advantage; second, a need to compensate for the inflationary effect of depreciation by a moderation of wage demands and pay settlements. The conventional response to the krona's new value is easily described. Workers would have been exhorted or obliged to hold down their salary claims. The extra profit would have been overlooked, welcomed as the harbinger of eventual greater output or, in the extreme case, frozen for a limited period as a gesture to the trades unions. In each of those cases, not excluding the dividend freeze, workers would have been left to ponder on the justice of a system which – for reasons wholly unrelated to the wisdom of management or the performance of employees – produces bigger profits for the one and lower wage increases for the other. They are entitled to be more than puzzled, for even if dividend payments are subject to statutory limitation the eventual result is extra wealth for shareholders. Dividend restraint and pay restraint are not symmetrical disciplines. A pay increase deferred is likely to be a pay increase lost for ever. A dividend deferred is, literally, money in the bank – an interest-earning investment to be cashed when either the government or economic conditions change.

The Swedish solution was to introduce both a special profits tax and a payroll levy. Workers and owners would lose an increment of their income for ever, but they would not lose it to the amorphous coffers of the Swedish Treasury. The proceeds of both the tax and the levy were allocated to an investment fund which was run by five regional boards, on each of which representatives of the workers were given a majority. The workers knew that high profits in themselves do not automatically generate investment which is beneficial to the interests of either the employees in the high-profit companies or the economy as a whole. The five regional investment boards gave the trades unions a chance to ensure that the new level of profits – by being reinvested in either improved employment opportunities or desirable social and infrastructure projects – actually benefited the workers whose energies and restraint had brought about the increase.

The scheme was created to meet an immediate need – a scheme which would persuade the trades unions to accept wage restraint and high profits at the same time. But it produced enormous additional long-term advantages. It contributed to a major shift in economic power, for over the years the new investment funds – largely controlled by representatives of the employees – will make up an increasing share of each company's equity capital. The scheme will help in the redistribution of wealth as well as power, for a growing control of investment income will be under the control of working men and women. It also makes more risk capital available to the types of project which do not always find new investment readily available; and it assists in the encouragement of workers – and the unions which represent them – to accept the high profit economy which is essential for industrial progress. To ask trades unions to acquiesce in the promotion of such an economy requires the government to ensure both the reinvestment of those profits and a trades union voice in how the reinvestment is distributed.

It is still sometimes suggested that mere employees will possess neither the knowledge necessary for successful management nor the commitment to the success of the whole enterprise which a manager requires, as distinct from concern with their ability to maximise the rewards which that enterprise pays. The question of ability is, in part, related to the tasks which the worker-owner is expected to perform. Employee ownership no more requires the employee-owner to take day-to-day management decisions than private ownership obliges the conduct of a registered company to be determined by the army of elderly widows who, when increases in taxes on unearned income are suggested, are always represented as the typical shareholders in public limited companies. As far as enthusiasm for and commitment to the success of the whole enterprise is concerned, John Stuart Mill said the last word in his famous assertion that the people most likely to further the interests of a business are those whose future is most directly and intimately concerned with its success. That notion has passed into our national subconscious. Together with our historic reverence for property, it resulted in a century of company law placing a statutory obligation on directors to meet the wishes and protect the interests of shareholders. The Company Acts of 1978 and 1985 imposed on directors obligations towards employees as well as shareholders. But the prejudices encouraged ever since limited liability was established in 1856 persisted. Shareholders' interests were thought to be synonymous with the interests of the company. But shareholders are not the participants in a company's activity who have the most direct and intimate interest in its success. The workers' interests are far greater. For, more often than not, the workers' future is concentrated exclusively in the future of a single firm. Mill was right in principle, but his judgment has been wrongly applied. The people to whom the future of an enterprise can be trusted with most confidence are its employees.

The neo liberals of the far right who have expropriated Mill and pronounced him one of their patron saints scoff at workers' influence, control and ownership. But Mill himself did not:

the form of association however, which if mankind continues to improve must be expected in the end to predominate, is not that which can exist between a capitalist as chief and workpeople without a voice in the management, but the association of labourers themselves on terms of equality: collectively owning the capital with which they carry on their operation, and working under managers elected and rewarded by themselves.[1]

We would call that 'form of association' a worker co-operative – a form of social ownership that has been scandalously neglected by a Labour Party which has been squeezed between the consumer co-operative obsession of the official Co-operative Party and the confusion between state and social ownership. We need now to begin the promotion of worker co-operatives – concerns which are owned by the workers within them, in which every worker holds a share of equal weight to every other share (which is relinquished on retirement) and in which the owner-ship and control of the business is inherited by future generations of employees in the company or by the community at large.

The co-operative is a company which is not only owned by its employees but which is organised in a way which enhances their general control over strategy and distributes the fundamental power equally among all the parties. Evidence of the extra economic strength created as a result of extensions is over-whelming – much of it provided from abroad because of Britain's failure to encourage the development of co-operative enterprise.[2] There are spectacular examples of success, like the municipality of Mondragon in which socialist fervour, Catholic discipline and preferential tax laws all combine to enable co-operative enterprise to dominate the output of a whole industry. But in France, Spain and Scandinavia individual worker co-operatives succeed within generally private sectors of the economy. Indeed, despite the neglect suffered by British co-operatives and the discrimination against them embodied in our laws, even in this country the record is impressive. Both the levels of productivity and the survival record of new co-operatives are vastly superior to that of new private companies of comparable size. The number of worker co-operatives set up each year has trebled during the last decade to an annual total of

[1] J. S. Mill, *Principles of Political Economy* (Longman, London, 1871), Vol. II, p. 352.
[2] For details of foreign co-operatives, see G. Hodgson, *The Democratic Economy* (Penguin, London, 1984).

more than two hundred. Moreover, they have achieved remarkable success in creating new jobs at a lower price than that at
which they are generated in the private sector. The co-
operatives established or assisted by local authorities have
produced jobs at an average cost of little more than £3,000 – far
less than the expenditure on other job-creation measures.

Yet co-operative development in Britain is held back by two
significant impediments: a tax system which discriminates
against them and a reputation which, no matter how unjust,
leads many consumers to believe that co-operatives are old-
fashioned, incompetent and slightly risible institutions. Tax
discrimination denies to co-operatives incentives which are
available to private companies. The benefits of the Business
Expansion Scheme cannot be enjoyed by co-operatives because
their share capital belongs to the workers within the company.
Losses made by individual workers on shareholdings cannot be
written off against tax because there is no ordinary share capital.
In addition, there is a tax disadvantage which, although less the
result of discrimination than the product of the co-operatives'
essential nature, still handicaps their progress. Schemes which
allow retained earnings to be shared among workers cannot be
employed in co-operatives because of the necessity for share
capital to be redeemable when a worker leaves co-operative
employment.

A government committed to a general extension of social
ownership ought to do more than remedy those specific
disadvantages. There is a whole swathe of fiscal measures by
which the development of co-operatives can be encouraged. For
co-operatives to flourish, there must be a tax régime expressly
intended to promote their creation and tax reforms explicitly
designed to encourage the flow of investment to co-operatives.
A second necessity is a series of new agencies which are willing
and able to finance new and socially owned enterprises. The
proposed British Industrial Bank – itself an extension of social
ownership since it will be a publicly owned alternative to the
private investment institutions – will, like its industrial banking
counterparts in other countries, encourage co-operative development. The BIB's principal task will be to provide an investment
institution which works with, understands and believes its future
to be inextricably linked to British industry. It will not seek to
make its profits outside Britain by speculating against sterling or

by channelling British investment abroad – it will be part of industry; and its freedom from the ideological prejudices of the City will enable it to look upon nascent social enterprise with an objectivity which does not always characterise private investment institutions. The BIB will ensure that funds are available for commercially viable projects to which the prejudices of private institutions deny investment.

Every regional enterprise board will provide examples of how the ignorance and prejudice of private investment institutions has jeopardised the prospect of economic expansion. At Warley in the West Midlands, Hammerley's now sells high quality men's clothing to New York's more expensive men's shops – Saks, Brooks Brothers and Bonwitt Teller. It was unable to finance the investment which allowed it to break into that market from traditional sources. Without the West Midlands Enterprise Board, far from expanding, Hammersley's would probably have gone bankrupt.

The local authority enterprise boards will perform a similar function – overlapping and co-operating with the British Investment Bank to produce a service which is essential to socialism's aims in two particulars. First, they will provide one of the alternative sources of capital which is essential to the promotion of autonomous social ownership. Second, by their nature and constitution they will allow both democratic control over, and regional concentration on, the investment projects which determine the prosperity of a local authority area.

The importance of what the GLC's Industry and Employment Committee called 'locally based, socially responsible and democratically accountable financial institutions'[3] is discussed at the end of this chapter. But their importance in relation to the development of new co-operatives needs explaining at once. It is unreasonable and unrealistic to expect worker co-operatives to thrive without support in an economic atmosphere which is structurally and psychologically geared to private ownership. The acquisition of shareholdings by employees – at least in a way which fulfils socialist aims – requires a bank ready to back approved schemes as well as a tax régime designed to encourage them. Unity Trust – the bank set up and owned by British trades unions – is beginning to provide that service. For the co-

---

[3] *The London Financial Strategy*, GLC, 1986.

operatives, much of the task must be performed by local enterprise agencies. The London Enterprise Board offered its services to co-operatives which found funds difficult to raise because it was 'difficult for a bank manager to find a leader or an entrepreneur in the group. And on top of that, the co-op is unlikely to have much, or indeed any, money of its own and no track record as a business and no individual in the group with a track record in business.'[4] If the bank manager feared that such a situation would be a recipe for failure, the bank manager would have been wrong. 'From 1982 to the end of February 1985, 94 loans were made by GLEB and the LCEB amounting to £2.9 million. This investment created 792 jobs at an average cost per job of £3,639. Only nine loans were lost during the period.'[5]

Ideally, the finance provided by the local enterprise agency will be raised from a variety of sources: private, municipal and government. The West Midlands Enterprise Board is already funding joint ventures with Lazards – a leading City merchant bank. Such collaborative ventures are an important part of the necessary integration of public and private enterprise. They are wholly consistent with the view that the dividing line between public and private enterprise is not so much variable as fluid. But without investment institutions that meet the specific needs of companies which bridge the public and private sectors, those new autonomous concerns will not prosper, for few enterprises – very few *new* enterprises – are wholly autonomous. But most socially owned enterprises can be autonomous from central government. To achieve that end, new ventures will need new institutions, beyond the Co-operative Development Agency, on which to rely. For the CDA is obliged by statute to provide advice but prohibited from providing investment. Those institutions will work best if they are predominantly public agencies which accept and welcome the extension of social ownership – and if they contain a substantial private element as proof and demonstration that autonomous social-owner companies are intended to be efficiently run and commercially viable.

Indeed, on the evidence of foreign experience, co-operatives are more efficient than comparable private concerns and the survival rate, the cost per new job created, and the productivity

---

[4] J. Thorney, *London Financial Strategy Conference*, May 1985.
[5] *ibid.*

record in Great Britain suggests that if our limited number of small co-operatives was to be extended, the same rule would apply here. Unfortunately, and this is the second impediment to their growth, they do not enjoy that reputation. The status of worker co-operatives was desperately damaged by the behaviour of the last Labour government, which gave its support to the Kirby soft drinks and night-storage heater enterprise and the Meriden motor-cycle venture. Both concerns were part of what the then Secretary of State for Industry called 'the right to work campaign'. During all the discussions of Kirby's future which I attended, the prospect of its ever becoming a commercial success was never considered. For better or worse, it was an item of outdoor relief. The damage it did to the reputation of co-operatives and co-opertaion was incalculable. The Meriden Motor Cycle Co-operative was, on the surface, a more sensible proposition. But whatever chance of independent life it possessed had been bought for it at the expense of the BSA Company – a better economic proposition which was forced into collapse in order to provide room in the market for Meriden. The destruction of BSA was indefensible. But the morality of the government's policy is not the central issue of our argument. In the cases of both Kirby and Meriden, co-operative organisation was thought to be a way of propping up firms which could not survive as independent private companies. Co-operative organisation is not and cannot be an economic retreat from the realities of the market and hope for industrial incurables. Co-operatives are institutions which, because they induce a justified feeling of real involvement, reduce the alienation which has been one of the most typical features of the relationship between British workers and the companies which employ them. By their nature, co-operatives should be more efficient than comparable private firms, for they are at once spurred on by the committed enthusiasm of their members and whipped forward by the pressures of markets. Employee co-operatives that either do not aspire to that aim or are incapable of achieving it are not worth support.

The same rule does not and cannot apply to consumer co-operatives. For even when employees stand for election to management boards, control still remains in the hands of customers. It is not to diminish the desirability of consumer co-operatives to say that while they provide a valuable alternative form of ownership – and, in consequence, a better distribution of profits – in terms of control over performance they simply substitute one form of sovereignty for another. Marks and Spencer is no less responsive to its customers' needs than is the Royal Arsenal Co-operative Society. It simply addresses them in a different way. Of course, the most successful consumer co-operatives are those which also respond to their customers not with appeals to socialist sentiment but, by price, quality and delivery. The efficiency of the co-operative retail store has increased immensely during the last twenty years. Indeed, the hypermarkets of the north-west are a model of commercial efficiency. It is impossible to avoid drawing a moral from the failure of the previous generation of co-op stores and their reluctance to move with the times. For years the local co-operative societies thought of themselves as distinct from the rest of the retail economy – relying on the ideological commitment of their customers-cum-owners and the enthusiasm and self-interest of their workers-cum-managers. Generations of shoppers were urged to buy CWS 'own brands' rather than more famous products and the dividend cheques helped the same families to pay for their annual week's holiday. That the one should finance the other was, in its time, an admirable arrangement. But it could not last. And the consumer co-operatives could not succeed when – in an increasingly cost-conscious world – they attempted to behave as if social ownership absolved them from the laws of economics. The moral is for autonomous firms within the public sector to maintain their special identity and purpose but to understand that their autonomy will last only for as long as they are commercially viable.

Local enterprise agencies, despite the caricatures that have been the inevitable result of their association with metropolitan counties, have pursued commercial efficiency with admirable zeal. Their practical task, in an age of accelerating unemployment and increased bankruptcy, was to protect as many old jobs and create as many new jobs as was possible – possible, that is, with the very limited public funds which they possessed. Of course, enterprise agencies have competed, often at great cost to themselves, for inward investment, augmenting local funds with EEC grants and money available for inner-city development. But they have operated most successfully when they have called upon local resources and local initiatives to meet the needs of the locality in which they operate. Like the worker co-operatives which they have helped to finance, they possess the intangible, but substantial, advantages which come with genuine accountability. They are of their regions, by their regions and, in consequence, for their regions and their regions alone. They have worked best when, in the words of the chairman of the GLC Industry and Enterprise Committee, they have wedded local accountability to the special needs identified by the minority report of the Wilson Committee on Investment Resources: 'Investment institutions that can link public and private sector funds but which, above all, have the capacity to plan, to structure and to prepare an investment package.'[6]

Since politicians are increasingly biased judges of their own achievements, it is worthwhile examining a more objective assessment of the achievement of the enterprise agency:

> It well illustrates the growing importance of introspection as a route to job creation: i.e., the concentration of effort within a community based on community resources as opposed to more traditional approaches aimed at bringing in jobs from outside the area by attracting inward investment . . . In terms of measuring enterprise agencies' results it is arguable that the process of raising the level of community concern is at least as important as the actual number of new jobs directly created.[7]

As described by the Economist Intelligence Unit, the local or regional enterprise agency seems to be part of the socialist ethos. The community combining, through self-help, to solve its own problems is part of the dream of the early socialists; and the need to find alternative sources of investment and investment advice has been a preoccupation with socialist parties of Western Europe ever since the end of the Second World War. The place such agencies will occupy in the organisation of a modern socialist economy is confirmed by the many young and enthusiastic councillors who have pioneered them in Britain during the last decade. For them to play their full part in the development

---

[6] ibid.
[7] Economist Intelligence Unit, *Creating New Jobs in Europe – How Local Institutes Work*.

of a new society they must themselves be given greater access to funds for investment within their regions. As many of them have already become the co-ordinators of private investment, they will become the local institution through which the funds of the British Industrial Bank are channelled. But for them to play their full part in the development of a more socially accountable economy, a number of prejudices have to be buried once and for all. Public ownership is not state ownership – and socialism which wants to build a society which is responsive to individual desires and needs will welcome a change in emphasis from centralised monopolies to local independent enterprises. The existence of those independent enterprises will require agencies which help in their creation and development – sometimes acquiring a (publicly owned) equity stake within them, sometimes simply providing loan capital. Those agencies will work best, and will perhaps only work at all, if we agree to private and public enterprise working in partnership.

The reluctance to blur the sharp distinction between social and private ownership has combined with the trades unions' traditional unwillingness to expand their rôle beyond the representation of employees to prevent the Labour Party from taking a cool look at the advantages of wider share-ownership. The acquisition by working men and women of small shareholdings is unlikely to change the nature of society. Conservatives may call it people's capitalism. But most of the capitalist people will see their small portfolios as another form of saving which may give them the feeling of middle-class prosperity which normally goes with a bank account but which does not emotionally commit them to support for the enterprise culture of stock exchange and commodity markets. For although the possession of a share certificate will provide a slice of theoretical power, the whole process of appearance or proxy (not to mention the likelihood of being swamped by institutional power) will diminish the feeling of real involvement. On the other hand, the possession of equity holdings which are organised to maximise the influence of employees within the company can produce a wholly different attitude, for the employee-shareholder is doubly involved with the company. That such schemes reduce alienation and increase the feeling that the employee-company relationship is more than the expenditure of the minimum effort necessary to ensure regular wage payment is beyond dispute. But, in the language of the hoary old question, are they socialist? If we define socialism as a more equal distribution of power, liberation and emancipation rather than state regulation, the answer must be 'yes'. But the answer has to be qualified according to the nature of the share-ownership scheme.

The extension of employee shareholding is wholly consistent with the aims of democratic socialism if, and only if, with it come the same rights enjoyed by other shareholders and, in particular, the right to elect the board of directors and to receive an account of its stewardship. That does not mean that share-ownership should provide workers with powers over the day-to-day management of the firm. To meet the aims of a socialism which seeks to give power to individuals rather than to institutions, share-ownership schemes must include genuine proposals for extensions of employee participation which carry with them influence as well as dividends. Cosmetic schemes, which are not available to all employees and amount to no more than executive bonus payments, will not do; nor will cheap alternatives to wage increases which are intended not to enhance employee rights but to divert their energy and interest away from the collective exercise of the rights which they already possess. The practical experience of such genuine schemes of worker-ownership parallels the history of the co-operatives with which they share common features. The Institute of Personnel Management reports that in America

> when ownership is spread widely through a firm, the company is likely to be more successful than a similar business without employee ownership. On the other hand, if an ownership scheme is confined to managers, this is usually counter-productive. The resentment of the other employees is likely to make the firm less successful in spite of the additional motivation given to managers.[8]

On the other hand, greater genuine participation in the general government of a company – the acquisition of shares and with them the normal voting rights that share-ownership provides – reduces the alienation which creates the greatest barrier to change and innovation in industry. That feeling of alienation is

---

[8] IPM, *Practical Participation and Involvement*, Vol. 5.

more pronounced in immobile and unequal British society than it is in any of our competitor economies. The progress made by those competitors towards greater employee involvement demonstrates what we could do. The German trades unions report an absolute increase in productivity per worker of 15 per cent after the introduction of greater employee participation. The American Center for Employee Ownership discovered from its study of 360 high-technology companies that those firms which shared ownership with all or most of their employees grew between twice and four times as fast as companies in which the employees owned no stock.

That should not surprise us. But in our hidebound society the obvious is not always readily accepted. It is not only socialists who find it difficult to amend all prejudices. Capitalists do not find it easy to accept that a dilution of their traditional power could improve the commercial performance of a competitive enterprise. So, despite the evidence, there is both formal and informal discrimination against genuine share-ownership schemes. Therefore, if we are to encourage and promote them we need – exactly as in the case of co-operatives – to do more than create a favourable tax régime. We need explicitly to organise financial institutions which meet their special needs.

One of the principal barriers to the extension of real share-ownership is the criterion laid down by the investment protection committees of the big industrial investors – the insurance companies, the pension funds and the unit trusts. They fear that, notwithstanding the evidence of improved performance, worker share-ownership will dilute the value of traditional holdings as new shares are issued to employees. Therefore they stipulate that the firms in which they invest should not allocate more than 5 per cent of their pre-tax profits or 1 per cent of their existing share issue to employee shareholders. That prejudice could be overcome by law, but even such a statute would have to be accompanied by the gradual education of slow learners. In the meantime, we need to establish trusts which can purchase existing shares on behalf of employees without diluting the value of the shares in general. Unless such new institutions are created, investment protection committees will inhibit the development of worker-shareholder schemes in a way which tax incentives do not possess the power to overcome.

Indeed, the extension of genuine share-ownership plans –

available to all employees irrespective of rank or grade and carrying with membership the normal rights of share-ownership – is wholly dependent upon the creation of institutions and structures which can give reality to the theoretical rights of share-ownership. America, the home of free enterprise, is, according to International Business Week, second only to Sweden – the paragon of democratic socialism – in the speed by which it has increased employee shareholdings. In the United States 7,000 companies operate schemes which enable their employees to acquire shares. The extension of these schemes has been encouraged by tax-assisted employee stock-ownership plans (ESOPs) – the creation of trusts which acquire shares in a company and then sell either the shares or a stake in the trust to that company's employees. Of course ESOPs, like any other form of share-ownership scheme, come in different shapes and sizes – some bad, some tolerable, some excellent. But without specialised schemes it is foolish to suppose that the mere existence of share options (or tax incentives which encourage them) will in themselves encourage widespread share owner- ship. Socialists who are serious about the extension and diffusion of power and ownership need to start thinking about the mechanisms by which it can be achieved. Unity Trust – the trades union bank – has begun the process. Extending it is a classic socialist cause. Ownership and wealth is being spread more evenly; the state is employed not to enhance its own power but to organise the distribution of power to the people – theoretical rights are changed into reality; the mechanisms of government, the tax system, the legislative process, are all being used to provide individuals with a greater influence over their daily lives. To fail to provide that process because of some half-digested notion about collective action, centralised planning or state ownership would be a denial both of the individual rights which ought to be at the heart of socialism and the long-held belief that the emancipation of the worker requires his relation-ship with his employer (and his relationship with the capital which provides his employer with power) to change. 'An employee of a capitalist firm is, in many senses, more free than a slave. But consent to managerial authority does not mean that the worker in enjoying the quintessence of liberty',[9] writes

[9] G. Hodgson, *The Democratic Economy* (Penguin, London, 1984), Ch. 6, 'Capitalism and Markets', p. 29.

Geoffrey Hodgson, who quotes Marx to explain (slightly less elegantly) why the participants in the market where labour is bought and sold can, with very few exceptions, never enjoy that quintessential mutual liberty: 'He who was previously the money owner now strides out in front as a capitalist. The possessor of labour power follows as his worker. The one smiles self-importantly and is intent on business, the other is timid and holds back, like someone who brought his own hide to market and now has nothing else to expect but a tanning.'[10] The acquisition of shares with voting rights changes all that. The worker owns some and controls more of the capital; his vote influences policy. And the more different schemes to extend worker control and influence proliferate – co-operatives, ESOPs, investment funds – the more the whole nature of society is changed. That is surely a more noble objective than the trans-formation of a few private monopolies into state monopolies.

The acceptance of that principle requires some socialists to revise their attitude towards individual, as distinct from collective, action. If we believe that the purpose of socialism is human emancipation, we cannot regard the liberation of the individual – through extensions of personal rights and powers – as a manifestation of free-market values, and the extension of corporate influence as the essence of socialism. Collective – indeed, class – action is necessary to obtain individual rights. Collective action is the means. Individual rights are the object – individual rights when properly defined as their extension to the largest possible number of citizens, and the provision, for those citizens, of the ability to make the theoretical rights a practical reality. We understand the principle perfectly well when we support the collective struggle for democratic rights, for the freedom to dissent or for the protection of free speech. All those personal freedoms are the product of collective action. Only in the tyrannies of Eastern Europe did the forces which fought against the old autocracies retain for themselves the collective powers which ought to have been passed out to individual men and women. The same rule has to apply in the campaign for economic reorganisation – collective action to secure new individual powers.

[10] K. Marx, *Capital* (Lawrence & Wishart, London, 1970), Vol. 1, p. 280.

In that process, the trades unions will be crucial. Traditionally antagonistic towards worker shareholdings, lacking all enthusiasm for worker co-operatives and, in some notable cases, positively opposed to the industrial democracy of trades union or employee-nominated directors until the 1970s, they have continually sought class, group or corporate solutions to the problems which faced their members. All that has begun to change. Trades union leaders are enthusiastic about ESOPs. Indeed, Unity Trust, the trades union bank, propagates and finances them. Even when the state has created the necessary institutional framework and put the helpful tax régime in place, schemes for extending workers' rights and powers will have to be negotiated company by company. It ought to be the trades unions which propose the adoption of employees' share-ownership, a workers' buy-out or conversion to a co-operative. It should be the trades unions which – negotiate for the introduction of such changes as they once negotiated for pension plans, redundancy agreements and sickness benefits, and which make sure that what the owners offer is available to all employees and not a substitute for earnings increases. It must be the trades unions which, through their insistence on the introduction of industrial democracy, the implementation of the Vredling and 5th Directives of the EEC and the acceptance of planning agreements (a helpful but neither sinister nor significant contribution to the power of individual workers), arm their members with the information which makes it possible for them to make authoritative judgments about the prospects for and terms of the buy-out or the conversion to co-operatives. The trades union rôle in all those matters is to expand the powers of their individual members, not of their corporate institution – and to make sure that they are expanded in a way which extends equality and increases the sum of liberty. That is why, for instance, when the Bill which requires a general extension of industrial democracy is published, the rights embodied therein must be provided for the workers, not for the trades unions. The right to information, the right to elect representatives to boards of directors and the right to question those directors' stewardship cannot be limited to card-carrying members of a specific trades union. Those rights must be available to all employees. It would be unworthy to suspect that the motives of those trades unions which persist in the pursuit of corporatist solutions are based on a desire to protect their collective power. Such a response would be ignorant as well as cynical. For unless the trades unions begin to respect the new individualism which is the product of the new prosperity – and work to translate it into changes in society which are consistent with ideologies which the trades union leadership supports – they will lose their power completely.

Chapter Eleven

A Socialist Supply-side

To the Labour Party, 'planning' has always been a magic word – magic in almost its literal sense for, like abracadabra, its importance lies not in its meaning but in the superstition that simply to intone its mystic syllables brings instant and beneficial change. Planning has, traditionally, been accepted as the alternative to the waste of competition, the method of resource allocation which satisfies wants rather than maximises profits and the process that responds to needs rather than to demand which is the product of nothing more socially acceptable than purchasing power. The truth is that planning – some forms of planning – can contribute to socialism's aims. But it can only assist in their achievement. It cannot, in itself, bring about the more equal and more free society which socialists seek. Further, in some of its more authoritarian manifestations, planning can be positively inimical to socialism's true aims. But the word 'planning' still casts its destructive spell over serious attempts to construct sensible systems of socialist economic management. With 'planning', as with 'nationalisation', history has bequeathed Labour a problem which is semantic as well as philosophical. Until we are clear about what we mean by planning, we will not begin to determine how it can be used in pursuit of our ends.

Socialism's concern for freedom, as well as its dependence upon the success of an efficient economy, requires support for the market system in a large part of the economy. If planning means the bureaucratic determination of prices or the administrative allocation of resources, socialists ought to be against it. Five-year plans, which announce how many houses will be built at the end of the quinquennium and then go on to organise the brick production and build the power stations necessary to generate the electricity which heats the kilns, have not, in the past, been universally successful. To socialists trying to promote both liberty and equality, planning cannot mean central regulation by which goods and services are distributed according to a national formula devised by politicians and implemented by civil servants. Such a system could sustain neither the buoyant economy which socialism needs nor the freedom of spirit which it hopes to promote. To democratic socialists, support for planning is not the advocacy of Soviet centralism with its queues, shortages, black markets and inefficiencies.

However, the unpopularity – as well as the inefficiency – of the managed market must be kept in perspective. There is a lesson to be learned from the way in which the theoretical advocates of unrestricted markets react to planning in practice. When managed markets produce the most beneficial results for their particular sector, passionate advocates of free enterprise moderate their passion. Despite the formal commitment of the Treaty of Rome to free-market economies, the EEC operates, through the Common Agricultural Policy, the most centrally regulated system of agricultural output and pricing since the Middle Ages. Neither the Free Liberal farmers of Bavaria nor their Conservative counterparts in Britain call for a return to the discipline of market-determined supply and demand. The Labour government of 1974–9 was supported in its determination to maintain the managed market in retail milk by the whole establishment of British industry and commerce. Its decision to end the statutory regulation of bread prices was attacked by the same pillars of capitalism with a fervour reminiscent of the Corn Law debates. To the devotees of private enterprise, the free-market mechanism is a system to be spoken about with reverence but only to be supported when it operates in their sectional interests. Socialists should apply the same rule. When the market serves our ends, it should be encouraged. When it does not, it should be discarded in favour of whatever process directly encourages the more equal – and therefore more free – society which we aim to create. It would be absurd to reject the Marxist notion that the form of economic organisation can, in itself, determine the nature of society and then insist that one system – free or managed markets – was invariably necessary for our purposes. The Labour Party must stop confusing means and ends. Economic organisation is means.

The arguments about economic planning which have raged in the past were often based on the clearly absurd proposition that we had to make a choice between planning and market price and resource allocation. There was – as there always should have been – general agreement about the public utilities and, until after the Second World War, financial institutions. Discussions about other sectors of the economy were complicated by two typical diversions. One was temporary, for it was based on the brief apparent success of the Soviet economy in Europe. The Webbs were typical:

> In the midst of the capitalist depression, they returned from Russia convinced of the superiority of the Russian economic system, *Soviet Communism: A New Civilisation?* The final intellectual fruits of their partnership in the collective cause, was first published in 1935. It was republished, this time without the question mark, in 1937.[1]

From then on, the enthusiasm for the Soviet system declined. But an equally damaging, if more honourable, impediment to clear thinking on the subject of planning persisted. It was called sentimentalism. Evan Durbin – author of *The Problems of Economic Planning* and normally one of Labour's most hard-headed economists – provides an example of the romanticism which inhibits rather than illuminates plain thinking:

> The efficiency of planning depends in the last resort upon the breadth and consistency of the Socialist faith which animates us . . . The interests of the whole are sovereign over the interests of the part. In society we are born: in society we must live. To the centralised control of a democratic community our livelihood and our security must be submitted. It is the business of society to secure the welfare of all. To do so it must be able to set limits to the welfare of each of us.[2]

It could be argued that Durbin was doing no more than restating the various contract theories of Hobbes, Rousseau and Locke in flowery language – or simply saying that no man is an island. The passage would make an admirable text for an Easter Sunday sermon or a noble statement of principle around which to build a close community. But as a statement of policy it does contain at least the implication that we must make socialists converts first and begin to build the socialist society afterwards –

[1] Elizabeth Durbin, *New Jerusalems* (Routledge & Kegan Paul, London, 1985), quoting 'New Fabian Plan for Socialism'.
[2] *ibid.*

on the historical evidence, a lengthy process. Nor does it help determine the answer to any of the hard questions. What sort of planning? How much planning? Planning by whom and against which criteria? These questions obsessed the distinguished economists who argued Labour policies between the wars. Few of them believed that there was a general rule which could be applied in all circumstances; they knew that 'planning' is not a single simple concept. Different sectors of the economy have to be planned in different ways and some of them should not be planned at all.

Between the wars the study groups of Fabians, the XYZ Club and all the other discussion groups, invariably produced statements of general principle which, by today's standards, would be regarded as extreme. Durbin – now regarded (especially by Social Democrats) as a paragon of moderation – demanded more than the 'intervention of the government in particular industries'. He wanted 'the general supercession of individual enterprise'. Hugh Dalton, criticising the budget of 1934 and preparing for the following year's election, announced that the constant fluctuations between boom and slump would be ended only by what he called Planning – a process which he did not define but to which he ascribed a capital 'P'. He was, of course, writing at a time when Keynes (although formulating his ideas on demand management) had yet to publish his *General Theory*. Undoubtedly some of the planning to which he – and his fellow socialist economists – referred was demand management. When the actual proposals which were agreed are carefully examined, they prove to be measures intended, not to create a regulated command economy, but policies meant to erect an economic framework within which the new society could be built. By planning the Labour Party has always meant, in practice:

1. The determination and the achievement of a level of demand which, when matched with suitable fiscal and monetary policies, encourages growth and full employment.

2. The structural reorganisation of the economy so as to provide the institutions which are necessary to promote long-term growth through high levels of investment, the financing of the socially owned sector of the economy and

the diffusion of power and prosperity between the social classes and amongst the economic regions of Great Britain.

3. The provision by government of those elements of infrastructure which are necessary to the achievement of a prosperous economy but which would not be provided by the actions of the market – railways to outlying towns, adequately trained craftsmen, energy and investment resources.

That does not mean, and cannot mean, that the items of planning which we espouse are purely technical devices unrelated to our political aims. The economy is not ideologically neutral and it will contribute to the creation of a socialist society only if we build within it institutions specifically focused on that objective. The lesson of the libertarian right is clear. It is impossible wholly to distinguish judgments about the economy from opinions about the nature of society. Virtually every quotation from Hayek which has appeared in previous chapters has contained an ideological element which was at least as great as its analytical content. Mises illustrates the point even more starkly:

> In the real world acting man is faced with the fact that there are fellow men, acting on their own behalf as he himself acts. The necessity to adjust his actions to other people's actions makes him a speculator for whom success and failure depend on his greater or less ability to understand the future. Every investment is a form of speculation. There is in the course of human events no stability and consequently no safety.[3]

That sentiment is worth contrasting with the passage from Durbin quoted above. Mises is saying – indeed boasting – that man *is* an island; when the bell tolls a knell for someone else it peals in joy for us. The socialist view of society is starkly different. To build a society in which the members are all 'one of another' requires the creation of institutions which make that achievement possible. Planning thus becomes not the imposition of regulations, but the creation of mechanisms by which the instinct for a fairer share of power and wealth can be transformed into action. Planning is the equivalent of the rules

[3] L. von Mises, in T. Mischel, *Human Action* (Yale University Press, London, 1949), p. 113.

213

drawn up for John Rawls's imaginary debating society: if everyone is allowed to speak without their liberties to give tongue being restricted, the best outcome will be that those with the loudest voices are heard. The worst will be that nothing of any value can be heard above the general hubbub.

The need to create the conditions within which a socialist economy can thrive is what makes socialists natural 'supply-siders', anxious to organise the economy in a way which meets their ideological objectives. The classic 'supply-side' position is that the economy prospers only when its organisation allows it to operate efficiently. Concern for that view of the 'supply-side' has recently become associated with free-market economists – partly because they have claimed it their own, and partly because it has been foolishly assumed that interest in demand precluded concern for the other side of the economic equation. The successful regulation of demand and its direction into the most desirable sectors of the economy require a supply-side revolution. The institutions and organisation of the present-day economy cannot meet socialism's needs. Socialist economies are, by definition, concerned with supply-side changes. There is no socialist level of interest, socialist exchange rate or socialist Public Sector Borrowing Requirement – unless socialism is taken to be synonymous with rational judgment on these issues. But there is a socialist view on patterns of ownership, on methods of investment finance, on control of monopolies and of means by which the exchange rates and interest rates are regulated in order to obtain the rational level. There is a socialist view on how to sustain the autonomous publicly owned sector and how to prevent the ideologists who pretend to be objective bankers and politically agnostic stockbrokers from sabotaging the creation of a system with which they do not agree. The socialist supply-side is about changing the ownership, management and organisation of the economy. We can call it planning for 'Auld Lang Syne' because it is the most euphonious of the available alternative descriptions. But we must not confuse this with government regulation of the whole economy.

The first necessity is to 'plan' the provision of the level of investment which is necessary to sustain growth and sustain or restore full employment. That requires more than simply the availability of what the private financial institutions insist is an adequate overall level of investment funds. Those funds have to be available to sustain the sort of enterprises which socialists want to see and to encourage new economic activity in the most neglected areas. In any case, the private institutions fail significantly to provide even the necessary overall level of investment. Unless a level of unemployment which remains well above 3.5 million is the natural point of equilibrium at which the economy comes to rest, the institutions of private investment have chronically failed to sustain activity at the optimum level. In fact, there is no 'natural' state. The economy is what its participants make it. But even if the alternative explanation were true, it would hardly be an endorsement for the present system. The causes of British industrial decline are many and numerous. They range from the complacency which was created in the nineteenth century by the invisible export subsidies of empire to the contempt for trade and commerce which infects so much of the British establishment. But the pattern of, and attitude towards, investment has played a crucial part in our failure. There has been too little concern with the home economy and too much excitement for the easy pickings of overseas activity. Of course, the City can boast a considerable record of success in its own terms and on its own behalf; and – as the decline in British manufacturing industry has accelerated – the financial services industry has made a larger relative contribution to our national income. Indeed, in recent years it has made an escalating absolute contribution, as government policy reflected acquiescence to or positive enthusiasm for the collapse of our manufacturing base. But the extent of the City's earning, the explosion in its size and scope of its operations which followed deregulation of its activities and the growing interdependence of domestic and foreign financial markets, which is the inevitable result of advances in information technology, should not prevent us from examining the detriments which all those benefits bring. Had the City been more concerned with the domestic economy, it might have been less successful in terms of the balance sheets of individual stock-brokers, merchant banks and insurance companies; but its contribution to the British economy would have been so much greater that the nation as a whole would have boasted a far healthier profit and loss account. Changes in the City's organisation would both increase the City's contribution to the whole economy and make Britain a freer and more equal society.

Of course, the City has done well for *itself* during the 1980s. Pay in the City has risen much more quickly than it has increased in other sectors. Whilst employment, in general, has fallen since 1979 by over one million, employment in the financial services sector has grown by 300,000. Financial services is one of the few areas of economic activity in which Britain is a world leader: we are the world's largest international banking centre and have the biggest foreign exchange market. This tradition of overseas business has its origins in our imperial past – the feature of our history which for a hundred years diverted our attention from domestic investment and therefore contributed to our more recent decline. It is a position which can be maintained now only by allowing overseas bankers and financial institutions to colonise London. The imperial past has become a colonial present, in which Britain is the colony. The involvement of Japanese, German and American stockbrokers and investment bankers emphasises the detachment of the City from the rest of the domestic economy. Its fortunes are not dependent upon the success of the whole economy; indeed, some of the conditions which help the City hinder other industries. The encouragement of the environment in which the City thrives has contributed to the long-term decline of the economy as a whole. In the immediate past the City has benefited from high interest rates, over-valued sterling and the end of exchange control. The City thrives on change and movement – floating exchange rates and free international flow of capital – whilst manufacturing industry needs stability.

It is possible to argue that the enthusiasm for the City and its interests is a transient feature of British politics; that for a moment, the decline in manufacturing industry, the vested interests of the financial services and the predilections of the government all combined to work in the interests of the City. But that is both too simplistic and too optimistic an explanation. Socialists who, like Tawney, believe in unyielding opposition to private as well as state tyranny must make a more fundamental judgment about the City's behaviour. The right of the City to behave in a way which enhances its own position but damages the interests of the community in general is wholly consistent with a philosophy which describes freedom as the absence of restraint and regards the pursuit of equality of outcome as sinful. But for socialists who want to distribute wealth more evenly and diffuse power to an increasing number of men and women, the *status* of the City within our society demonstrates the ability of the rich and powerful to manipulate even governments. The arguments against an economic policy geared to the needs of financial institutions and known to damage other sections of industry and commerce are not concerned with output and income alone. They demonstrate a fundamental objection to society as presently organised. The existence of centres of unrestricted and unregulated power results in society being coerced into acting on behalf of those unrestricted and unregulated power centres.

Raymond Plant was describing the unintentional coercion by one individual of another when he wrote about 'action . . . which lowers the value of liberty for others'. But his analysis could easily apply to the rôle of the whole City within the whole economy – except for the fact that the financial institutions damage other sectors of industry not so much without knowing as without caring.

> . . . [if] in my intentional activity in buying and selling in an unconstrained market I have no intention to act coercively [but] if as a routine consequence of my exercising my freedom in this way some persons are put in the position of lacking the conditions for effective agency, then I am by my action, although not my intention, supporting a system which lowers the value of liberty for others and thus is coercive.[4]

It is that aspect of the debate about City fraud and City corruption which ought to cause most concern. The crime wave which sweeps, largely unchecked, through the City is in itself a national scandal. The widespread insider-dealing on the Stock Exchange, the insurance frauds at Lloyds, as well as less well publicised bogus commodity deals and phantom export-credit schemes, are now so frequent and involve such large sums of misappropriated money that the failure to deter further offences and the apparent inability to prosecute many known offenders amounts to a major breakdown in law and order. But the way in which the government is prepared to stand aside whilst the City

---

[4] R. Plant, *Journal of Comparative Politics*, Government and Opposition, Vol. 20, No. 3, p. 311.

crime wave continues is indicative of a deeper malaise. It illustrates the double standards of the establishment: its determination to prosecute one class of crime and its willingness to tolerate another. It also demonstrates the fact about British life which the City epitomises. There are some parts of our society which regard themselves as separate and superior – required neither to make a full contribution to the life of the nation nor to care about the consequences of their actions on others.

The double standards can be easily illustrated. In 1986, the government had 31 specialist Claims Control Units (made up of 175 staff) to combat social security abuse. In the same year there were 21 qualified investigators in the Director of Public Prosecution's Fraud Investigation Group.[5] Not surprisingly, Social Security frauds (although, usually, involving comparatively small sums) are far more likely to result in prosecution than are City frauds through which immense sums are misappropriated. Of the 324 serious UK City frauds detected in 1983, only 37 led to prosecution. In the City the chances of getting caught are small, the chances of prosecution (when caught) are slim and the chances of conviction (if prosecuted) are slight. Successful prosecutions usually lead to sentences which are shorter than those imposed for similar crimes outside the City. But the problem is the low priority which the authorities give to the prosecution of financial corruption. 'The City of London has long been policed by bumbling Inspector Clouseaus, always several steps behind those sleek pink panthers and their crafty frauds.'[6] But equally significant in the story of undetected crime is the City's own attitude. After the Parliamentary Under-Secretary at the Department of Trade and Industry described the record of malpractice at the Stock Exchange, a reckless politician rashly referred to evidence of 'Stock Exchange fraud'. The Parliamentary answer was explicit. There were 25 prima-facie cases of insider-dealing reported; 80 cases were referred to the Department of Trade and Industry under Section 2 of the Companies Act.[7] The response of the chairman of the Stock Exchange, Sir Nicholas Goodison, to my reference to 'fraud' was disturbingly revealing. He wrote a brief letter containing a

[5] From a letter from DHSS Headquarters to all Controllers, 15 May 1986, and *Hansard* 13.1.86, pp. 768–69.
[6] *The Economist*, 7.12.85, p. 15.
[7] *Hansard*, 12 March 1986, 'Financial Services in the City of London'.

rhetorical question: 'to what frauds' did the rash Member of Parliament refer?

It seems inconceivable that Sir Nicholas Goodison was not aware of the facts revealed to the House of Lords by Baron Lucas of Chilworth. The only possible explanation of his apparent ignorance is the belief that the conduct described by the Parliamentary Under-Secretary did not amount to fraudulent conduct. Yet the government persists in its apparent belief that the City must be allowed to regulate the conduct of its members.

Self-regulation is the panacea of the public school. It is the insider's remedy, the solution which prevents the disgrace from being publicised beyond the family. It is also a practice which allows the family – if the family so decides – to protect its errant member against outsiders and to choose the pretence of perfection rather than to admit the reality of crime. It is a relic of the days when the City was a gentlemen's club and it has been perpetuated long after the passing of the old genteel standards because it is to the convenience of the City and the City has the power to ensure that its will prevails.

The problem is illustrated by the spate of scandals which provoked Lloyds into a brief examination of its own regulations and conduct. At Lloyds – where self-regulation was carried out by insiders who were themselves operators in the market – it was impossible to avoid conflicts of interest. The regulators could only identify unacceptable behaviour by risking the reputation of Lloyds as a whole and, by so doing, both diminishing the prospects of an institution in which they had a vested interest and prejudicing their own position within it. Known offenders were not prosecuted. Lloyds were advised that it had no right or powers to hand over to the police documents which were essential to a thorough investigation. The release of documents necessary for legal action was, in itself, illegal. The establishment looks after its own.

Even after a chief executive of undoubted probity (and appointed from outside the magic circle) had completed all the reforms of procedure and practice which he thought possible, the problems still persist:

> Some of the market structures which led to the past abuse are still in place and will need careful and impartial supervision: for example, there is no central auditing system for Lloyds' market . . . So far the commercial penalties for regulatory and

management failure have been few. But unless the fragile
regulatory structure is partly supervised by an independent
outsider there could be a recurrence of scandal in future . . .[8]

This is not the place to argue in any great detail the form of
government supervision which should be exercised over the
financial institutions of the City. The pattern which seems right
in principle and works most effectively in practice is likely to be
made up of a statutory framework within which self-regulation is
allowed to work as long as it works effectively – spurred on by
the knowledge that if internal discipline fails an outside
authority will impose external sanctions. For a system which is
entirely statutory may be slow to react to the pace of change in a
dynamic industry and may, therefore, be more easily side-
stepped by ingenuity and innovation than would be the case with
a flexible régime based on self-regulation but underwritten by
statute. Some practices, particularly in new and fast changing
areas, may turn out to be wholly consistent with legal requirements which are, by necessity, narrowly defined. But they may
be outside the spirit of the law and only susceptible to control by
more broadly constructed ordnances. An entirely statutory
system may become excessively litigious – as is certainly the case
with the United States Securities and Exchange Commission
where the nature of the powers and the character of the
American people combines to produce constant litigation. But
the details of an acceptable regulatory system are less important
to the consideration of the promotion of freedom and equality
than are the necessity to provide effective regulation of some
sort and the ability of powerful institutions to insulate themselves from any sort of public or democratic control – control
which would ensure that they operated in the wider national
interest rather than to their own narrow sectarian advantage.
There are strong pragmatic reasons for advocating more outside
regulation of the City: its success depends on its experience,
expertise and integrity, and if its integrity is rendered suspect by
publicised scandals which it takes no steps to eradicate only the
competing financial institutions of Tokyo, New York and
Frankfurt will benefit.

Yet the City institutions which (left unregulated) would
certainly neglect or ignore the full discharge of all those duties

[8] *Financial Times*, 20.11.85.

think of the imposition of statutory regulation as infractions of their natural liberties. They will be right to claim that their freedoms have been restricted. They will no longer be free to overlook the misappropriation of clients' funds. They will no longer be free to use their insider knowledge in a way which gives them special benefits within the market. The need to regulate the City is analogous to other rights of which Margaret Thatcher often speaks. If there is a right not to be burgled, there is a right not to be swindled. That such freedoms are so often denied to the small operator within the financial sector is a profoundly disturbing revelation about Britain in the 1980s. There are still institutions too powerful to be constrained by the rules which govern the weak.

The weak have their commercial and industrial conduct – as well as their social behaviour – governed by law. And under the 1979 and 1983 new-libertarian governments, which wanted to see a more flexible labour market, the power of workers to combine in or collectively to pursue common ends was consciously and consistently diminished. Combination is, however, neither frowned upon nor forbidden on the other side of industry. Britain suffers the penalties of being burdened with one of the world's most concentrated economies – very largely the product of one of the world's most feeble anti-competition policies. Those penalties are, in part, material. Competition is suppressed in favour of the inefficient, highly profitable and easy life which market domination can provide. But the economic detriments are only part of the price which society has to pay. The domination of whole sectors by a single firm or the spread of ownership by a single conglomerate through a group of interdependent industries puts at risk the democracy of the society in which such power exists. That risk does not have to be demonstrated by dramatic, indeed melodramatic, examples of pre-war German cartels undermining that nation's nascent democracy or South American mining companies preventing the election of dangerously representative radicals. We acknowledge the danger in British monopolies and merger legislation – without taking adequate power to protect society from its consequences. It is, for example, accepted that the concentration of newspaper ownership is a threat to political freedom. Yet the merger regulations contain a specific escape clause which enables weak-minded or corrupt governments to permit a single owner to purchase title after title. If the future of a paper is threatened – or said to be threatened – all the rules governing newspaper mergers are suspended. It was in such circumstances that Rupert Murdoch acquired *The Times* and the *Sunday Times*, backing up his application to the Monopolies Commission with figures about the commercial prospects of the newspaper which he wished to acquire which turned out, on a charitable interpretation, to be mistaken.

> Mrs Thatcher wanted Rupert Murdoch's acquisition of Times Newspapers to avoid a reference to the Monopolies Commission. The Minister who had to take the decision, John Biffen, is regarded by all sides of the House of Commons as a fair and pleasant man, but not a Minister with an iron grip, nor one to stand up to the Prime Minister. Times Newspapers was the subject of his first major decision as Secretary of State for Trade and he made it with surprising dispatch. When he was Chief Secretary of the Treasury, he agonized where Ministers like Nigel Lawson wielded the axe with pleasure and he did have a reputation for detailed application. The case of the *Sunday Times* and its capacity to survive as a separate newspaper required this, but his consent to Murdoch's takeover was swift. A newspaper merger unprecedented in newspaper history went through in three days. In such a rapid process it is perhaps understandable that he overlooked, or his officials allowed him to overlook, £4.6 million of revenue and £7,000,000 of *Sunday Times* profit, so that as regards the *Sunday Times* he failed to apply the provisions of the Fair Trading Act of 1973.[9]

The bogus figures were backed up by meaningless promises about editorial freedom and the editor's independence to appoint the senior staff of his choice. The 'undertakings' were never kept. Such undertakings rarely are. In 1976, the Labour government allowed the absorption of Manbray-Granton into Tate and Lyle on the strict understanding that there would be no redundancies in the new sugar-refining giant. When, in just over a year after the merger, the redundancies were made, the government did not possess the power to insist that the promise must be kept. To their credit, monopolies are usually frank

[9] H. Evans, *Good Times, Bad Times* (Weidenfeld & Nicolson, London, 1983), Ch. 7, 'Biffen's Missing Millions', p. 141.

about the advantages they enjoy from their monopoly status. In 1979, British Oxygen (then supplying almost 90 per cent of this country's industrial gas) explained to the government that its near monopolisation of the industry solved all its pricing problems. Large wage increases posed no problems: they were automatically passed on to consumers with the invitation to take it or leave it and the confidence that came from knowing that if the consumers left it, they had nowhere else to go. The trades unions endorsed their employers' judgment about the advantages of the way the industry was organised, confirming that it was a great help during pay negotiations. Monopoly is as much, perhaps more, about power than it is about efficiency. Yet the right in British politics, for all their recent talk of liberty, allows a monopoly to flourish. The reason is clear: they have no objection to the concentration of power when it is concentrated in the hands of their friends and supporters.

The concentration continues and accelerates. Ten years ago, the British economy was already the most concentrated in the industrial world. In Britain the 100 largest firms accounted for 42 per cent of net manufacturing output whilst in America the figure was 32 per cent and in Germany 22 per cent. Since then the merger boom has exploded into merger mania. In 1985, the total value of mergers and takeovers was £7 billion – well over 50 per cent of the total value of all capital investment in firms. At the end of 1985, 52 of the top 300 companies (with combined value of £30 billion and covering 15 per cent of the total market) were threatened by takeovers. In 1986, the total annual value of mergers increased from the previous year's level of £7 billion to £10 billion. The economic, as well as the democratic, penalty is enormous.

The growth in asset sales does not create wealth. All it does is transfer existing wealth. The effect of these massively expensive takeovers is deeply damaging to our long-term industrial health. Not only does it result in the direction of resources into wholly unproductive purposes, it also concentrates the minds of owners and managers on essentially short-term objectives – resisting takeovers, making takeover bids, maximising the advantages of being taken over. Takeovers are justified in theory by the hope that they result in the more efficient use of resources. In practice the opposite is often the case. David Walker, a director of the Bank of England, has described – in the *Bank of England*

Review[10] – the growth in takeovers as creating obsession with the short-term prospects of dividends and share prices to the detriment of the long-term performance of both individual companies and the economy as a whole. Large-scale investment in research and development and retaining profits or borrowing for investment – all desirable activities in themselves – are likely to hold down quoted share prices relative to the underlying asset value and make a company more vulnerable to takeover. Indeed, the absurd paradox is that companies which use available resources wisely are both more attractive to takeovers and more easily taken over than companies that simply maintain high share prices.

The boom in takeover activity is an extension of the City's enthusiasm for short-term speculation. The motivation for takeovers is often the immediate profit which can be made during, or shortly after, the takeover, rather than the creation of more efficient firms. Indeed, when there is long-term motivation, the takeover is often carried out to avoid the necessity of improving efficiency, for the elimination of competition removes the necessity to provide a lower price or better product than other firms in the market. It is no longer simply City institutions which think of takeovers as a profit-generating activity *in themselves*. Some giant companies have built up such large cash surpluses that they are beginning to assume the characteristics of financial institutions. The increased profitability of these companies should create the right environment for expansion. Using surplus funds for acquisition reduces the likelihood of profits being used for new investment. Some City firms are actually seeking out prospective takeovers, telling the putative predator of the profits that can be made and hoping to earn large fees for themselves.

The massive changes in British market structure and balance in industrial power which are taking place in the United Kingdom, with little or no reference to the United Kingdom's interest, is wholly consistent with the neo liberals' support for the free for all, as distinct from the free market. What we need now is a complete review of our attitude towards competition and takeovers.

The new policy which emerges must be consistent with our

[10] *Bank of England Review*, Vol. 25, No. 4, December 1985, pp. 570–5.

broader aims. What we need is not just a competition policy. We need a policy for competitiveness – of which the maintenance of competition, where it is appropriate, is an important ingredient. For competition is not an end in itself. The object of all economic policy should be the welfare that competition sometimes, but not invariably, provides.

It is, for example, possible to cite instances of where domestic competition undermines the international competitiveness of British products. In such cases we should not be constrained by a slavish commitment to the theory rather than to its outcome in practice. Similarly, there are some industries – the public utilities are the obvious example – that need to be organised as national corporations. Such inevitable monopolies are best run as public monopolies and subject to stringent regulations which oblige them to pay proper regard to the interests of their consumers. The new policy must be built on the presumption that competition is to be promoted and encouraged. But its operation cannot be built on some rigid formula which automatically relates to the structure, conduct and performance of a market. The degree of concentration *may* be the criterion against which the government measures the desirability of action, but it cannot be the only test. There is, of course, a particular attraction in operating a mergers policy which has the neat consistency of the formula based on concentration and market share. It protects ministers from having to make difficult individual decisions. But it often inhibits mergers which are necessary to create companies which enjoy the economies of scale and sometimes allows mergers which are, by any standards, undesirable, but which are legal within the arbitrary framework of numbers on which the Act is now based. One of the essential objections to takeovers – particularly the creation of larger and larger conglomerates – is that they concentrate power in too few hands. The prohibition of such a concentration of power cannot be based on any formula which simply reflects market share in one particular sector.

A London Business School Survey[11] showed that in half of the mergers which they examined the shareholders in the acquiring firm would have been better off if the merger had not taken place. Evidence from the Liesner Committee[12] (set up by the

[11] London Business School Survey, *The Times*, 7 April 1986.
[12] Liesner Committee Reports: May 1979, Cmnd 7198 and March 1979, Cmnd 7512.

Labour government of 1978), later confirmed by American experience, suggests that most mergers do not produce the increases in profits and efficiency their proponents promised. That is because (despite all the fine talk about economies of scale) most mergers are not concerned with industrial performance.

The motivation for a high proportion of all mergers is an increase in monopoly power and a reduction in competition. Yet only 3 per cent of mergers are referred for investigation. Given the poor record of many mergers and the undesirable side effects of merger activity, the discouragement provided by the uncertainties of a case-by-case approach was clearly desirable. Yet in 1984 the government declared its intention to remove that uncertainty. Even before 1984, the presumption on which an investigation was carried out, was that – in the absence of proof to the contrary – the merger was desirable. Any company which, in those circumstances, lacked the confidence to risk an investigation was clearly short of rational justification for its merger proposal.

For socialists there are three main reasons why a tougher merger and monopolies policy is necessary:

1. The classic objection to market concentration: the abuse of monopoly power, diseconomies of scale and the costs of integrating two companies.

2. The record of mergers over the recent past which demonstrate that, at best, they have had a neutral effect on growth and efficiency.

3. The increasing emphasis – in the City and some major companies – on merger activity rather than real growth with the consequent shortening of time horizons which diverts managerial resources and acts to the detriment of new investment and research and development.

But, of course, these points do not justify a general prohibition of mergers. We have to devise a system which prohibits those which are undesirable, and allows those which are beneficial to proceed. It is not – and never can be – possible to set out rigid criteria against which every merger can be judged or every merger reference determined. Monopolies policy demonstrates the need for *selective intervention*, the right of society to make judgments about the actions of its most powerful institutions – to encourage them when they are beneficial to the community's accepted aims but to discourage them when they are inimical to those goals. If our goal is a greater liberty, a tougher monopolies policy is essential.

The control of financial institutions and the 'organisation of competition' are both essential to the creation of a more equal and more free society. Control by itself is not enough. A Labour government should prevent undesirable mergers and control monopoly practices when a monopoly exists but cannot be divided, by legislative action, into more competitive parts; but if the intention is the creation of a socialist society in which power and wealth are more equally distributed, it is necessary to create the institutions which can finance the new sort of economy which we mean to build. The early socialists dreamed of and planned to abolish the Stock Exchange – though those who did not believe in Soviet centralism were not altogether clear how they would provide capital for new investment. They proposed the nationalisation of the Bank of England as an essential element of central planning, never dreaming that when the Bank of England did come into public ownership, instead of acting as the agent of the government in the City it would become the agent of the City within Whitehall. In a more realistic age we have to limit our aspirations to curbing the City's power and to directing its enthusiasms in a socially desirable direction. That involves regulation and control, but it also involves something positive. It requires us to create alternative institutions which are prepared for, and capable of, financing the sort of society that we want to see.

By their nature, the financial institutions set up within the capitalist system cater for that system. They do so with the confidence which comes from hundreds of years of uninterrupted supremacy. Conversations with the City of London concerning the need for some sort of exchange control always prove philosophically revealing. They begin with complaints about reduced return on investment which is brought home to Britain and invested within the domestic economy. They continue with complaints about the insecurity of investing within one country. When, on the established and accepted evidence, both of those

227

arguments are proved to be false, representatives of the City fall back on philosophy. In a free society, they say, individuals and institutions must be allowed to do whatever they choose with their own money. We must develop a similar ideological certainty.

That certainty must be translated into the creation of new financial institutions which subscribe to our views and reinforce our aims. There is nothing revolutionary or exclusively socialist about industrial banking. The Kreditanstalt für Wiederaufbau (KfW) distributed loan capital of DM 15.7 billion in 1983; in the same year the Long Term Credit Bank of Japan has an asset base of Y 14,430 billion. Industrial banks work closely with industry. They offer loans and investment of various patterns for various periods and at various rates of interest. It is possible to argue that the establishment of a similar institution in Britain – in part organised in conjunction with regional development agencies and local authority development committees – is no more than industrial common sense. But common sense has a great deal to do with socialism.

It is similarly necessary to build on the work already done by the Unity Trust to provide special finance for ESOPs and to create a Co-operative Development Agency which specialises in providing development funds for new co-operatives. All these schemes will be described by our critics as doctrinaire profligacy – institutions designed to waste public money and risk private savings. We need to develop a confidence that disregards such nonsense. On the evidence, the financial institutions that support a wider distribution of industrial power finance companies with better industrial records than firms in which the employees feel no commitment to the undertakings' success. Here is John Stuart Mill's point again: companies are best run by those with a vested interest in their success. Since such people are the workers within the companies, it is reasonable as well as right to provide them with the structures and institutions which make a reality of increased involvement. Once again philosophic theory and economic necessity coincide.

Chapter Twelve

To Them That Hath . . .

To achieve the objectives which are the proper aim and purpose of democratic socialism it is necessary to redistribute wealth by reducing the income of the rich and increasing the earnings of the relatively poor. That process will improve the efficiency of the economy as well as increase the ability of society to meet as many of the needs of as many citizens as any one level of resources makes possible. There will, however, be arguments about the popularity of that proposition and even some suggestion that a party committed to such a process cannot expect to be elected. But it is beyond dispute that democratic socialism requires such a process and it is necessary for us to be absolutely explicit about our object, in order to fulfil the obligations of political honesty and to provide the party with the moral impetus and popular credibility which it would otherwise lack. Previous chapters have documented the accusation of Hayek that democracy will unavoidably lead to a demand for redistribution. Socialists must hope that the allegation is well founded, for a belief in effective liberty – as well as in equality itself – requires an increase in both the absolute and relative levels of income received by those members of society who now earn the least. During the earlier discussion of that moral imperative, passing attention (which was all that was deserved) was given to the two clichés which so often demean the arguments about redistribution. It is convenient briefly to dismiss both of them again before we examine the ways in which redistribution can be brought about.

The first sophistry is built around an image involving loaves, cakes or pies and it amounts to the notion that political bakers should be more concerned about the total volume of their confection than about the size of individual portions. In some ways, the cake metaphor is no more than a vulgarisation of what is called the 'trickle-down effect' – the idea that only if the rich do very well will the poor do any better than before. The trickle-down effect (like the related concept of 'echelon advance') is a consciously cultivated myth propagated by people who have a vested interest in pretending that there is some moral justification for their greed. It is as absurd as the notion that, for economic progress, the highest paid need constant financial incentives whilst lower-paid workers will do their best without a similar cash inducement. There will be those who judge that, if the incentive theory holds good, moral superiority lies with the lower-income groups, who are expected to work without the constant stimulus of bonus and increment, rather than with the more prosperous members of society who can only be expected to do their best when offered ever increasing incentives. But that is not the point that the proponents of the competitive society intend to make. Further, since their theory is demonstrably wrong in terms of the knock-on effect it is said to have for the incomes and standard of living of the lower paid, there is no need to spend much time on considering the moral slur it casts on the public spirit and altruism of the highly paid. It was John Rawls who advised that we should pursue egalitarianism up to the point at which the least well-off judged that their long-term interests were best served by an unequal redistribution of resources. It is difficult to disagree with that judgment and impossible to believe that our society has yet reached a point at which material benefits are so equally spread that it would be dangerous for society as a whole – and even for the lowest paid – were equality to be extended any further. It may well be that some financial incentives are necessary to encourage effort and stimulate ambition; but it is still impossible to argue that one man needs £100,000 a year to make him work effectively as a company executive whilst a woman can be expected to become a successful nursing auxiliary for £60 a week.

The second cliché accuses those who preach equality of peddling the 'politics of envy'. Matthew Arnold, R. H. Tawney, Archbishop Temple are, no less than Mahatma Gandhi, all encompassed in the allegation that to describe the inequalities in our society and to argue that they be removed or diminished is to unleash a wave of covetousness and greed. It cannot be wrong to tell a poor man that he is poor whilst others are rich and to explain that, at least in part, his poverty is the product of their riches. For once we abandon the sentimentality of the trickle-down effect and the arrogance of the insistence that progress depends on the provision of special rewards for the specially talented, the ethics of inequality are put into their proper perspective. If the argument is to be carried on in such terms, the moral inadequacy lies with those people who not only possess and enjoy a disproportionate share of society's wealth but also use the power at their disposal – their control of the newspapers in particular – to invent a spurious ethical justi-fication for their selfishness. The whole pattern of income distribution is made up of interrelated items. A society is less likely to pay poor families an adequate child benefit if it is obsessed with the need to reduce income tax, and it is more likely to depress the wages of local authority manual workers if it insists on cutting down public expenditure in order to reduce capital transfer tax or the additional tax on unearned income. The opponents of redistribution persist in saying that 'there are no free lunches' – rightly implying that everything must eventually be paid for. Sensible socialists know that; but they also know that the rich should pay for metaphorical lunches consumed by the poor. We have to decide whether to pay more towards the National Health Service or to cut taxes. Those who choose tax cuts should openly and honestly argue that reducing the standard rate is more important than financing the extra dialysis machines which would save the lives of renal failure patients. To accuse those who question the present distribution of income as breeding envy reveals extraordinary values. Their arguments need not detain us long from the crucial question: what is the best way in which we can achieve a more equal distribution of income?

Within the Labour Party, the first and easiest answer to that question has always been 'taxation'. We have believed in a progressive taxation system in which the income of the very rich contributed to the welfare of the poor. That belief has not been reinforced during the years of Margaret Thatcher's government – the first time in recent history when the lower-earning groups continually paid more tax whilst the higher earners have regularly paid less.[1] Certainly – even without the massive tax

[1] *Hansard*, 21 March 1986, Columns 607 and 608.

concessions which were granted to the rich between 1979 and 1986 – the case for requiring the highest paid to make a larger contribution to the welfare of society as a whole would have been overwhelming. The way in which that contribution might have been paid is open to debate. Certainly marginal rates of tax which amount to 90 per cent or more are not the most desirable option. That is not to say that the pop group guitarist who earns £200,000 per year is entitled – by any rule of natural justice – to receive, in net income, any more than 10p of the final pound of what appears in his alternative to a pay packet. The problem is that few pop group guitarists (or for that matter many of the super-rich of any sort) ever paid 90p in the pound – unless they were advised by accountants of monumental incompetence. The very rich manipulate the tax system through a variety of 'allowances', the application of which allows them to avoid paying any tax at all on too large a part of their earnings. It is by the reorganisation of those allowances that their proper share of tax must be collected.

Indeed, we need to regear the whole tax system with the explicit and overt intention of making it an instrument of redistribution.

> . . . the British system of taxation is only mildly progressive . . . the average single wage earner now (1986) pays about one-third of his/her income (32.5 per cent) in direct tax, compared with 26.1 per cent of the earnings of the low paid and just over half (52.7 per cent) that of the very highly paid (earnings ten times the average) . . . Of all the countries in the EEC and seven other main advanced industrial countries in the OECD only New Zealand and Australia impose such a high rate of tax on such a low level of income as the UK.[2]

And whilst the theoretical incidence of direct taxation results in the lower paid contributing a share of their income which is relatively and absolutely too high, in practice the burden is piled even more heavily upon them. For the allowance system provides the more highly paid with two special advantages. First, by their nature, allowances enable the richest members of society to claim the largest tax exemptions and their exemptions exclude from tax liability income which would otherwise bear the top rate. Second – and equally because of the character and

[2] *Low Paid Review* (Low Pay Unit), 'The Great Tax Divide', pp. 17–19.

condition of top earners – they exploit to the full the exemptions open to them. There are no figures to demonstrate either the quality or quantity of tax advice available to the lowest paid as compared with that employed by the top 10 per cent; but there is no doubt that 'them that hath' make absolutely sure that they contribute no more than the law allows – and that they possess the resources to employ the professional services which make it possible to reduce their tax liability to the lowest legal pound.

Tax avoidance (as compared with tax evasion which is illegal and less common, though not unknown) combined with the opportunities to exploit the allowance system results in the lower paid contributing a far higher proportion of government revenue than a superficial analysis of the system suggests. That bias against the poor has to be removed, and so does the bias in the benefits system. Successive governments have boasted that pensioners and the unemployed are insulated against increases in the cost of living. In fact, they are protected against the escalation in prices *which affects the community* as a whole, and the cost-of-living index which could be appropriately applied to the poor moves at a different speed and in a different way from that which reflects price changes within the entire nation. The poor spend their income almost entirely on basic necessities; and in Britain during the last twenty years, inflation has risen more rapidly when calculated on the price of necessities than when it is computed for a package of purchases which includes goods and services which the lowest paid rarely, if ever, buy.

> To apply an overall cost of living index, such as the RPI, to benefits received by the poor will be to over-estimate the change in their real value . . . For the poorest 10% of households, the apparent 5% rise in supplementary benefit over the period (January 1982 to January 1984) relative to the RIP was in fact negligible: similarly, indexation of benefits to the RPI implies a fall in their real value.[3]

Of course the rich, always benefiting more than the system intended, find that it is their income group that suffers inflation less than the official index registers – and, therefore, as well as preserving the overall statistical balance, receive (if, for instance, they are retirement pensioners) greater annual increases than are justified by the changes in their personal price index:

[3] Institute of Fiscal Studies, *The Retail Price Index and the Cost of Living*, p. 20.

householders with half the average expenditure have experienced a 5½% higher cost of living index compared with those on average expenditure. The opposite is true for households with twice the average expenditure.[4]

We learned, in 1978, of what the National Consumers' Council called 'double detriment': the extra expenditure incurred by the lowest paid as a result of their low income. The poor cannot buy in bulk and do not own freezers; for the poor, credit is more expensive than it is for the rich. The actual – as distinct from the theoretical – effect of our tax and benefit system shows that, in our divided society, a third detriment exists. The poverty of the lower paid does not come from low pay alone. It is in part caused, and in every way intensified, by the inhibitions it places on their patterns of consumption and by a tax system which – whilst in theory mildly progressive – contains such a bias towards the highest-income earners which dilutes even its mildly redistributive effect.

This is not the place to set out even part of a Labour budget, but some examples of how the tax system could be geared to greater redistribution illustrate two important truths. If we choose to help the worse-off and lower paid, we could do so even through the tax system. A reduced rate band of tax on the first tranche of taxable income concentrates relatively the largest relief on the lowest paid. The restriction of pension contribution and mortgage interest relief to the basic rate of income tax would provide extra revenue (contributed by the most highly paid) to finance schemes which alleviate poverty; so would the calculation of employees' national insurance contributions on all income rather than upon earnings up to an arbitrarily determined ceiling. There are an infinite number of ways in which the tax and benefit system can be used to promote equality.

Changes in taxation cannot, however, in themselves either achieve the level of equality which we seek or provide an adequate income for the lowest paid. For the highest paid, the increases in tax which they are required to pay will always be compensated, at least in part, by additional emoluments added to their primary salaries by their employers; and no taxation

[4] *ibid.*, p. 30.

system can be devised which, in itself, adequately redistributes to the point that meets the needs and aims of socialism. In 1979, (before the Thatcher administration's tax policies helped the rich at the expense of the poor) 95 per cent of the national total marketable wealth was owned by 50 per cent of the population, leaving 5 per cent for the other half of society. When occupational and state pension rights (the major source of wealth amongst the lower-income groups) were added to the calculation the richest 50 per cent still owned 83 per cent.[5] The calculation of income distribution shows a similar pattern. Taxes and benefits *can* reduce the degree of the inequality, but not very much and certainly not enough. Taxation policy – even progressive taxation policy – would have found it difficult to reduce materially the divergence in earnings levels between 1976 and 1983, when the share of original income enjoyed by the lower-paid fifth of the population fell from 0.8 per cent to 0.3 per cent and that of the top fifth grew from 44.4 per cent to 48 per cent.[6] In fact, during that period inequalities, even in final incomes, increased. To increase equality we need to create more equal primary incomes. For the 20 per cent of the population who receive between them only one three-hundredth of total disposable income, hope rests in increasing their share of primary earnings. For the lowest paid, the receipts in benefit will never be sufficient to enable them to approach, even in terms of total income, an acceptable earnings level. To improve their position it is necessary to organise a radical change in the level of pre-tax income which they receive.

Traditionally the Labour Party (whilst opposing and denouncing the free market) insists that the state has no part to play in wage determination. The market for labour is not, of course, free. That has long been the complaint of neo liberals who would like to see the individual employee negotiating his wages with the individual employer. But the theory of wage determination which has historically commended itself to British democratic socialists is the combination of workers in trades unions which then pit their wits and strength against the combined power of owners and managers. Clearly in the unequal struggle between manager and man it is right and necessary for the

[5] *Social Trends* (1986 Edition), p. 91 table 5.21, p. 92 table 5.22.
[6] *ibid.*

collective power of workers to be used to enhance the prospects of the individual members of their group. But that is only part of the story. What is called free collective bargaining does not and cannot, in itself, provide an acceptable pattern of income allocation. Since it is dependent on the strength of the opposing parties, it gives most to the strong and least to the weak. Indeed, it so inadequately meets the demands of a just society that even its strongest proponents within the TUC accept the need for some limitation and modification. The unorganised workers in low-pay industries must, by general socialist consent, be protected by Wages Council and Fair Wage legislation. The extremes of wealth and poverty must, they argue, be reduced by progressive tax and social security régimes which take from the rich and give to the poor.

The notion that wages should be determined by a mixture of measures is clearly right. Since each element of economic management should be regarded as one of the methods by which equality and freedom are extended, the structure and form of income allocation must – like the organisation of other parts of the economy – be accepted as no more than a means by which the desired end is achieved. Democratic socialists ought to be wholly ideological about the sort of society which they hope to create and wholly empirical about the way in which it is created. Thus the case for free enterprise is balanced, according to circumstances, by the arguments against planning. Markets and monopolies are encouraged or prohibited according to their results in specific sectors. The division between public and private ownership is determined by the advantages which each system produces in individual industrial sectors. If it is sensible to make empirical judgments about the way in which other economic activities are organised, it must be equally reasonable to support free collective bargaining on some occasions but to develop other forms of wage determination to meet different circumstances.

Described in such detached terms, the need to mix the various techniques by which personal incomes are determined is widely accepted within the Labour movement. It is when *cases* are considered that pragmatic necessity is ignored. That is as much the product of human optimism as of human greed – the belief that, left to themselves, the workers can do the best deal possible for each negotiating group, and that the best deal possible for the group is what is best for each particular industry at any particular time and for the economic prospects of the whole community. The unions themselves know perfectly well that free collective bargaining is not, alone, enough. But the right of collective bargainers to carry on their business free from outside influence or interference is defended, by many demo-cratic socialists, with a *laissez-faire* passion which is wholly inconsistent with their enthusiasm for the regulation of other forms of economic activity. For that mistake there are many varied reasons. One is a romantic attachment to trades unions themselves, the working-class institution around which free collective bargaining is built. Another is a proper suspicion of and resistance against bureaucratic intrusion into areas of life to which the bureaucracy has little to contribute. A third is the feeling that for workers – with very little power over their daily lives – the wage negotiation is one ritual over which power can be exercised. Each of those pressures is in favour of keeping the wage negotiation process in the form that it has operated for the last 100 years. But to do so ignores the essential question. Does so-called free collective bargaining meet the needs of economic efficiency and social justice?

Government intervention in wage negotiations is at its most unpopular when it is actually taking place and is most appreciated when it is not happening. The 'social contract' of 1974–9 provided substantial benefits to millions of union members – in many cases, benefits which they would not have obtained through their own bargaining strength. But the experiences of that period so prejudiced the Labour Party against 'incomes policy' that socialists who believed in that system had to search desperately for another name with which to describe the object of their enthusiasm.

Conversely, government involvement in pay negotiations was most vocally demanded, and its need was most dramatically demonstrated, when the Thatcher government of 1985 removed Wages Council protection from young workers and abolished the Fair Wages resolution. The explanation with which the government attempted to justify its decision was the need to increase flexibility and reduce distortions in the labour market. If wage rates were determined by competition, the argument ran, the over-pricing which reduced demand would be avoided.

The argument was almost certainly doctrinaire nonsense. Many Wages Council industries were already paying below the statutory rates, yet employment continued to fall as the level of real wages deteriorated. In a wage-cutting competition most of the Wages Council industries would certainly lose to their rivals in South East Asia. The only certain effects of the end of statutory protection were the deterioration in the wage levels of the affected sector, and the realisation that, by definition, the badly paid cannot negotiate a decent wage. The lower paid suffer that unhappy condition either because they work in industries insufficiently profitable to afford decent rates of pay or because they lack the bargaining strength to obtain better rates when higher pay is practicable. In theory the workers in retail distribution, agriculture and textiles could be persuaded to join their appropriate trades unions in larger numbers and then make a successful collective demand for a living wage. But had the structure of those industries – and the character of the people who work within them – been capable of sustaining such solidarity they would not have become low-wage sectors in the first place. Perhaps there was a time when the employers in those sections could not afford to pay. But that period passed, when the revolution from corner shop to supermarket made retailing one of the most efficient and one of the most profitable industries in the country. In most of agriculture the years of farming poverty ended with the managed market of the Common Agricultural Policy. In both industries, when high profits came in, low wages did not go out. They remained because of the difficulty of organising effective union action within industries which contain thousands of small concerns which each employ a handful of workers; and low rates persisted because of the nature of the workers in those industries – women working part-time and men, tied by temperament and necessity, to the one area, one employer and one occupation which they, and their families, had always known.

To provide a fair deal for the very poor, government intervention is essential. Indeed, since income depends upon the chance to work as well as the earnings which work provides, government involvement is often necessary to ensure that the least privileged members of society earn anything. For an unregulated labour market certainly denies jobs to the black and Asian British. An imperfectly regulated labour market does exactly the same. The PSI study of 1984[7] showed that racial discrimination in employment was just as great as it had been before the Racial Discrimination Act was passed ten years earlier. The Department of Employment and the Commission for Racial Equality estimate that between 50,000 and 100,000 Black and Asian young workers who are now unemployed would have jobs were they white. It is for that reason that those who genuinely believe in freedom are willing – indeed anxious – to impose on employers the obligation to recruit and promote irrespective of an applicant's race or colour. Such legislation is a perfect example of a limitation on the freedom of the powerful being necessary to extend the liberties of the weak.

The parallel with the Irish Land Act (see Chapter 4) is exact: the rights of property are curtailed so that the opportunities of labour can be enhanced. The parallel applies both to the chance to work and the hope of receiving a decent wage for whatever work is available. There are groups within society on whose behalf the state has to intervene because those groups cannot command or organise sufficient collective support to provide adequate self-protection. Those groups are not simply minorities; the majority of the population is at risk because discrimination against women in work persists. The problem now only applies to the professional classes in one limited way: restricted promotion opportunities. Although in the recent past they were denied equal pay for equal work. The wages of unskilled women remain intolerably low. Only legislation will provide for them a decent level of earnings.

The unions may rally round and give their support to the cause of those least advantaged groups, recruiting them to membership wherever they can and advocating the protection of their interests. Indeed, the unions are now generally committed to fair employment legislation and they are the natural and inevitable representatives of the low paid on Wages Councils. But whilst in the areas both of employment opportunities and fair wages organised labour can help, it cannot solve the problem on its own. The task will only be done successfully if government and unions act in partnership. The argument for involving workers in ownership and management is also the argument for their continued direct involvement in wage

---

[7] C. Brown and P. Gay, *Racial Discrimination Seventeen Years after the Act of 1968*, (Policy Studies Institute, London, No. 646, 1985), p. 51.

negotiation. That argument concerns the need to make employees feel engaged and involved in the decisions which effect their daily lives. But – again as with cases of industrial democracy, share options and workers' buy-outs – the operation has to be conducted within the guidelines of public interest and the government has to provide the structures by which workers can first balance their sectional claim against wider considerations and then give effect to the conclusion to which they come.

The whole business of wage determination has to be seen as part of a general drive to create a participatory democracy. It is not possible to argue rationally for greater worker participation in all those aspects of industrial life from which the influence of employees is now excluded and, at the same time, lay down wage rates by the edict of some central authority, thus removing the representatives of workers from the one area of management in which their voices are heard. In any event, a party which is opposed to the bureaucratic allocation of steel and cement cannot advocate the rigidity of imposed patterns of wage and salary payments which totally destroy the labour markets and impose on workers the tyranny of all working for the same employer. The same rule must apply to decisions affecting the use of labour as that which applies to the allocation of other commodities. Sometimes the market will be the most effective way of deciding the price of labour, and then, what we have come to call free collective bargaining will approximate to a system which balances supply and demand. Sometimes the market will have to be replaced with a system which provides a greater overall utility and a higher level of social justice. In wage determination, as in other aspects of economic management, it is necessary to ask which structures most serve our ends of increasing equality and extending the sum of liberty. There is no simple formula that meets our needs.

The simple formula of which we want to be most wary is the insistence that to leave individual unions free to pursue their own interests is essential to socialist democracy. That cannot be true. The ways in which free collective bargaining might prejudice progress towards a further distribution of wealth are easy to describe. Powerful managerial and technical trades unions, which recruit and represent highly skilled workers whose expertise and experience are in short supply, could negotiate for themselves a disproportionate share of whatever additional money is available during the annual wage negotiations. Less skilled and lower paid workers would, in consequence, receive less than their legitimate share. Unions representing members in work could negotiate pay deals which would prevent an expansion of the economy, which in turn would produce the extra jobs which are necessary to make any real impact on the level of unemployment. Only sentimentalism leads to the notion that as long as trades unions are empowered to negotiate in the way they choose, even the interests of the least well paid workers will be properly recognised and protected.

Fortunately fewer and fewer trades union leaders would now suggest such a state of affairs. Trades union *laissez faire* is the favoured doctrine of the old guard and the new revolutionaries. There is an increasing determination to find procedures by which proper trades union rights are maintained within the guidelines of responsibility. The pursuit of that solution has to begin with a firm statement of why *some* income planning is necessary and the clear and categorical assertion that the system which socialists devise should not be an incomes policy of the old model, with its norms, ceilings and acceptable exceptions. Such a system will not work and does not deserve to work, for it can only be introduced, and would only be temporarily accepted, as a desperate expedient. Income planning cannot be used as the heroic surgery which hacks away at the national economy when all other remedies have failed. Still less must it be – or be seen to be – a way of piling the cost of financial recovery on the backs of weekly paid workers. A national view on the overall level and general distribution of wages must become a permanent part of both our economic and social strategy, advocated and accepted on its own merits. That is one of the reasons why Labour governments cannot involve themselves in complicated horse-trading with the trades union movement. An agreement which ends with reluctant acquiescence to temporary wage limitation by the TUC and the unhappy acceptance of undesirable industrial relations legislation by ministers is not a foundation on which the New Jerusalem can be built. 'You scratch my back and I will scratch yours' is not an acceptable battle cry for a reforming and radical party.

Just as important, promises to sweeten the pill naturally

confirm the fear that without the sugar the pill would be very bitter indeed. The truth is quite the opposite. Some degree of planning is directly and wholly in the interests of trades unions and their members. That truth will not be accepted if we allow ourselves to fall into the weak-minded habit of talking as if incomes policy is an act of sacrifice made by workers on behalf of the country as a whole. One of the errors of the 1974–9 Labour government was the persistent use of language – 'give a year for Britain' and the rest – which was far too reminiscent of economic blood, industrial sweat and financial toil. If there is to be a permanent element of planning, it has to be used to secure a continual growth in real earnings and their more acceptable distribution.

Its effect on distribution is crucial. We will not mobilise the essential support for income planning unless we make it clear that its contribution to economic success is only one of its objectives. Income planning must be used as a positive contribution to the creation of a fairer society. It must have that explicit aim. It can be no more comprehensive than competition policy; it can be no more dependent on direction and regulation than investment policy. But it must have the same overt and explicit purpose. It must create the environment, the conditions and the formal structures within which individuals are offered the opportunity to choose freedom for themselves and equality for their communities. Since both those conditions are essentially dependent on providing a higher standard of living (or greater degrees of economic power) for the families at the bottom of the income scale, wage planning must be directly concerned with relieving the condition of the low paid.

It is inevitable that within an unregulated economy, where inflation is controlled only by fiscal and monetary techniques, the lowest paid will always fare badly. If money incomes rise at rates which bear little or no relationship to output and productivity, inflation – with its desperate consequences for living standards and employment – will certainly escalate. No government can allow uncontrolled inflation to continue for long. The free market remedy is bound to damage the interests of the lowest paid, for the cure will contain as an essential ingredient a reduction in public expenditure. The cuts will come in the services on which the lowest paid rely. The health service will deteriorate; housing costs will increase; pensions and benefits will be held down; schools' capitation allowances will be cut; public transport costs will escalate. Anyone with real concern for the welfare of the lower paid will co-operate in creating the economic conditions in which public expenditure can be sustained at a higher proportion of national income. It is fatuous to argue that, given the will, high levels of welfare and security can be sustained, even in economic crisis, by taxation-financed redistribution. The need to maintain international confidence will not allow high levels of social expenditure in conditions of incipient collapse. If we want high levels of public spending we have to create the conditions which make them possible. Concern for the poor and badly paid requires us to agree some sort of income planning.

Without some agreement on the distribution of money income, governments will inevitably use the fiscal and monetary weapons which are at their disposal to hold the aggregate level down – leaving the protagonists in the wages process to fight each other for shares of the total available amount. Inevitably, that process will lead to the lions receiving the lions' share. Workers in successful and prosperous companies who enjoy strong bargaining power will obtain large increases. Employees in barely profitable companies – particularly if those firms are small and barely unionised – will get small increases, if they get any increases at all. The philosophers of the wholly free market will argue that the glory of the unregulated system is the way in which its hidden hand allocates resources in a way which encourages the survival of the fittest and ensures the death of the weak.

But that is not a process which should be encouraged by socialists, for, as we have already seen, the market system does not always maximise efficiency – unless efficiency is defined by the self-fulfilling criteria of free enterprise success. It has nothing whatever to do with social justice. Socialists cannot accept a system in which men and women who work – through no choice of their own – in old or low-profit industries, are automatically required to survive on wages which are gro-tesquely different from those workers who are paid to perform similar tasks in expanding and more profitable sectors. Of course, the realities of change and decline have, in part, to be reflected in wage rates. What remains of heavy industry in the north-east is unlikely to finance the earnings common in the new technologies. To expect an equalisation of earnings in those different economic conditions would be as unrealistic as to pretend that the market will somehow right all the wrongs by encouraging the low-paid labourers of heavy industry to become computer programmers and information-technology engineers. There are going to be substantially different levels of earnings in different industries. But, remembering Tawney's definition of equality of outcome as a system which minimises rather than encourages disparities of wealth, socialists ought at least to set the parameters of economic policy in such a way as to reduce the risk of the poor doing worse whilst the rich (as always) at least protect their position. The lowest paid have the strongest vested interest in an economy which sustains high levels of public expenditure and maintains continual growth. That economy is most likely to be achieved if there is, at least, some planning of aggregate income levels and general agreement about the rough pattern by which that aggregate is distributed.

What is more, there is, for socialists, a special problem of income allocation within the unregulated economy which arises because the apparently unregulated economy is never wholly unregulated. Whatever governments may say, there is always an incomes policy within the public sector. Violently ideological administrations may argue that the ceilings which they impose on public-sector pay are the product of no more than prudent management – the government as employer paying no more than it can afford. But the truth is that the less regulated the private sector, the more the public sector will be expected to compensate for the excessive wage claims that the government cannot control. Industrial costs, pushed up by free collective bargaining, will be held down by minimal rate increases which are made possible by low public-sector pay settlements. The government will be anxious to set a slow pace in the wage round (and reduce the expectation of renewed inflation) by making an example of public employees. Most important of all, governments of all persuasions and philosophies will possess the power and procedure to regulate the pay of half the workers within the economy. Any public-sector union leader who believes that the government will resist that temptation is incurably naïve. The best for which they can hope – and it is a very good best, for it offers public-sector workers a prospect which no other system provides – is an overall view of income determination which does justice to the public sector. The low paid and the publicly employed have everything to gain from wage planning – as the £6 flat-rate weekly increase of the 1978 pay policy proved. The low-paid public employees have a double interest in breaking out from the system which has kept them in poverty for years. In the past, they have sacrificed the prospect of that escape for two wholly unworthy reasons: national leaders have wanted to respond to the half-thought-out ideas of unrepresented political activists and local leaders have feared a loss of influence and authority.

The next time at which the opportunity arises, the interests of trades unionists must not be jeopardised by attempts to preserve the power of trades unions. It is important to maintain the influence and authority of the organisations which reflect and represent the collective strength of working men and women. Sacrificing that authority for some trivial or temporary purpose would be a scandalous long-term betrayal of trades unions' interests and of the interests of trades unionists. But there are issues of principle, as well as questions of immense practical importance, which transcend such considerations. One is the right of *all* employees to be properly represented in any scheme to extend industrial democracy; another is the right of low-paid workers to receive a living wage. The introduction of that moral and social necessity requires the abandonment of the notion that collective bargaining – freed from all other constraints than the determination to strike the best immediate bargain – is the only acceptable method of wage determination.

For it is *impossible* to introduce a statutory minimum *real* wage unless other wage bargains and bargainers take account of it. In theory, a statutory minimum wage, if introduced into an irreversible buoyant economy, could have the effect of putting up the levels of all earnings. The lowest paid would, in such circumstances, remain the lowest paid and receive relatively low wages; but the absolute level of their real income would improve as workers who traditionally occupied higher positions in the earnings league negotiated to maintain their own differentials. But in the real world, not even that limited improvement would be achieved. If the law requires employers to pay a statutory minimum rate, and if workers in more highly paid industries successfully negotiate to preserve their relative position, there can be only one possible outcome. The low paid remain low paid at a higher level of inflation. The truth is that assistance for the lowest paid can only be achieved as part of a concerted campaign for redistribution. It is vain to preach the virtues of greater equality without accepting the disciplines that greater equality provides.

Of course, it is possible to provide help for some of the lowest paid without the introduction of a statutory national minimum wage. Wages Councils – re-equipped with the power to determine rates for whole sectors – can judge what is socially just and economically possible for individual industries. The largely ineffective Wages Council inspectorate can be replaced by a system which enables trades unions to police the payment of stipulated wage rates. The government itself can oblige its suppliers to observe Fair Wages Regulations and can conduct negotiations with its own employees with the deliberate intention of biasing the distribution of available funds towards the lowest paid. But, desirable as all those expedients are, none of them quite make up for the absence of a minimum wage which, because its purchasing power is not eroded by retaliatory claims in other sectors, maintains its real value.

That can only be achieved by the establishment of a general consensus that the poor must be helped and that the price of help has to be paid, in different degrees, by society as a whole. The obstacles in the path which leads to a statutory minimum wage are many and various. Some trades unions may fear – wrongly but understandably – that, if the law sets minimum wage rates, the union is itself redundant. Many trades unionists will fight to preserve both their higher than average rates of pay and the higher than average status which goes with them. And the economists who speak for the employers in the low-wage industries will claim – irrespective of the facts – that higher pay in each and every sector can only lead to the triumph of low-cost exporters in South East Asia and Eastern Europe. But the response to the call for a statutory minimum wage which is most likely to prevent its implementation is not an open objection to its introduction. The real danger comes from the pretence that a national minimum wage could be introduced cheaply or easily. Minimising the cost and the difficulty is the popular political option. But those who do not face the full consequences of such a fundamental change are – whether they know it or not – the most dangerous enemies of the campaign for a nationally enforceable living wage. The situation which their sentimentality and partiality will preserve was described by Peter Townsend in 1979. If the condition of the poor has changed since then, it has changed for the worse.

> Low pay has a direct, immediate effect on the numbers in or on the margins of poverty. But it also has specific indirect effects. It may influence future life chances . . . Low pay in the past can cause indebtedness for years to come, prevent the accumulation of assets, reduce capacity to overcome such sudden adversity as sickness or unemployment when it arises, result in under-nutrition, restrict activities and social experience, and hence leaves permanent scars.[8]

To alleviate that condition a statutory minimum wage is necessary. In order to introduce a statutory minimum wage, it is necessary to determine pay by some other way than the crude operation of an imperfect market which is called free collective bargaining. The real case for planning incomes concerns social justice. We will never develop a fair system of wage determination, for we have no idea how to calculate the value of a worker's labour or how to measure the relative deserts of different trades and occupations. But we do know that workers at the bottom of the pay scale receive far too little, and that their existence is often made tolerable only by the level and quality of the public services which they receive. To determine wages in a way which prevents the lowest paid from receiving the benefit of a statutory minimum wage and also jeopardises the prospects of increased and improved public service is the antithesis of socialism.

The question for socialists cannot be whether or not collective bargaining needs to be augmented. The answer to that question – to those who are in serious pursuit of a more equal and free society – is obvious enough. The real question concerns how wages can be properly planned and what system can be introduced to ensure that free collective bargaining assists in the creation of the sort of society that socialists want to see.

Some of the alternatives to the present system can be quickly ruled out. A government-determined and implemented incomes policy is wrong in principle and unworkable in practice. It is no

[8] P. Townsend, *Poverty in the United Kingdom* (Penguin, London, 1979), p. 631.

more sensible to allocate wages through a state bureaucracy than it is for the apparatus of government to determine levels of output and attempt to achieve them by administrative allocation of resources. In any case, in a free society, such a system cannot work for long and cannot, even for the briefest of periods, work effectively. Nor is it sensible to suggest a wages policy which, whilst voluntary in theory, is by any practical test sustained and supported by coercion. Penalising companies which pay larger increases than the government regards as reasonable may work as a brief expedient and may be justified in times of crisis, but it cannot bring into wage negotiations the elements of fairness and justice that socialists should want to see. Nor can some complicated apparatus of tax penalties imposed on companies which pay salaries above the stipulated limit offer a practical alternative. If such a system is intended to solve economic problems, it would probably have the opposite effect to that which its proponents believe – resulting in the increased wages *and* the tax penalties which they incur all being passed on to consumers. Coercion is bound to destroy the element that income planning must contain if it is to be a permanent feature of a socialist society.

It is necessary to persuade those who determine wages and those on whose behalf the wages are determined that an element of planning is right and desirable; that it is not a penalty to be resisted until the forces of the state ensure embittered acceptance, but a measure to be welcomed as an instrument of social improvement which ought to be implemented with good grace and in the expectation of general benefit. Some of those benefits will, for most groups within the economy, be direct and material: wage increases which are not eroded by inflation or, in the case of the lowest paid, wages that allow a decent standard of life. For others they will be equally material but less direct. It may be that for these groups planned wages offer them no more, or even less, than they would have previously received. But the benefits which they obtain through living in a full employment society in which the levels of public services are adequately maintained will be enormous.

Income planning can only work if people believe in it. But people will believe in it only if the case for income planning is argued with clarity and conviction. That requires socialists to be absolutely explicit about the sort of wage levels which are consistent both with accepted economic aims and with acceptable social priorities. It requires a party preparing for an election and government after the election is over to set out the numbers around which acceptable wage limits can be negotiated – not norms enforceable in law or supervised by a special committee of the TUC, but figures about which the government can say two things: first, that if the parameters they set are generally accepted then the proper aims of a socialist government can be fulfilled; and second, that if they are ignored those who ignore them must take responsibility, not simply for the standards of modified free enterprise being applied in wage determination, but also for the standards of living that such a system provides for various groups within society. In short, we have to persuade trades unions and trades unionists that they have a vested interest in socialism and they should conduct themselves in a way that socialism requires.

Because trades unionism and socialism are inextricably linked within Great Britain, socialists are disinclined to say to trades unions and trades unionists what they are willing to say to others. It is perhaps offensive and patronising to preach to members of the true religion about that religion's obligations. But occasionally the tenets of theology are forgotten and the practice of the good life ignored. Then it is necessary to evangelise. The gospel we have to spread is clear. It is what Matthew Arnold, a hundred years ago, called 'the Gospel of equality'. The text of his sermon was, 'Choose equality and flee greed'. The equality he sought provided the power that makes the generality of men and women truly free. That is why socialists must choose equality and in doing so choose freedom.

The Prospect

The Labour government of 1945 was elected to power on the most radical programme which the Labour Party has ever offered to the electorate. The radicalism of the Attlee manifesto was not in itself the sole reason for Labour's landslide victory, but the contents of Labour's programme and the size of vote cast in its support make one fact undeniable: electoral success and ideological commitment are not incompatible. It may well be that in 1945, after the Second World War, Labour would have won whatever it had promised in its programme. But it was, at least in part, socialism's moment because Labour made it so. It was a time when the national mood was instinctively sympathetic to egalitarian aspirations and democratic ideals, and the Labour Party was brilliantly successful in convincing the men and women who were emotionally on Labour's side that they could, with safety, allow their votes to follow their hearts.

The world has changed since 1945 and the circumstances of the Attlee victory can never be recreated. Indeed, if Labour is to win the next, or any subsequent, election it is essential to understand that the next campaign will be different from any which we have fought in the past. But the Attlee campaign and the Attlee triumph has a fundamental lesson to teach us. To win, the Labour Party has to offer a reasonable revolution which both catches the country's enthusiasm for change and allays the fears that change might cause disruption.

The Labour Party managed in 1945 – perhaps for the only time in its history – to reconcile the two imperatives of policy formation which R. H. Tawney has outlined in *Equality*. The Labour Party has to maintain its commitment to the creation of a new society. For it 'forgets its mission' when it seeks 'not a social order of a different kind . . . but a social order of the same kind in which money and power will be somewhat differently distributed'. But the new social order has to be pursued with reality as well as with passion. 'The important point' for socialists 'is not that they should express – or even hold – opinions as to policy which attract attention as extreme. It is that they should show extreme sense in reaching them, extreme self-restraint in keeping their mouths shut until their opinions are worth stating and extreme resolution in acting upon them when stated.' That combination of philosophy and pragmatism creates a genuinely united Labour Party – an indispensable ingredient of victory. For balancing the two elements of Tawney's formula satisfies both the ideologists who believe in the abiding values of socialism in principle and their more down-to-earth comrades and friends who seek merely to ameliorate the social conditions of the time. The requirement, for the Labour Party to achieve united success, is not the reconciliation of conflicting obligations but the construction of a policy and programme which simultaneously serves both ends.

Committed socialists will argue that socialism is always the right remedy for the sickness of the time and that it can be prescribed with advantage to the fit, as a certain stimulus to even more health and vigour. But the special achievement of the Party which Mr Attlee led was its persuasion – of people who had never voted Labour in their lives – that socialism was the one relevant remedy for the problems of 1945. The ideologues proposed planning, public ownership and the welfare state and their policies made obvious sense. The visionaries advocated a more equal society and their evangelism was accepted as the advocacy of a practical improvement in the way in which the country was organised and run. And, at the same time, the actual items in the programme could be endorsed by party members and potential supporters who asked only for a policy relevant to the needs of the time. The coalition of objectives was complete. Its supporters could choose to support the nationalisation of gas and electricity because such basic utilities belonged to the people as of right or because public ownership would 'lead to the reforming of uneconomic areas of distribution'. The health service could be advocated as a way of providing free medicine for the ailing poor or a step towards the social emancipation of the working classes. The programme, despite its clearly 'socialist' basis, was generally acceptable to radicals and reformers of many different sorts. Indeed, some of its far-reaching proposals were adaptations of the work of Keynes and Beveridge – both liberals either by inclination or formal party membership.

The creation of the coalition of objectives enabled a united party to speak for a wide spectrum of national opinion – far wider than anything that the Conservatives (who looked increasingly like a party of outdated theories and sectional interests) could claim to represent. Attlee could write to his brother with absolute conviction and unusual sentimentality that

> Forty years ago the Labour Party might with some justice have been called a class party, representing almost exclusively the wage earners. It is still based on organised labour but has steadily become more and more inclusive . . . The Conservative Party remains as always a class party . . . It represents today, as in the past, the forces of property and privilege. The Labour Party is, in fact, the one Party which most nearly reflects in its representation and composition all the main streams which flow into the great river of our national life.[1]

At the moment of its historic triumph, the Labour Party rejoiced that it had a wider base than the support of a single class. It did not see itself as a party united by the narrow pursuit of the interests of one sector of society. It certainly believed in its duty to help the dispossessed and the disadvantaged, but it realised that it could not discharge its duty to the poor if it relied on their votes alone. The Party triumphed in 1945 because it drew its support from and reflected the ideas and ideals of every section of the community. In 1945 Labour was elected because it was a party of wide appeal: it possessed the cohesion and the *élan* that came from ideological self-confidence and the popular attraction of a programme which seemed directly relevant to the nation's needs. The summer of 1945 was the Labour Party's historic moment. For the next forty years the coalition of objectives did not exert its special appeal again.

During the Wilson years the ideological climate turned sharply against the sort of remedy with which the Labour Party seemed to be associated. Collective action went out of fashion; the very idea of co-operation seemed decent but dull; steady

---

[1] K. Harris, *Attlee* (Weidenfeld & Nicolson, London, 1984), Ch. 17, 'Into Power 1945', p. 257.

growth had become boring. The new individualism of Margaret Thatcher, advocated with fanatical enthusiasm, offered different and exciting solutions. There was a new philosopher's stone which might, if pointed at or rubbed on the economy, turn lead into gold. The Labour Party could only argue for moderation, safety and the security of the familiar. For the first time this century, conservatism seemed novel and socialism a continuation of the status quo. An ideologically based party of the right made a pragmatic party of the left seem dull and unadventurous.

Meanwhile, the revolutionary left, still, despite all evidence to the contrary, unflinchingly convinced that capitalism contains the seeds of its own destruction, and still determined to live out the Marxist paradox by making the inevitable happen, abandoned ineffectual isolation in favour of a policy of the co-ordinated infiltration of established parties. On the new right, the fear of the 'socialist ratchet' confirming the permanent existence of welfare socialism evolved into a messianic contempt for consensus. The belief in redemption by individual effort found its modern prophets and in Britain the Conservative Party gladly became the publicists and popularists of what was represented as the freedom to be unequal. The world was full of abrasively challenging ideas. The Labour Party had nothing with which to challenge them except its ancient remedies for old ills. The lack of an ideological foundation on which to build a coalition of objectives lay at the root of the election failures of 1979 and 1983.

The recreation of the coalition of objectives requires a fundamental change in our attitude towards the Party's ideology – not in the ideology itself but in the clarity with which it is expressed. If we leave the ideas to be argued out in small groups at Fabian teas and *New Statesman* seminars, we will fall again into the abyss which engulfed us after 1945.

It is now essential to rebuild the moral and intellectual confidence which makes a real renaissance possible. We cannot evangelise without a creed. And it will be necessary in the new world of proliferating political positions, to possess, as well, a catechism by which belief in the true faith can be tested.

The circumstances which made Labour irresistible in 1945 cannot be reproduced, but every ten or fifteen years a moment comes when the principles of democratic socialism are particularly appropriate to the time. That time has come again. Labour will only take advantage of its historic moment if it makes unequivocally clear the ethical framework on which its policy is built.

By the time of the next election, the doctrine of economic *laissez faire* will have visibly failed to provide the certain solutions which its proponents promised; and a naturally compassionate people will have recoiled from the suffering which the free market has created – whilst failing to produce the benefits which were offered as justification for the sacrifice. The Tories will still argue that the solution to our late twentieth-century problems is the economic system which sentimental Victorians wrongly believed existed in the market places of medieval England. Moreover – until the ghost of Thatcherism is exorcised from Central Office – the Conservatives will continue to fight the ideological battle. They are on the brink of defeat; but they will only be beaten by a party which is sufficiently confident of its own ideology to proclaim it as an alternative to Tory philosophy. Included in that confidence must be the conviction that a programme based on that ideology will produce in a wide spectrum of voters the simple response: 'it makes sense to me'.

It is in that form that the old coalition of objectives can be recreated. The policies which flow from it must appeal to political agnostics, but they must have the consistency that comes from a sound philosophical foundation. We know – indeed we have always known – what that foundation should be. Tony Crosland encapsulated it in a single sentence during that weekend I spent with him six days before the onset of his fatal illness. 'Socialism,' he said, 'is about the pursuit of equality and the protection of freedom – in the knowledge that until we are truly equal we will not be truly free.' Establishing that precept as the bedrock of Labour Party belief and accepting it as the yardstick by which every item of policy is measured would enable the recreation of the coalition of objectives which, in 1945, produced the greatest victory in the history of British socialism.

Index

257

Index

Index

Index

Gray, John, 32, 46–7, 48, 63
GLEB, 198
Green, T. H., xvii, 76n, 77, 79

Habermas, J., 62
Hansson, Per Albin, 16–17
Hardie, J. Keir, 8
Hardy, Thomas, *Jude the Obscure*, 34
Hayek, F. A., xvi, 16, 19, 32, 39, 46, 51, 66–72, 76–7, 87, 95, 141, 155, 158, 213
  on coercion, 68, 70, 71, 83
  The Constitution of Liberty, 48, 55–6
  on democracy, 55, 71–2, 91, 142, 229
  on freedom, 55–6, 66–8, 72, 81, 84, 88, 91, 104
  on inequality, 48–9, 69–70, 81–2
  on market system, 61–2, 64, 110, 169
  The Road to Serfdom, 46
  on social justice, 68, 70–1, 91–2
health service, 57, 64, 85, 90–1, 93, 104, 136, 142, 161, 165, 170, 171, 242, 251
  distribution of resources, 47, 165–7
  NHS, 5, 28, 51, 67, 90, 99, 136, 145, 165–6, 231
  pay beds, 67, 145
  private, 93, 112, 120, 145–7, 166
  and social class inequalities, 27–9, 39
Heine, Heinrich, 9
Helvetius, 87–8, 89
Herzberg, Professor Frederick, 109
Hirsch, Fred, 42–3, 48, 63, 115
  Social Limits to Growth, 57–8, 59, 94, 98, 113–14, 122
Hobbes, Thomas, 87, 211
Hodgson, Geoffrey, 206
Hobhouse, John, xvii
home ownership, 15, 16, 30, 93
House of Commons select committees, 137
housing, 30, 36, 57, 63, 64, 78, 79, 85, 92, 93, 165, 170, 242
  of black immigrants, 37–8
  council home sales, 134
  home-ownership, 15, 16, 30, 93
  market distribution of, 47

public-sector, 140, 142
tenant management committees, 142–3
human blood, organs and tissue, free market in, 99–101
Hutt, 155

incentives, 108, 109, 112–13, 114, 122, 149, 155, 192, 196, 230
income(s), 50, 64, 133, 165
  determination of, 235–49
  differentials, 108
  equality, 124, 135–7, 169, 235
  market allocation, 110, 111
  planning, 241–9
  redistribution, 51, 55, 64, 136, 138–9, 167, 231–49
incomes policy, 133, 237, 241–9
Independent Labour Party, 4, 8
  inaugural conference (1893), 7
individual advance, theory of, 113–14, 122
industrial banks, 196–7, 198, 202, 228
inequality:
  difference principle, 52–4, 94, 98, 165
  disparities between social classes, 27–32, 37
  in education system, 114–19
  incentives argument, 112–13
  justification for, 24, 46, 48–9, 54, 69–70, 81–2, 98, 106–7, 230
  legitimacy of, 54–5, 69
  and market system, 45–50, 55, 57, 60–5, 109–10, 111
  and politics of envy, 230–1
  and private sectors in health and education, 145–7
  and 'trickle-down effect', 29, 42, 49, 51, 54, 57, 107, 112, 147, 230, 231
  see also equality
infant mortality, 27, 28, 29
inflation, 233, 242, 244, 246, 248
inner city, 62, 118, 200
  deprivation, 28, 37–8, 138, 161
Institute of Economic Affairs, 19
Institute of Personnel Management, 203
Institute of Policy Studies, 46
investment, 214–15, 223–4
investment agencies, 196–8, 200–2, 204–5, 227–8

260

Index

investment funds, workers', 174, 175, 193, 206
investment protection committees, 204
Irish Land Act (1870), 76–7, 79, 239
Islamic Fundamentalists, 95

Joseph, Sir Keith, 4, 54, 143
Jowett, Fred, 7
junk food industry, 154

Keynes, J. M., 16, 22, 78, 123, 212, 252
Kirby co-operative, 199

Labour government:
1945–51 (Attlee administration), xv-xvi, 5, 6, 9, 14–15, 17, 18, 176, 177, 250, 251–2, 253
1974–9: 181–2, 210, 226, 237, 242
labour market, 79–80, 237, 238–9, 240
Labour Party, xvii, xviii, xix, 110, 141, 149, 231, 250
and the Alliance, 19–21
changing support for, 15, 17–18, 20
Clause IV of Constitution, xvii, 12, 172
coalition of objectives, 5–6, 14, 251–2, 253, 254
conferences, 15, 174
ideology, 3–23, 250–4
membership, 17–18
NEC, 175, 177
and planning, 209–15, 224–8
social contract (1974–9), 237
Labour Party manifestos, 17–18
Labour and the New Social Order (1918), xvii, 11–12
Let Us Face the Future (1945), 5, 177, 178, 250
Labour Representation Committee, 6, 7–8, 15
Lawson, Nigel, 222
LCEB, 198
Legal freedom, 75, 76–7, 92
Lenin, V.I., 159
Lewis, Arthur, xvii
Liberal/SDP Alliance, 19–21
libertarian right *see* new libertarian right
liberty *see* freedom

Liesner Committee Reports (1979), 225–6
linear theory of politics, 10
Lloyds insurance scandals, 217, 219–20
local authorities, 103, 131, 133–4, 131, 132, 133, 173, 190–1, 196
local authority development committees, 228
local authority enterprise boards, 197, 198
local enterprise agencies, 191, 198, 200–2
Locke, John, 211
London Business School Survey (1986), 225
London Passenger Transport Board (LPTB), 14, 174
Lucas of Chilworth, Baron, 219

Macallum, G., 83
Macleod, Iain, 49
Macmillan, Harold, 18, 25, 49, 56
Manning, Cardinal, 76
manufacturing industry, decline of, 215, 216
marginal utility, 107, 135
market allocation of income, 110, 111
market system of distribution, 11, 148–71, 236
allocation of rewards, 60–2, 68
and consumer sovereignty argument, 154
democratic socialists' view of, 64–5, 110–11, 149–51, 152, 158–71, 209
and efficiency, 50, 68, 110, 155, 157, 163, 169, 243
and inequality, 45–50, 57, 60–5, 81–2, 109–10, 111, 121
moral legitimacy, 48, 55, 60, 61, 62, 64
regulation of, 149, 150, 152, 160, 170, 171, 210
and social justice, 45–6, 51, 57, 63, 68, 90, 91–2, 97, 111
and social ownership, 150–1, 158, 169, 171, 186–7
and supply-side, 214
unpredictability of, 61, 82
Marshall, Alfred, 59, 153

261

Index

Marx, Karl, 4, 11, 13, 14, 166
   Critique of the Gotha Programme, 168
Marxism, xv, 4, 10, 11, 18, 19, 21, 95, 168, 172, 210, 253
Menger, C., 155
mergers and takeovers, 221–4, 225–7
Meriden Motor Cycle Co-operative, 199
Militants, 18
Mill, James, 162
Mill, John Stuart, xvii, 95, 98, 194–5, 228
   On Liberty, 73–4, 84, 103–4, 112
Mises, L. von, xvi, 155, 213
monopolies, 110, 129, 131, 149, 150, 151, 154, 160, 161–3, 164, 169, 181, 221–4, 225–7, 236
   'natural', 159, 170, 171
   privatisation of, 156–7
   state, 14, 109, 157, 159, 171, 173, 177–89, 206, 225
Monopolies Commission, 222
Morrison, Herbert, 3, 14, 174–5
mortality rates, 27, 28 &n, 29, 39
mortgage interest relief, 234
municipal enterprise, xiv, 150, 174, 187, 190, 191
Murdoch, Rupert, 222

National Children's Bureau, 36
   Born to Fail, 30, 39
   From Birth to Seven, 30, 39
National Consumers' Council, 234
National Enterprise Board, 189
National Executive Committee, Labour Party, 175, 177
National Health Service (NHS), 5, 28, 51, 57, 67, 90, 99, 136, 145, 165–6, 231
national insurance, 5, 234
National Union of Railwaymen political fund ballot (1983), 15
nationalisation *see* public ownership
neo liberalism, 19, 21, 32, 65, 66, 67, 70n, 78, 79–80, 83, 87, 89, 97–8, 99, 100, 101, 136, 138, 140, 148–9, 151, 153, 160, 162, 194, 224, 235
new libertarian right, 24, 25, 45, 54, 55, 56, 87, 91, 93, 94–5, 100, 102, 138, 153, 213, 221

new right, 46, 47–8, 49, 50, 51, 52–3, 55–6, 73, 140, 148
newspaper mergers, 221–2
non-elective government, 55
North Sea oil, 157, 176
Nove, Alec, *The Economics of Feasible Socialism*, 163–4, 167–8, 180–1
Nozek, R., 83, 84
oligopoly, 150, 163
opportunity costs, 182
Orwell, George, 8–9
Owen, Dr David, 67, 152, 158
Oxford Social Mobility Survey, 31, 59

parent power, 143–4
paternalism, 96, 130, 141
pensioners' bus passes, 136, 137
pensions, 234, 235, 242–3
   earnings-related, 57
'personal coercion' school of philosophy, 87
planning for human need, 165–7
   see also economic planning
Plant, Raymond, 83, 217
police powers, extension of, 140
political freedom, 53, 72, 75–6, 79, 92, 129
politics of envy, 230–1
positional goods, 58, 59, 115
positive discrimination, 11, 67
postal balloting, 132
poverty, the poor, 47–51, 64, 89, 98, 106, 114, 140, 229, 230–1, 233–4, 236, 238, 245–7
Powell, Enoch, 90, 152, 158
privatisation, 119, 120, 156–7, 160, 171, 189
Proudhon, Pierre Joseph, 173
PSBR (Public Sector Borrowing Requirement), 157, 180, 182, 214
public expenditure, 139
   cuts, 242–3
   patterns of, 29–32
   v. private spending, 119–21
Public Health Act (1848), 29
public schools, fee-paying, 93, 112–13
public ownership (nationalisation), 3, 10, 11, 12–14, 22, 109, 124, 157, 172–89, 190, 191, 202, 236, 251

Index

Index

Index